# Post-Colonial T

In his new book Bill Ashcroft gives us a revolutionary view of the ways in which post-colonial societies have responded to colonial control.

The most comprehensive analysis of major features of post-colonial studies ever compiled, *Post-Colonial Transformation*:

- demonstrates how widespread the strategy of transformation has been
- investigates political and literary resistance
- examines the nature of post-colonial societies' engagement with imperial language, history, allegory and place
- offers radical new perspectives in post-colonial theory in principles of habitation and horizonality.

*Post-Colonial Transformation* breaks new theoretical ground while demonstrating the relevance of a wide range of theoretical practices, and extending the exploration of topics fundamentally important to the field of post-colonial studies.

**Bill Ashcroft** teaches at the University of New South Wales and is the author and co-author of several books and articles on post-colonial theory, including *The Empire Writes Back*; *The Post-Colonial Studies Reader*; *Key Concepts in Post-Colonial Studies*; and *Edward Said: The Paradox of Identity*.

# Post-Colonial Transformation

**Bill Ashcroft**

London and New York

First published 2001
by Routledge
11 New Fetter Lane, London EC4P 4EE

Simultaneously published in the USA and Canada
by Routledge
29 West 35th Street, New York, NY 10001

*Routledge is an imprint of the Taylor & Francis Group*

Typeset in Baskerville by
BC Typesetting, Bristol
Printed and bound in Great Britain by
TJ International Ltd, Padstow, Cornwall

*British Library Cataloguing in Publication Data*
A catalogue record for this book is available from the British Library

*Library of Congress Cataloging in Publication Data*
Ashcroft, Bill, 1946–
    Post-colonial transformation/Bill Ashcroft.
       p.   cm.
    Includes bibliographical references and index.
    ISBN 0–415–23829–3 (alk. paper)–ISBN 0–415–23830–7 (pbk.: alk. paper)
    1. Postcolonialism.   2. Decolonization.   3. Social change.
    4. Globalization.   I. Title.

JV51.A75 2001
325′.3–dc21                                                              00-062760


ISBN 0–415–23829–3 (hbk)
ISBN 0–415–23830–7 (pbk)

# Contents

# Introduction

From the Renaissance to the late nineteenth century, European colonial powers invaded, occupied or annexed a huge area of the globe. That movement outwards, seldom wholeheartedly supported by those countries' domestic populations, plagued by political opposition and by controversy over the morality or even the practicality of colonial occupation, nevertheless advanced so relentlessly that it has come to determine the cultural and political character of the world. The predominance of Western civilization by 1914 was unprecedented in the extent of its global reach, but it had been relatively recently acquired. The centuries-long advance of European modernity had been radically accelerated during the eruption of capital-driven, late-nineteenth-century imperialism. The huge contradiction of empire (which also reached its most subtle expression in that period) between the geographical expansion, designed to increase the prestige and economic or political power of the imperial nation, and its professed moral justification, its 'civilizing mission' to bring order and civilization to the barbarous hordes, is a contradiction which also continues in subtler forms in the present-day exercise of global power. There may have been much good, in medical, educational and technological terms, in the colonial impact upon the non-European world. But the simple fact remains that these colonized peoples, cultures and ultimately nations were prevented from becoming what they might have become: they were never allowed to develop into the societies they might have been.

As Basil Davidson points out, the legacy of this colonial control for newly independent governments in Africa 'was not a prosperous colonial business, but in many ways, a profound colonial crisis' (1983: 182). As he puts it, in a discussion of the charismatic Kwame Nkrumah, who led Ghana into independence, the 'dish' the new leaders were handed on the day of independence was old and cracked and little fit for any further use. Worse than that, it was not an empty dish. For it carried the junk and jumble of a century of colonial muddle and 'make do,' and this the new . . . ministers had to accept along with the dish itself. What shone upon its supposedly golden surface was not the reflection of new ideas and ways of liberation, but the shadows of old ideas and ways of servitude.

(1973: 94)

For this reason, and because colonial structures were often simply taken over by indigenous élites after independence, the central idea of resistance rhetoric – that 'independence' would be the same thing as 'national liberation' – was inevitably doomed to disappointment.

But the striking thing about colonial experience is that after colonization post-colonial societies *did* very often develop in ways which sometimes revealed a remarkable capacity for change and adaptation. A common view of colonization, which represents it as an unmitigated cultural disaster, disregards the often quite extraordinary ways in which colonized societies engaged and utilized imperial culture for their own purposes. This book is concerned with how these colonized peoples responded to the political and cultural dominance of Europe. Many critics have argued that colonialism destroyed indigenous cultures, but this assumes that culture is static, and underestimates the resilience and adaptability of colonial societies. On the contrary, colonized cultures have often been so resilient and transformative that they have changed the character of imperial culture itself. This 'transcultural' effect has not been seamless or unvaried, but it forces us to reassess the stereotyped view of colonized peoples' victimage and lack of agency.

A common strategy of post-colonial self-assertion has been the attempt to rediscover some authentic pre-colonial cultural reality in order to redress the impact of European imperialism. Invariably such attempts misconceive the link between culture and identity. Culture describes the myriad ways in which a group of people makes sense of, represents and inhabits its world, and as such can never be destroyed, whatever happens to its various forms of expression. Culture is practised, culture is used, culture is made. 'Culture has life,' says Mintz, speaking of the Caribbean, 'because its content serves as resources for those who employ it, change it, incarnate it. Human beings cope with the demands of everyday life through their interpretative and innovative skills . . . not by ossifying their creative forms, but by using them creatively' (1974: 19). All cultures move in a constant state of transformation. The attempt to understand how post-colonial cultures resisted the power of colonial domination in ways so subtle that they transformed both colonizer and colonized lies at the heart of post-colonial studies.

In 1912 the leader of the French Socialist Party, Jean Jaurès, spoke out in Parliament at the acquisition of Morocco:

> I have never painted an idyllic picture of the Muslim populations, and I am well aware of the disorder and oligarchic exploitation by many chiefs which takes place. But, Sirs, if you look deeply into the matter, there existed [before the French takeover] a Moroccan civilization capable of the necessary transformation, capable of evolution and progress, a civilization both ancient and modern . . . There was a seed for the future, a hope. And let me say that I cannot pardon those who have crushed this hope for pacific and human progress – African civilization – by all sorts of ruses and by the brutalities of conquest.
>
> (cited in Aldrich 1996: 112)

The most interesting word in this speech is 'transformation'. Jaurès acknowledges that all cultures transform themselves, this is the natural movement of cultural existence. How they do so is another matter. He condemns the colonization of Morocco, and, by implication, all colonization, for its crushing of the hope of progress and, specifically, the hope for progress into an African civilization. According to him, Morocco had been robbed of its capacity to become what it might have become. If we think of the case of Morocco magnified many times over, we must see the European colonization of the world as a cultural catastrophe of enormous proportions. But what Jaurès did not expect, any more than the proponents of the *mission civilatrice*, was that colonial societies' capacity for transformation could not be so easily truncated. Although the European view of the civilizing process was nothing less than enforced emulation – colonial cultures should simply imitate their metropolitan occupiers – the processes of imitation themselves, the 'mimicry' of the colonizers, as Homi Bhabha has famously suggested (1994), became a paradoxical feature of colonial resistance. The ambivalence of post-colonial mimicry and the 'menace' which Bhabha sees in it are indicators of the complexity of this resistance.

This complexity is linked directly to the transformative nature of cultural identity itself. In his celebrated essay 'Cultural Identity and Diaspora' (1990), Stuart Hall suggests there are two ways of conceiving such identity: 'The first position defines "cultural identity" in terms of one shared culture, a sort of collective "one true self", hiding inside the many other, more superficial or artificially imposed "selves", which people with a shared history and ancestry hold in common' (1990: 223). Such identity searches for images which impose 'an imaginary coherence on the experience of dispersal and fragmentation' (224). Images of a shared 'Africanness', for instance, provide such a coherence, although that Africanness may exist far in the past. But there is a second view of cultural identity which explores 'points of deep and significant *difference*' (225) and which sees the longed-for, and possibly illusory, condition of 'uniqueness' as a matter of 'becoming' as well as being.

> Cultural identities come from somewhere, have histories. But, like everything which is historical, they undergo constant transformation. Far from being eternally fixed in some essentialised past, they are subject to the continuous 'play' of history, culture and power. Far from being grounded in mere 'recovery' of the past, which is waiting to be found, and which when found, will secure our sense of ourselves into eternity, identities are names we give to the different ways we are positioned by, and position ourselves within, the narratives of the past.
>
> (225)

The struggle between a view of identity which attempts to recover an immutable origin, a fixed and eternal representation of itself, and one which sees identity as inextricable from the transformative conditions of material life, is possibly the most deep-seated divide in post-colonial thinking. Hall goes a long way towards arbitrating this divide when he suggests that cultural identity is not a fixed essence at all but a matter of *positioning* – 'Hence, there is always a politics of identity, a politics of position, which has no absolute guarantee in an unproblematic, transcendent "law of origin"' (226).

Positioning is, above all, a matter of representation, of giving concrete form to ideological concepts. Representation describes both the site of identity formation and the site of the *struggle* over identity formation. For the positioning of cultural identity has involved the struggle over the means of representation since colonized peoples first took hold of the colonists' language to represent themselves. Today the means of representing cultural identity includes the whole range of plastic and visual arts, film and television and, crucially, strategies for *consuming* these products. Hence, transformation, which describes one way of viewing cultural identity, also describes the strategic process by which cultural identity is represented. By taking hold of the means of representation, colonized peoples throughout the world have appropriated and transformed those processes into culturally appropriate vehicles. It is this struggle over representation which articulates most clearly the material basis, the constructiveness and dialogic energy of the 'post-colonial imagination'.

Creative artists often seem to express most forcefully the imaginative vision of a society. But artists, writers and performers only capture more evocatively that capacity for transformation which is demonstrated at every level of society. 'When I was growing up in the 1940s and 1950s as a child in Kingston,' says Hall, 'I was surrounded by the signs, the music and rhythms of this Africa of the diaspora, which only existed as a result of a long and discontinuous series of transformations' (231). The imaginative and the creative are integral aspects of that process by which identity itself has come into being. Cultural identity does not exist outside representation. But the transformative nature of cultural identity leads directly to the transformation of those strategies by which it is represented. These strategies have invariably been the very ones used by the colonizer to position the colonized as marginal and inferior, but their appropriation has been ubiquitous in the struggle by colonized peoples to empower themselves. This suggests that 'resistance' can be truly effective, that is, can avoid simply replacing one tyranny with another, only when it creates rather than simply defends. Post-colonial writing hinges on the act of engagement which takes the dominant language and uses it to express the most deeply felt issues of post-colonial social experience. This form of 'imitation' becomes the key to transforming not only the imitator but the imitated. The engagement of post-colonial writing is one which had transcultural consequences, that is, dialectic and circulating effects which have become a crucial feature of the world we experience today.

Given the positive and productive effects of this capacity in post-colonial society, the question must be asked: does the fact of transformation, the capacity of colonized peoples to make dominant discourse work for them, to develop economically and technologically, to enjoy the 'benefits' of global capitalism, mean that the colonized have had a measure of 'moral luck' as philosopher Bernard Williams puts it (1981: 20–39)? This would be comparable to saying that the political prisoner has been fortunate because he has been able to write, in prison, an autobiography which caught the imagination of the world, as Nelson Mandela has with *Long Walk to Freedom*. One might even say that such imprisonment has even been a crucial factor in the ultimate overthrow of the apartheid regime. How do we assess the moral dilemma of such a possibility? If we gained advantages from imperial discourse – even if it was only the pressure to focus on our own freedom, to concentrate on the things which we value most, not to mention the material and technological advantages of metropolitan society – was colonization ultimately good for us?

Or, to take another example: consider the human and social catastrophe caused by the colonial development of the sugar plantation economies of the Caribbean. The obliteration of the indigenous Amerindians, the capture and disinheritance of millions of Africans transported as slaves, the dislocation of hundreds of thousands of South Asian indentured workers, the wholesale destruction of the landscapes of islands turned into virtual sugar factories, the institution of endemic poverty and the destruction of economic versatility. The effects of the colonization of the Caribbean appear to be an unprecedented disaster. Yet the creole populations of the Caribbean proceeded to develop a culture so dynamic and vibrant that it has affected the rest of the world. How is one to judge the cultural effects of imperialism under these circumstances? Spivak calls this the deconstructive moment of post-coloniality.

> Why is the name 'post-colonial' specifically useful in our moment?
> Those of us . . . from formerly colonized countries, are able to communicate with each other, to exchange, to establish sociality, because we have access to the culture of imperialism. Shall we then assign to that culture, in the words of the ethical philosopher Bernard Williams, a measure of 'moral luck'? I think that there can be no question that the answer is 'no.' This impossible 'no' to a structure, which one critiques, yet inhabits intimately, is the deconstructive philosophical position, and everyday here and now named 'post-coloniality' is a case of it.
>
> (1993: 60)

The concept of 'moral luck' is a strategic suppression of the liberatory capacity of colonized societies. Much more interesting than the ethical conundrum, the 'deconstructive moment', in which the post-colonial subject lives within the consequences of imperial discourse while denying it, is the political achievement. In post-colonial engagements with colonial discourse there has been a triumph of the spirit, a transformation effected at the level of both the imaginative and the material, which has changed the ways in which both see each other and themselves. Agonizing over the benefits of colonization is like asking what the society might have become without it: the question is unanswerable and ultimately irrelevant. This book focuses instead on the resilience, adaptability and inventiveness of post-colonial societies, which may, if we consider their experiences as models for resistance, give us insight into the operation of local engagements with global culture. By eluding the moral conundrum and simply investigating how transformation affected the imaginative and material dimensions of post-colonial life, we arrive at a form of resistance which is not so much deconstructive (or contradictory) as dynamic, not so much ethically insoluble as practically affirmative.

## The term 'post-colonial'

This book uses the terms 'post-colonial' and 'transformation' quite deliberately, for the kinds of cultural and political engagements it examines are characterized by the unique power relationships operating within European colonialism. Post-colonial studies developed as a way of addressing the cultural production of those societies affected by the historical phenomenon of colonialism. In this respect it was never conceived of as a grand theory but as a methodology: first, for analysing the many strategies by which colonized societies have engaged imperial discourse; and second, for studying the ways in which many of those strategies are shared by colonized societies, re-emerging in very different political and cultural circumstances. However, there has hardly been a more hotly contested term in contemporary theoretical discourse. Since its entry into the mainstream in the late 1980s with the publication of *The Empire Writes Back* there has been a constant flood of 'introductions' to the field, most of them focusing on the work of the 'colonial discourse' theorists: Edward Said, Homi Bhabha and Gayatri Chakravorty Spivak.

Post-colonialism means many things and embraces a dizzying array of critical practices. Stephen Slemon surveyed the situation evocatively when he remarked in 'The Scramble for Post-Colonialism' that the term has been used in recent times

> as a way of ordering a critique of totalising forms of Western historicism; as a portmanteau term for a retooled notion of 'class', as a subset of both postmodernism and post-structuralism (and conversely, as the condition from which those two structures of cultural logic and cultural critique themselves are seen to emerge); as the name for a condition of nativist longing in post-independence national groupings; as a cultural marker of non-residency for a Third-World intellectual cadre; as the inevitable underside of a

fractured and ambivalent discourse of colonialist power; as an oppositional form of 'reading practice'; and – and this was my first encounter with the term – as the name for a category of 'literary' activity which sprang from a new and welcome political energy going on within what used to be called 'Commonwealth' literary studies.

(1994: 16–17)

Even the term 'postmodernism' cannot claim to be a repository of such a wide and contradictory variety of critical practices. Those in least doubt about its meaning are invariably its opponents. Shohat and Stam's complaint is that 'Despite the dizzying multiplicities invoked by the term "postcolonial," postcolonial theory has curiously failed to address the politics of location of the term "postcolonial" itself' (1994: 37). One might well wonder where Shohat and Stam had been. For at times it seems as though no other contemporary discourse has been so obsessed with the politics of its location. This comment demonstrates the way in which a particular form of post-colonial study, one that focuses on the work of celebrated theorists operating from the metropolitan academy, can be assumed to *be* the whole of post-colonialism. Such a construction of post-colonial practice patently fails to address the emergence of the term in the cultural discourse of formerly colonized peoples, peoples whose work is inextricably grounded in the experience of colonization. Not all forms of post-colonial practice can be constituted as 'transformative', but that discourse which has developed the greatest transformative energy stems from a grounding in the material and historical experience of colonialism.

Arif Dirlik, while narrowing down the categories of the term, sees problems emerging from the identification of post-colonial intellectuals.

The term *postcolonial* in its various usages carries a multiplicity of meanings that need to be distinguished for analytical purposes. Three uses of the term seem to me to be especially prominent (and significant): (a) as a literal description of conditions in formerly colonial societies, in which case the term has concrete referents, as in postcolonial societies or postcolonial intellectuals; (b) as a description of a global condition after the period of colonialism, in which case the usage is somewhat more abstract and less concrete in reference, comparable in its vagueness to the earlier term *Third World*, for which it is intended as a substitute; and (c) as a description of a discourse on the above-named conditions that is informed by the epistemological and psychic orientations that are products of those conditions.

Even at its most concrete, the significance of *postcolonial* is not transparent because each of its meanings is overdetermined by the others. Postcolonial intellectuals are clearly the producers of a postcolonial discourse, but who exactly are the postcolonial intellectuals? . . . Now that postcoloniality has been released from the fixity of Third World location, the identity of the postcolonial is no longer structural but discursive. Postcolonial in this perspective represents an attempt to regroup intellectuals of uncertain location under the banner of postcolonial discourse. Intellectuals in the flesh may produce the themes that constitute postcolonial discourse, but it is participation in the discourse that defines them as postcolonial intellectuals. Hence it is important to delineate the discourse so as to identify postcolonial intellectuals themselves.

(1994: 331–2)

The contention that 'the identity of the postcolonial intellectual is no longer structural but discursive' illuminates the need for some signifier of the difference between post-colonialisms which distinguishes the different locations and different orientations of its practice. If 'the conditions in formerly colonized societies' have any bearing on a 'global condition after the period of colonialism', this relationship needs to be analysed. Although Dirlik considers these to be simply variant meanings of the term, there are determinate, historical ways in which the material, political and cultural conditions of formerly colonized societies have impacted on global culture. Indeed, it is in assessing these that we may understand the transformative impact of post-colonial cultural strategies on global cultures.

An investigation of the emergence of the term 'post-colonial' reveals how and why such a range of meanings has come to surround its use. Employed by historians and political scientists after the Second World War in terms such as the post-colonial state, 'post-colonial' had a clearly chronological meaning, designating the post-independence period. However, from the late 1970s the term has been used by literary critics to discuss the various cultural effects of colonization. The study of the discursive power of colonial representation was initiated by Edward Said's landmark work *Orientalism* in 1978 and led to the development of what came to be called 'colonialist discourse theory' in the work of critics such as Gayatri Spivak and Homi Bhabha. However, the actual term 'post-colonial' was not employed in the early studies of colonial discourse theory, rather it was first used to refer to cultural interactions within colonial societies in literary circles. The second issue of *New Literature Review* in 1977, for instance, focused on 'post-colonial literatures', and this was the recognition of a widespread, though informal, acceptance of the term amongst literary critics. The term had emerged as part of an attempt to politicize and focus the concerns of fields such as Commonwealth literature and the study of the so-called New Literatures in English which had been initiated in the late 1960s. The term has subsequently been widely used to signify the political, linguistic and cultural experience of societies from the former British Empire.

A simple hyphen has come to represent an increasingly diverging set of assumptions, emphases, strategies and practices in post-colonial reading and writing. The hyphen puts an emphasis on the discursive and material effects of the historical 'fact' of colonialism, while the term 'postcolonialism' has come to represent an increasingly indiscriminate attention to cultural difference and marginality of all kinds, whether a consequence of the historical experience of colonialism or not. Perhaps more telling is the relationship of these forms of analysis to the contemporary European philosophical cultural discourses of poststructuralism and postmodernism. The spelling of the term 'post-colonial' has become more of an issue for those who use the hyphenated form, because the hyphen is a statement about the particularity, the historically and culturally grounded nature of the experience it represents. Grounded in the practice of critics concerned with the writings of colonized peoples themselves, it came to stand for a theory which was oriented towards the historical and cultural experience of colonized peoples, a concern with textual production, rather than towards the fetishization of theory itself. The hyphen in 'post-colonial' is a particular form of 'space-clearing' gesture (Appiah 1992: 241), a political notation which has a very great deal to say about the materiality of political oppression. In this respect the hyphen distinguishes the term from the kind of unlocated, abstract and poststructuralist theorizing to which Shohat and Stam object.

Admittedly the hyphen can be misleading, particularly if it suggests that post-colonialism refers to the situation in a society 'after colonialism', an assumption which remains tediously persistent despite constant rebuttals by post-colonialists. Anne McClintock suggests that

> the term postcolonial . . . is haunted by the very figure of linear development that it sets out to dismantle. Metaphorically, the term postcolonialism marks history as a series of stages along an epochal road from 'the precolonial', to 'the colonial', to 'the post-colonial' – an unbidden, if disavowed commitment to linear time

and the idea of development. If a theoretical tendency to envisage 'Third World' literature as progressing from 'protest literature' to 'resistance literature' to 'national literature' has been criticized for rehearsing the Enlightenment trope of sequential linear progress, the term postcolonialism is questionable for the same reason. Metaphorically poised on the border between old and new, end and beginning, the term heralds the end of a world era but by invoking the same trope of linear progress which animated that era.

(1995: 10–11)

This seems to be a ghost which refuses to be exorcized. Undoubtedly the 'post' in 'post-colonialism' must always contend with the spectre of linearity and the kind of teleological development it sets out to dismantle. But rather than being disabling, this radical instability of meaning gives the term a vibrancy, energy and plasticity which have become part of its strength, as post-colonial analysis rises to engage issues and experiences which have been out of the purview of metropolitan theory and, indeed, comes to critique the assumptions of that theory.

More pertinently perhaps, the term has expanded to engage issues of cultural diversity, ethnic, racial and cultural difference and the power relations within them, as a consequence of an expanded and more subtle understanding of the dimensions of neo-colonial dominance. This expanded understanding embraces the apparently ambiguous situation of Chicano experience in the USA. Alfred Arteaga explains that

> Chicanos are products of two colonial contexts. The first begins with the explorer Colón and the major event of the Renaissance: the 'old' world's 'discovery' of the 'new.' Spanish colonization of the Americas lasted more than three centuries, from the middle of Leonardo da Vinci's lifetime to the beginning of Queen Victoria's. . . . The second colonial context begins with the immigration of Austin's group from Connecticut to Texas, Mexico.
>
> (1994: 21)

Engaging the actual complexity and diversity of European colonization, as well as the pervasiveness of neo-colonial domination, opens the way for a wide application of the strategies of post-colonial analysis.

However, one of the most curious and perhaps confusing features of post-colonial study is its overlap with the strategies of postmodern discourse. Asking the question, 'Is the post in post-colonialism the same as the post in postmodernism?' Anthony Kwame Appiah says:

> All aspects of contemporary African cultural life including music and some sculpture and painting, even some writings with which the West is largely not familiar – have been influenced – often powerfully – by the transition of African societies *through* colonialism, but they are not all in the relevant sense *post*colonial. For the *post* in postcolonial, like the post in postmodern is the *post* of the space-clearing gesture I characterised earlier: and many areas of contemporary African cultural life – what has come to be theorised as popular culture, in particular – are not in this way concerned with transcending – with going beyond – coloniality. Indeed, it might be said to be a mark of popular culture that its borrowings from international cultural forms are remarkably insensitive to – not so much dismissive of as blind to – the issue of neocolonialism or 'cultural imperialism'.
>
> (1992: 240–1)

This is an astute perception. But the post-colonial, as it is used to describe and analyse the cultural production of colonized peoples, is *precisely* the production that occurs *through* colonialism, because no decolonizing process, no matter how oppositional, can remain free from that cataclysmic experience. Once we determine that post-colonial analysis will address 'all the culture affected by the imperial process from the moment of colonization to the present day' (Ashcroft et al. 1989: 2), our sense of the 'space-clearing gesture' of which Appiah speaks becomes far more subtle, far more attuned to the transformative potential of post-colonial engagements with imperial discourse. It is *quite distinct* from the space-clearing gesture in postmodernism. Post-colonial discourse is the discourse of the colonized, which begins with colonization and doesn't stop when the colonizers go home. The post-colonial is not a chronological period but a range of material conditions and a rhizomic pattern of discursive struggles, ways of contending with various specific forms of colonial oppression. The problem with terminology, the problem with the relationship between post-colonialism and postmodernism, lies in the fact that they are both, in their very different and culturally located ways, discursive elaborations of postmodernity, just as imperialism and Enlightenment philosophy were discursive elaborations of modernity.

Crucially, words such as 'post-colonial' do not describe essential forms of experience but forms of talk *about* experience. If the term 'post-colonial' seems to be homogenizing in the way it brings together the experiences of colonialism in a wide variety of situations, it must also be remembered that these experiences are just as various *within* particular national or linguistic communities. Once we see the term 'post-colonial' as representing a *form of talk* rather than a *form of experience* we will be better equipped to see that such talk encompasses a wide and interwoven text of experiences. For instance, what is the *essential* experience of oppression, of invasion, of domination? These involve various forms of material experience, located in their specific historical and political environments. Just as the experiences of colonization within colonized societies have varied from the most abject suffering to the engendering of filiative feeling, the responses of those colonized societies to colonialism have occupied a continuum from absolute complicity to violent rebellion, all of which can be seen to be 'post-colonial'. If we see post-colonial discourse in the Foucauldian sense as a system of knowledge of colonized societies, a space of enunciation, the rules which govern the possibility of statements about the field, we must still confirm the discursive significance of language, of talk about experience. If it is the potential of the political subject to intervene, to engage the power of the modern imperial state, post-colonial writing testifies to discourse in which this may occur, and interpolation the strategy by which it may occur.

## Modes of transformation

The following chapters address some of the fundamental issues which arise in post-colonial responses to imperial discourse. The Western control over time and space, the dominance of language and the technologies of writing for perpetuating the modes of this dominance, through geography, history, literature and, indeed, through the whole range of cultural production, have meant that post-colonial engagements with imperial power have been exceptionally wide-ranging. The one thing which characterizes all these engagements, the capacity shared by many forms of colonial experience, is a remarkable facility to use the modes of the dominant discourse against itself and transform it in ways that have been both profound and lasting.

The question of resistance lies at the forefront of this analysis because the concept of resistance has always dwelt at the heart of the struggle between imperial power and post-colonial identity. The problem with resistance is that to see it as a simple oppositionality locks it into the very binary which Europe established to define its others. Very often, political struggle is contrary to the modes of adaptation and appropriation most often engaged by post-colonial societies. This discussion reveals that 'resistance', if conceived as something much more subtle than a binary opposition, has always operated in a wide range of processes to which post-colonial societies have subjected imperial power. The most sustained, far-reaching and effective interpretation of post-colonial resistance has been the 'resistance to absorption', the appropriation and transformation of dominant technologies for the purpose of re-inscribing and representing post-colonial cultural identity.

One of the key features of this transformative process has been the entry, aggressive or benign, of post-colonial acts and modes of representation into the dominant discourse itself, an interpolation which not only interjects and interrupts that discourse but changes it in subtle ways. This term 'interpolation' ironically reverses Althusser's concept of 'interpellation' by ascribing to the colonial subject, and, consequently, to the colonial society, a capacity for agency which is effected within relationships that are radically unequal. Interpolation recasts our perception of the trajectory of power operating in colonization. Rather than being swallowed up by the hegemony of empire, the apparently dominated culture, and the 'interpellated' subjects within it, are quite able to interpolate the various modes of imperial discourse to use it for different purposes, to counter its effects by transforming them.

Language is the key to this interpolation, the key to its transformative potential, for it is in language that the colonial discourse is engaged at its most strategic point. With the appropriation of language comes the persistent question of how texts mean. For if the meaning were to be limited to either the writer or the reader, or indeed, somehow embodied in the language itself, then the radical communication, which post-colonial writing itself represents, could not occur. The question of transformation, and the phenomenon of communication between cultures, therefore, lead us into a recognition of the constitutive processes of meaning. The constitutive theory proposed here is one which emphasizes the acts of writing and reading as social rather than solitary, a sociality within which language is appropriated and transformed. It is upon the foundation of this particular transformation that post-colonial writing is built. But its capacity to stand as a model for a wide range of appropriations is almost unlimited.

Historiography has been one of the most far-reaching and influential imperial constructions of subjectivity, and post-colonial histories, responding to the power of this discourse, have interpolated the narrativity of history while disrupting it by blurring the boundaries that would seem to separate it from literature. Representations of human time and human space have been the most powerful and hegemonic purveyors of Eurocentrism in modern times. History, and its associated teleology, has been the means by which European concepts of time have been naturalized and universalized. How history might be 're-written', how it might be interpolated, is a crucial question for the self-representation of colonized peoples. Ultimately, the transformation of history stands as one of the most strategic and powerfully effective modes of cultural resistance. By interpolating history through literary and other non-empirical texts, post-colonial narratives of historical experience reveal the fundamentally allegorical nature of history itself.

The issues surrounding the concept of place – how it is conceived, how it differs from 'space' or 'location', how it enters into and produces cultural consciousness, how it becomes the horizon of identity – are some of the most difficult and debated in post-colonial experience. Where is one's 'place'? What happens to the concept of 'home' when home is colonized, when the very ways of conceiving home, of talking about it, writing about it, remembering it, begin to occur through the medium of the colonizer's way of seeing the world? The Eurocentric control of space, through its ocularcentrism, its cartography, its development of perspective, its modes of surveillance, and above all through its language, has been the most difficult form of cultural control faced by post-colonial societies. Resistance to dominant assumptions about spatial location and the identity of place has occurred most generally in the way in which such space has been inhabited.

Habitation describes a way of being in place, a way of being which itself defines and transforms place. It is so powerful because the coercive pressures of colonialism and globalization have ultimately no answer to it. Whether affected by imperial discourse or by global culture, the local subject has a capacity to incorporate such influences into a sense of place, to appropriate a vast array of resources into the business of establishing and confirming local identity. To what extent is inhabiting a place not only a statement of identity but also a means of transforming the conditions of one's life? The conceptual shift from 'space' to 'place' which occurs as a result of colonial experience is a shift from empty space to a human, social space which gains its material and ideological identity from the *practices* of inhabiting. Habitation, in its reconfiguration of conceptions of space, also engages the most profound principles of Western epistemology: its passion for boundaries, its cultural and imaginative habits of enclosure.

It is, ultimately, in the capacity to transcend the trope of the boundary, to live 'horizontally', that post-colonial habitation offers the most radical principle of transformative resistance. It is in horizonality that the true force of transformation becomes realized, for whereas the boundary is about cultural regulation, the horizon is about cultural possibility. The concept of 'horizon' proposes a theoretical principle for that movement beyond epistemological, cultural and spatial boundaries to which post-colonial discourses aspire. The horizon is a way of reconceiving the bounded precepts of imperial discourse, a principle which defines the dynamic and transformative orientation of those myriad acts by which post-colonial societies engage colonial power.

The question which must be faced ultimately is: does the concern with colonization involve an intellectual orientation that is inescapably backward-looking? Do we find ourselves looking back to the effects of power relationships which no longer seem relevant? The answer to this is twofold: the effects of European imperialism and the transformative engagements it has experienced from post-colonial societies are ones that have affected, and continue to affect, most of the world to the present day. This engagement has come to colour and identify the very nature of those societies in contemporary times. But the other answer suggests that the very *dynamic* we are analysing here, the dynamic of the power relationships which characterize colonial experience, has now achieved a global status. The issue of globalization recasts the whole question of post-colonial identity. Both imperialism and globalization are consequences of the onrushing tide of European modernity. But while we cannot see globalization as a simple extension of imperialism, a kind of neo-imperialism, as early globalization theory proposed, the engagement of imperial culture by post-colonial societies offers a compelling model for the relationship between the local and the global today.

The ways in which local communities consume global culture continually disrupt the 'development' paradigm which has characterized the representation of the Third World by the West since the Second World War. Whereas 'development' acts to force the local into globally normative patterns, 'transformation' acts to adjust those patterns to the requirements of local values and needs. This capacity to adjust global influences to local needs disrupts the simple equation of globalization and Westernization, the idea that globalization is a simple top-down homogenizing pressure.

Post-colonial transformation emerged from a power relationship – between European imperial discourse and colonial societies – that was in many ways unique. Different colonies were inevitably oriented towards a particular empire, a particular metropolitan centre and language, and led to particular kinds of discursive transformations. But the range of strategies which has characterized those transformations can be seen to operate on a global scale. It is tempting to suggest that this is because the consequences of European imperialism itself have ultimately reached global proportions. But it is the range of strategies, the tenacity and the practical assertiveness of the apparently powerless with which we are most concerned, not with the relationship between imperialism and globalism. When we project our analysis on to a global screen we find that the capacity, the agency, the inventiveness of post-colonial transformation help us to explain something about the ways in which local communities resist absorption and transform global culture itself. In the end the transformative energy of post-colonial societies tells us about the present because it is overwhelmingly concerned with the future.

# 1   Resistance

In her celebrated *testimonio*, *I, Rigoberta Menchú*, the author gives an account of an appalling atrocity in the 1970s in which Guatemalan government soldiers force villagers from several villages to watch as their relatives, arrested on suspicion of subversion, are systematically tortured, degraded and burnt alive. The incident stands as a symbol of that cruelty and abuse, that terrorism of power, which colonized societies have continually resisted. It also focuses some exceptionally complex, and controversial, questions of truth and representation, as we shall see in Chapter 5. Yet what it means to resist effectively is a key question, perhaps *the* question to emerge from her account. When we compare Menchú's response with that of her father, we discover two models of resistance between which post-colonial societies have continually alternated in their reaction to colonial dominance.

Observing her father's response Menchú says: 'My father was incredible; I watched him and he didn't shed a tear, but he was full of rage. And that was a rage we all felt' (1983: 178). Her father's stoicism during this act of barbarity was like a rock against the power of the government's terror, and the passage offers him as an example of the Indians' spirit of resistance. '[I]f so many people were brave enough to give their lives, their last moments, their last drop of blood,' he says, 'then wouldn't we be brave enough to do the same?' (181). The experience politicized him completely. He became an organizer of resistance groups throughout Guatemala but was killed in the occupation of the Spanish embassy. But we are left with lingering doubts about what he achieved. If Menchú's father was a rock, then the rock was smashed by the sledgehammer of the state, along with all resistance which reduces the struggle to one of brute force.

On the other hand, Rigoberta Menchú's resistance was more elusive and covert, as she organized communities of Indians against the government. In this respect her *testimonio* demonstrates the fine balance between resistance and transformation in revolutionary activity – opposition is necessary, but the appropriation of forms of representation, and forcing entry into the discursive networks of cultural dominance, have always been a crucial feature of resistance movements which have gained political success. The co-operation of the Indian groups was made possible only by using the colonizing language as well as other culturally alien structures of organization. But Menchú's most effective resistance to the overt brutality of the state, the most resilient opposition to material oppression, is the discursive resistance which gained her a global audience, the resistance located in her *testimonio* itself. Rigoberta Menchú and her father shared a deep anger against the terrorism of power. But the radically different strategies emerging from that anger compel us to examine the concept of resistance itself.

Resistance has become a much-used word in post-colonial discourse, and indeed in all discussion of 'Third World' politics. Armed rebellion, inflammatory tracts, pugnacious oratory and racial, cultural and political animosity: resistance has invariably connoted the urgent imagery of war. This has much to do with the generally violent nature of colonial incursion. In all European empires the drain on resources to fight wars of rebellion was great. Algerians, for instance, fought a sustained war against French conquest for two decades after 1830, led by Abd El-Khader. Although colonial wars were usually of shorter duration, such protracted hostilities were not uncommon, and often led to profound cultural consequences, such as the Treaty of Waitangi in 1840 in New Zealand which concluded the Maori wars, falsely ceding Maori *mana* to the Crown.[1] Armed rebellion began in the Caribbean as early as 1501, and, according to Julio Le Riverend, the Governor of Cuba, Ovando, 'asked for the complete prohibition of the [slave] trade, for, in previous years, the Negroes had shown an open tendency towards rebellion and conspiracy' (Riverend 1967: 82). The often unabashedly exploitative nature of colonial economic ventures, the actively racist attitudes of colonists – even those from France, which was determined to assimilate colonial societies into French political and administrative structures – and the overweening assumption of moral authority for colonial expansion, meant that political resentment, the motive for armed resistance, was constant. Indeed, such armed rebellion, from the 'Indian Mutiny' to the resistance movements in Kenya, Zimbabwe and other African states, became the very focus of indigenous demands for self-determination.

But we might well ask whether this armed or ideological rebellion is the only possible meaning of resistance, and, more importantly, whether such a history leaves in its wake a *rhetoric* of opposition emptied of any capacity for social change. Observing the way in which colonial control was often ejected by national liberation movements only to be replaced by equally coercive indigenous élites, we might well ask: What does it really mean to *resist*? Does the term 'resistance' adequately describe cultural relationships, cultural oppositions or cultural influences in the era of globalization? Given the widespread feelings of opposition in colonized communities, 'resistance' enacted as violent military engagement, a national liberation struggle, or, for that matter, even as a programme of widespread social militancy, is surprisingly rare. Ultimately, 'resistance' is a word which adapts itself to a great variety of circumstances, and few words show a greater tendency towards cliché and empty rhetoric, as it has become increasingly used as a catch-all word to describe any kind of political struggle. But if we think of resistance as any form of defence by which an invader is 'kept out', the subtle and sometimes even unspoken forms of social and cultural resistance have been much more common. It is these subtle and more widespread forms of resistance, forms of saying 'no', that are most interesting because they are most difficult for imperial powers to combat.

One question this raises is: can one 'resist' without violence? Can one even resist without obviously 'opposing'? The answer to this is obviously 'yes!' Gandhi's 'passive resistance' to the British Raj is a famous and effective example. But the most fascinating feature of post-colonial societies is a 'resistance' that manifests itself as a refusal to be absorbed, a resistance which engages that which is resisted in a different way, taking the array of influences exerted by the dominating power, and altering them into tools for expressing a deeply held sense of identity and cultural being. This has been the most widespread, most influential and most quotidian form of 'resistance' in post-colonial societies. In some respects, as in the debate over the use of colonial languages, it has also been the most contentious. Consequently, this engagement with colonial discourse has rarely been regarded as 'resistance', because it is often devoid of the rhetoric of resistance. While the soldiers and politicians have gained most attention, it is the ordinary people – and the artists and writers, through whom a transformative vision of the world has been conceived – who have often done most to 'resist' the cultural pressures upon them. In most cases this has not been a heroic enterprise but a pragmatic and mundane array of living strategies to which imperial culture has no answer. In this respect 'transformation' is contrary to what we normally think of as 'resistance' because the latter has been locked into the party-political imagery of opposition, a discourse of 'prevention'. But post-colonial transformation has been the most powerful and active form of resistance in colonized societies because it has been so relentless, so everyday and, above all, so integral a part of the *imaginations* of these societies.

Resistance which ossifies into simple opposition often becomes trapped in the very binary which imperial discourse uses to keep the colonized in subjection. As Coetzee's protagonist, Dawn, puts it in *Dusklands*:

> The answer to a myth of force is not necessarily counterforce, for if the myth predicts counterforce, counterforce reinforces the myth. The science of mythography teaches us that a subtler counter is to subvert and revise the myth. The highest propaganda is the propagation of new mythology.
>
> (1974: 24–5)

The most tenacious aspect of colonial control has been its capacity to bind the colonized into a binary myth. Underlying all colonial discourse is a binary of colonizer/colonized, civilized/uncivilized, white/black which works to justify the *mission civilatrice* and perpetuate a cultural distinction which is essential to the 'business' of economic and political exploitation. The idea that 'counterforce' is the best response to the colonialist myth of force, or to the myth of nurture, both of which underly this civilizing mission, binds the colonized into the myth. This has often implicated colonized groups and individuals in a strategy of resistance which has been unable to resist *absorption* into the myth of power, whatever the outcome of their political opposition. Dependency theorists who re-write the story of Europe as 'developer' into the story of Europe as 'exploiter' remain caught in the binary of Europe and its others. The subject of the new history is still Europe. Ironically, the concept of 'difference' itself may often be unable to extricate itself from this binary and thus become disabling to the post-colonial subject.

Intellectuals who set so much store by independence in the post-war dissolution of the British Empire were uniformly doomed to disappointment. National élites simply moved in to fill the vacuum. In most cases 'resistance' has meant nothing less than a *failure to resist* the binary structures of colonial discourse. But a difference which resists domination through the transformative capacity of the imagination is one which, ultimately, moves beyond these structures. The importance of transformation should not be regarded as diminishing the struggle for political freedom and self-determination, or refuting the active 'resistance' to imperial power. Nor should it be regarded as contrary to the spirit of insurgence. Rather it demonstrates the fascinating capacity of ordinary people, living below the level of formal policy or active rebellion, to foment change in their cultural existence. It is this change which makes active resistance meaningful.

The fixation upon the defensive interpretation of resistance stems from a tendency to homogenize the colonial experience. D. A. Masolo makes the point that, while a family might live under the tyranny of an authoritarian figure, the experiences of that relationship by both parents and children, depending on their age, gender and social role, could be entirely different from each other. Similarly, people could give entirely different interpretations of historical episodes based on how they want to identify themselves. 'They could take a group stand for political or moral reasons on a matter of which they themselves might never have had a direct experience or from which they might have in fact benefited' (Eze 1997: 284). While Masolo uses this example to demonstrate the difficulty of defining 'the postcolonial', we may also use it to indicate the absurdity of locking post-colonial experience into a simple opposition to colonialism.

The emancipatory drive of post-colonial discourse, the drive to re-empower the disenfranchised, is too often conceived in terms of a simplistic view of colonization, of post-colonial response, and of post-colonial identities. The consequent exhortatory tone of decolonizing theory runs the risk of theorizing how the world should be rather than how the world *is* in the ordinary actions of individuals. Horkheimer and Adorno argue, somewhat crankily, that classical Marxism had falsely imputed truly emancipatory potential to the proletariat, having failed to understand the social reality of the very people who were its object (1975). But in fact, the example of ordinary people in colonized societies reveals that the proletariat operates constantly in a dialectical and transformative mode. It might not be the emancipatory potential of organized ideological resistance as Marx perceived it, and it certainly doesn't include everybody. But transformation is a dominant mode in the post-colonial response to those colonizing forces which appear constantly to suppress and control. Recognizing this fact is all the more urgent given the complete failure of Marxist programmes of 'liberation' in post-colonial states in Africa and elsewhere.

The activity of transformation gives us a different way of looking at what Bhabha calls the ambivalence of colonial discourse. For rather than a kind of flaw in the operation of colonial discourse, a self-defeating need to produce in the colonized subject an imitation which must fail, because it can never be an exact copy, ambivalence may be regarded as a much more active feature of post-colonial subjectivity. It may be seen to be the *ambivalent* or 'two-powered' sign of the capacity of the colonized to 'imitate' transformatively, to take the image of the colonial model and use it in the process of resistance, the process of self-empowerment. Ambivalence is not merely the sign of the failure of colonial discourse to make the colonial subject conform, it is the sign of the agency of the colonized – the two-way gaze, the dual orientation, the ability to appropriate colonial technology without being absorbed by it – which disrupts the monologic impetus of the colonizing process.

Fundamentally, transformation is based on *sui generis* conceptions of modernity which evade the culture of 'development', which is, more or less, a simple euphemism for Westernization. While the term 'development' came into the English language in the eighteenth century conveying a sense of unfolding over time, 'development', understood as a preoccupation of public and international policy to improve welfare and to produce governable subjects, is of much more recent provenance (Watts 1993b). It is generally recognized that, because of their deep Eurocentrism and dismissal of the colonized world as 'lacking', Western development models have all but completely collapsed. However, constructing new conceptions of modernity represents, in global terms, the most far-reaching and enterprising goal of post-colonial transformation. Modernity is itself the expansive and persuasive signifier of the dominance of Western culture since the Renaissance. Yet new conceptions of modernity lie at the heart of the process of transformation itself, for the modern can be 'used' and 'resisted' at the same time. Strategies and techniques may be used without necessarily incurring the wholesale absorption into the *culture* of Western modernity. As Sri Aurobindo puts it, 'we must hold the past sacred, but the future even more so' (cited in Verhelst 1987: 62).

There is perhaps no more striking demonstration of the link between resistance and transformation than the culture which developed in the Caribbean. African slaves were unable to transport their culture with them to the plantations in any coherent way. Members of different language groups were placed together on plantations either through the exigencies of the system or to prevent conspiracy. The resulting heterogeneity limited what could be shared culturally. Yet Afro-American cultures took on a form generated from this heterogeneity, a dynamism adapted to the physical and social conditions with which they had to deal. In this process, both the various slave and non-slave populations absorbed aspects of the various African heritages. What developed was a culture of such creative adaptation that its trans-formative capacities were able to resist absorption into the dominant culture.

Ralph Ellison puts this situation very convincingly, in regard to music:

Slavery was a vicious system, and those who endured it tough people, but it was *not* (and this is important for Negroes to remember for the sake of their own sense of who and what their grandparents were) a state of absolute repression.

A slave was, to the extent that he was a *musician*, one who expressed himself in music, a man who realized himself in the world of sound. Thus, while he might stand in awe before the superior technical ability of a white musician, and while he was forced to recognize a superior social status, he would never feel awed before the music which the technique of the white musician made available. His attitude as a 'musician' would lead him to possess the music expressed through the technique, but until he could do so he would hum, whistle, sing or play the tunes to the best of his ability on any available instrument. And it was, indeed, out of the tension between desire and ability that jazz emerged . . .

. . . Negroes have taken, with the ruthlessness of those without articulate investments in cultural styles, whatever they could of European music, making of it that which would, when blended with the cultural tendencies inherited from Africa, express their own sense of life – while rejecting the rest.

(1964: 247–9)

This description of black music is true for every act of cultural engagement between a colonized person and the range of apparently awesome cultural technologies with which he or she is faced. Every one of those technologies is open to appropriation and transformation, whether in technique, location of use, social utility or cultural significance. Yet one gets a clear sense, from Ellison's description, of the integrity, the agency, the *resistance* involved in the process by which colonial subjects take hold of any imperial technology, and make it work for them. The consequences of the 'transformative resistance' of black music throughout the world have been strikingly obvious. It is a prominent example of what we mean by the term 'transcultural'. Indeed, if we think carefully, it is impossible to talk sensibly about culture without invoking this concept of transculturation, of a 'contact-zone' between cultures. Individual cultures are never cocooned from the dynamic flow of cultural interchange. 'Culture has "life"', says Mintz,

> because its content serves as resources for those who employ it, change it, incarnate it. Human beings cope with the demands of everyday life through their interpretative and innovative skills,

and their capacity for employing symbolism – not by ossifying their behavioral forms, but by using them creatively.

(1974: 19)

If we believed that African culture had been 'polluted' by its contact with other cultures in the Caribbean, for instance, we might be inclined to advocate, as many have, the rejection of all polluting influences of imperialism, capitalism and modernity. However, we would more than likely discover that that 'original purity' included forms no longer practised in Africa. The purity of a transported African culture lies in the certainty of its ability to absorb and reform both itself and the apparently dominant influences working upon it. Salman Rushdie puts the case much more provocatively when he asks:

> do cultures actually exist as separate, pure defensible entities? Is not mélange, adulteration, impurity, pick 'n' mix at the heart of the idea of the modern, and hasn't it been that way for almost all this shook-up century? Doesn't the idea of pure cultures, in urgent need of being kept free from alien contamination, lead us inexorably towards apartheid, towards ethnic cleansing, towards the gas chamber?

(1999: 21)

Indisputably the very illusory nature of this intensely desired state of purity underlies much of the disillusion of post-colonial resistance writers.

The critical problem with most concepts of 'resistance' in African literature is that decolonization was never initiated with a coherent agenda. Colonial structures and administration handed over to indigenous élites were unfit for any further use. This is not only sobering but extremely important in any discussion of the concept of 'resistance'. Neil Lazarus suggests that the expectations of independence 'were unrealistic from the very beginning, even as they were first being articulated' (1990: 23). We cannot make sense of post-independence literature in Africa unless we understand the depth and fervour of the initial expectations of independence among intellectuals. 'In spite of the positive rhetoric of anticolonialism, and the bitter lamentations of dismayed intellectuals in the independence era, the decolonizing process was not a revolutionary one' (23). Speaking from a Marxist perspective, Lazarus sees this as a crippling failure. But the failure is not so much a collapse of the will, or a betrayal of revolutionary values, as a failure inherent in the simple binary stereotype of resistance.

Consequently, those novels such as Armah's *The Beautyful Ones Are Not Yet Born* (1968), *Fragments* (1970) and *Why Are We So Blest* (1972), which have been characterized as 'disillusioned' because they focus on the failures of independence to deliver freedom, are, according to Lazarus, very much 'illusioned', because 'their preoccupation with subjects of betrayal, blindness, corruption, and decadence was rooted in expectations that right from the start had been drastically inflated' (23–4). If 'resistance' amounts to a massive miscalculation, in a decolonizing Africa, of the political reality, the state of the revolutionary consciousness of the people and the difference between independence and national liberation, then 'resistance' literature must share this failure. However, it is difficult to see how literature could have avoided the ambiguities and contradictions of decolonizing rhetoric.

The experience of a decolonizing Africa disrupts our understanding of 'resistance' itself. What exactly is resistance resisting if it cannot adequately conceive the nature of its object? On 6 March 1957, when Ghana achieved its independence from Britain, Kwame Nkrumah gave a speech which is not only historic but emblematic of the assumptions and the conflation of hope with actuality that accompanied decolonization.

> At long last the battle has ended! And thus Ghana, your beloved country, is free for ever. And here again, I want to take the opportunity to thank the chiefs and people of this country, the youth, the farmers, the women, who have so nobly fought and won this battle. Also I want to thank the valiant ex-servicemen who have so co-operated with me in this mighty task of freeing our country from foreign rule and imperialism! . . . from now on we are no more a colonial but a free and independent people.
>
> (1962: 106–7)

The ceremonies which accompanied independence were important for all African countries. As Lazarus puts it: 'The ceremony allowed the newly independent to reimagine their past in a meaningful way, to reconceive the defeats they had borne as positive events. The notion of defeat could give way to the notion of conflict; and conflict, in turn, was a notion that spoke of resistance' (1990: 2). This is an astute perception. The *idea* of conflict itself invokes resistance. Thus Nkrumah's speech begins with the assumption that there had been a battle, and not only that, but it was a battle which had been won *by everybody!* Furthermore, the winning of the battle, the end product of resistance, was another elusive commodity – 'freedom', *simply because there has been a battle!* The speech excluded nobody, and the victory invoked by Nkrumah belonged to all people. 'In retrospect,' comments Lazarus, 'there was surely something ominous about Nkrumah's Independence Day evocation of "chiefs" and "people," "farmers" and "ex-servicemen," which was so embracingly inclusive that it tended to reconstruct even active collaboration with colonialism as a form of anticolonial resistance!' (1990: 5). The speech demonstrates how in even the most triumphant and ebullient moments of liberation the temptation to reconstruct a force/counterforce binary almost inevitably diffuses the meaning of resistance. This was not just an accident, for abstraction was actively sought as a preventative to factionalism, with the consequence of its reduction to a rhetorical oppositionality.

> The general rhetoric of anticolonialism was reductive. It implied that there was only one struggle to be waged, and it was a negative one: a struggle *against* colonialism, not a struggle *for* anything specific . . . The register of anticolonialism actively sought abstraction, desiring above all to remain free of ideological factionalism.
>
> (5)

Whatever the failures or disillusionment of resistance movements, the transcultural effects of colonization, the changes brought about in the imperial culture, were profound. It is rarely noticed that these transcultural effects had, by the eve of the First World War, made the unprecedented dominance of Western culture quite insecure. At the very time when European expansion was approaching its climax, the foundations of Western European civilization had been broken up by an elemental inward change brought about by industrialization and democracy, and external pressures from those societies it had colonized. At the point of its zenith Europe was no longer a centre whose power radiated outwards but a centre on which the forces of the non-European world converged. This was a transformative effect brought about regardless of the nature or intensity of resistance movements in postcolonial societies. Arguably, it was this effect which paved the way for the national independence movements which gained such success after the Second World War. This is not to underplay the significance of those resistance movements but to suggest that the effects of transcultural change (along with the economic exhaustion of Europe) may have been the basis upon which their success was assured.

## Situating literary resistance

According to Barbara Harlow (1987: 2), 'resistance' (*muqāwamah*) was first applied in a description of Palestinian literature in 1966 by the Palestinian writer and critic Ghassan Kanafani. For Kanafani, resistance literature invoked a distinction between an 'occupied' people and a people in exile. Such literature was seen to be an identifiable, and significant, accompaniment to the project of political, military and social striving for national liberation. The writer gets himself into an impasse, however, when he claims that no research into such literatures 'can be complete unless the researcher is located within the resistance movement itself inside the occupied land' (Harlow 1987: 3). This invocation of critical exclusivity and insider knowledge is familiar in post-colonial criticism, and raises similar questions about the capacity of the literature itself to communicate 'outside the occupied land'. For whom and to whom, we might ask, does any writer write? However, for such writers, and for Harlow herself, resistance literature is an identifiable accompaniment to the activities of resistance *movements*.

For Selwyn Cudjoe, in *Resistance and Caribbean Literature*, resistance is 'an act or complex of acts designed to rid a people of its oppressors, be they slave masters or multi-national corporations' (1980: 19). It is something which so thoroughly infuses the experience of living under oppression that it becomes an almost autonomous 'aesthetic-political' principle. Literary resistance, for Cudjoe, is a category of literary writing which emerges as an integral part of an organized struggle for national liberation. As such its standard of value is entirely measured in terms of its social and political utility. He quotes Fidel Casto approvingly:

> Our evaluation is political. There can be no esthetic value where the human content is absent. There can be no esthetic value in opposition to man. Esthetic value cannot exist in opposition to justice, in opposition to the welfare or in opposition to the happiness of man. It cannot exist!
>
> (56)

The direct political function of resistance literature is emphasized by African poets such as Agostinho Neto, 'Angola's greatest poet and first president', or Marcelino do Santos, the president of Mozambique and 'one of Mozambique's finest poets' (Cudjoe 1980: 58). The concept of resistance literature arises from the central role of cultural expression in political struggle. Amilcar Cabral states that:

The study of the history of national liberation struggles shows that generally those struggles are preceded by an increase in expression of culture, consolidated progressively into a successful or unsuccessful attempt to affirm the cultural personality of the dominated people, as a means of negating the oppressor culture.

(1973: 69)

For Cudjoe the relationship between literature and political struggle is much more specific, direct and functional: 'In literature, caught up in the struggle, words must be like bullets: sharp, straight-shooting and to the mark. To miss is literally to lose one's life in the process. With the crushing urgency of the revolution, literature becomes functional in that it has a very real task to perform' (Cudjoe 1980: 64). According to this description, resistance literature, and hence resistance *in* literature, must inevitably accompany the broader programme of political resistance, because it has a specific material function. Although it is clearly politically focused, it becomes a historically circumscribed, and an imaginatively limited, aesthetic principle since it cannot account for the kind of subtle 'resistance' which may continue after the gaining of independence, that cultural resistance which is not accompanied by any clear political agenda.

This conflict between the imaginative and the didactic power of resistance literature, and the question of the authenticity of its cultural basis, re-emerges wherever this issue of resistance is broached. Cabral sees more potential for development in the form, when he says that at 'any moment, depending on internal and external factors determining the evolution of the society in question, cultural resistance (indestructible) may take on new forms (political, economic, military) in order to fully contest foreign domination' (1973: 40). Yet this indestructible cultural resistance is apparently unable to take on new forms of expression even when circumstances change. According to Cabral the masses are those who retain the culture of the people, remaining untouched by the culture of the colonizer, a view which might find some difficulty with Caribbean people's culture, a fluidly syncretistic African-based form which absorbed influences from many sources.

The conceptual problems which complicate the potential of resistance literature (and resistance *in* literature) to develop and transform itself, stem entirely from the defensively oppositional agenda in which notions of resistance find themselves. Such an agenda inevitably privileges a construction of culture, that is, the culture of the 'masses', as 'pure', as distinct from what Cudjoe calls the 'cultural renaissance' undertaken by intellectual élites (1980: 67), who somehow find themselves stranded between the cultures of the colonized and colonizers. This binary view of colonization and resistance is by no means uncommon yet its problems are obvious: only the masses are colonized and only the masses have a pure culture which can contest the culture of the colonizers. The desperate need to claim authenticity leads to contradictory and illogical assumptions about the nature of cultural production itself.

Paradoxically, this idea that the intelligentsia may be somehow 'uncolonized' and exist *between* the colonizers and the colonized replicates Lord Macaulay's proposal in his 1835 Minute to Parliament that the riches of English learning should be imparted by 'a class of interpreters between us and the millions whom we govern – a class of persons Indian in blood and colour, but English in tastes, opinions, in morals and in intellect' (Macaulay 1835). Yet when we view the role of English-educated intellectuals in the eventual achievement of independence, we begin to understand how deeply intertwined complicity and resistance can be. Furthermore, if 'cultural purity' is class-based, how do the cultures of the different classes avoid influencing each other? One only needs to observe the extent of the consumption of global popular culture by the 'masses' to see how threadbare the claim to cultural purity becomes. If we consider the contemporary vernacular film industry in India, for instance, we see very clearly how a demand for indigenous self-expression, although by no means obviously 'resistant', can appropriate and transform a global technology.

Constricting though it may be, the tight linkage between resistance literature and national liberation gives the genre clear boundaries. But we might ask, in that case: How does literary 'resistance' operate in the absence of organized struggle? What, exactly, constitutes 'literary' resistance? What is the relationship between figurative language and the intention to resist? How 'real' must resistance literature be? The strangely untheorized yet ubiquitous use of the term means that it fails to address three critical problems: the extent to which centre/periphery notions of resistance can actually work to *re-inscribe* centre/periphery relations, trapping resistance in the binary established by imperial discourse; the question of exactly how resistance can be said to exist within the text; and the problem raised by Foucault that power itself inscribes its resistances, and thus seeks to contain them (Slemon 1990: 37). The concept of literary resistance, because it is absorbed into a general typology of political acts, assumes a transparent sender–receiver theory of communication, while completely disregarding the function of reading in the resistance process. But as Chambers has indicated in *Room for Maneuver: Reading (the) Oppositional (in) Narrative* (1991), reading is an important, and fruitful, aspect of the resistance process. The consumption of culture can be so tied up with its pro-duction and reproduction that it becomes a transformative species of resistance.

The tendency to typify resistance as an act of militant opposition obscures the actual complexity, and sometimes the ambivalence, within which resistance is situated. Jenny Sharpe's demonstration of the difficulty in situating resistance is a good example. She discovered, in the India Office Library in London, the draft of a letter from a British judicial officer, F. J. Shore, describing an imaginary dialogue between two Bengalis – purportedly written by Rammohun Roy, a well-known proponent of Western education – in which Baboo Must Hathee explains to his friend, Baboo Dana, why the English would benefit from learning Bengali. This conversation, which parodies Macaulay's famous 1835 Minute on Indian Education propounding the benefits of learning English, seems to contradict Rammohun Roy's public position on the learning of English. It is a subversive mimicry of Macaulay's imperialist position which appears to signify a secret, and perhaps wide-spread, resistance to English domination.

The initial triumph with which Sharpe discovered this letter was quelled somewhat by the reminder that 'the binary opposition between colonizer and colonized is not so easily reversed; the entire power struc-ture of colonialism itself stands in the way of such an improbable exchange' (1989: 146). She concluded that it was more likely that Shore himself invented the dialogue as evidence of a native desire for vernacular education. We might see this as the extension, in a different guise, of the patronizing power of the colonial administrator. But, on the other hand, it is a fascinating demonstration of the difficulty in situating resistance. For if the letter did not emanate from a 'native' it nevertheless transcribes the reality of native desire. 'Do we identify, as the native response,' asks Sharpe, 'Rammohun's actual demand for English education or his alleged demand for a vernacular one? This double demand reveals Rammohun Roy as a contested site that cuts across the binary opposition of colonizer and colonized' (147).

There is nothing ambivalent, of course, about the cotton weavers who starved to death because of the importation of cheaper English cloth, or about the poverty induced by the economic system generated by imperialism, or about the many who died in military reprisals. We also encounter the endemic problem that the 'resistance' we find in this document may be, in any case, the province of an élite. But the difficulty in *situating* resistance also introduces the difficulty in *typifying* resistance as a transparent act of opposition. This is particularly true for acts of 'literary resistance'. Stephen Slemon's conclusion is that 'a *theory* of literary resistance *must* recognize the inescapable partiality, the incompleteness, the untranscendable *ambiguity* of literary or indeed *any* contra/dictory or contestatory act which employs a First World medium for the figuration of a Third-World resistance' (1990: 38). A 'spectacular' conclusion to this inevitable ambiguity, reached by Timothy Brennan in his book *Salman Rushdie and the Third World*, is that 'the Third World resistance writer, the Third World resistance text, is necessarily self-produced as a doubly emplaced and *mediated* figure' (Brennan 1989: 38). It is only when this mediation is embraced rather than furtively obscured that the transformative potential of resistance may be realized.

If resistance is *never* a simple and transparent polarity, if textual resistance is necessarily a mediated act, then our notion of what resistance actually means, what it entails, what kind of act it implicates, must undergo a radical readjustment. We may extend this to include any kind of 'textual' resistance which appropriates a First World medium, such as the astonishing phenomenon of Indian cinema. If resistance is sometimes ambivalently situated, it is also open to a wide horizon of possible forms, forms which often look very different from resistance but which stem from the desire for indigenous self-empowerment. While we may have difficulty viewing the stereotyped, parodic and repetitious action and characters of Indian cinema as 'resistance', we might consider the extent to which Hollywood is being 'resisted' in this astonishingly popular mass-produced South Asian commodity. Whereas the lack of a programme seems fatal to a national liberation struggle, unprogrammed change is the very heart of that form of resistance which is realized in cultural transformation.

## Counter-discourse

The effectiveness of a resistance which operates transformatively is demonstrated very well by the term 'counter-discourse' coined by Richard Terdiman in 1985. Although Terdiman was talking about symbolic resistance in nineteenth-century France, the term has been eagerly embraced by post-colonial critics such as Slemon (1988) and Tiffin (1988). The concept of *counter*-discourse seems confusing at first. Discourse, in Foucault's formulation, intimates a system of social knowledge with well-bounded rules of inclusion and exclusion: one is either in a discourse or not; one either adheres to it or not, in which case one might subscribe to an *opposing* discourse. But no discourse is seamless and totalitarian, no discourse is immune to doubt and reflexivity, and the fractures which open up within it allow for forms of resistance which operate *within* discourse, on many of its own terms. A discourse such as imperial discourse may be so pervasive and embracing in post-colonial life that the notion of any discourse beyond it seems remote. A powerful Eurocentric discourse such as literature represents itself as 'natural', universal and timeless, and yet it exposes itself, by virtue of such claims, to continual resistance and contradiction.

This is particularly clear in the form of counter-discourse called 'canonical counter-discourse' or 'writing back', which operates within the discourse of literature itself. Canonical literary texts are 'consumed' in such a way that they become the basis for resistant, appropriated versions which subtly subvert the values and political assumptions of the originals. The significance of the texts that are re-read is that they offer powerful allegories of European culture, allegories through which life in post-colonial societies has itself been 'written'. One of the most protean of these texts is *The Tempest*, in which the relationships between Prospero and Caliban and Prospero and Miranda can be seen to provide endlessly adaptable models for the relationship between empire and settlers, or between colonizers and indigenous inhabitants. Contemporaneous reproductions and re-readings such as Aimé Césaire's *Une Tempête: d'après 'La Tempête' de Shakespeare – Adaptation pour une théâtre nègre* in 1969 and George Lamming's discussion of the play from the point of view of Caliban in *The Pleasures of Exile* in 1960 show how intertwined consumption and production can be, a relationship that is best described by the concept: resistance *as* transformation.

Re-writings of *Robinson Crusoe* which illuminate both the relationship between Crusoe and Friday and the mercantile ethic enacted in Crusoe's civilization of the island; re-writings and re-readings of Jane Austen which focus on the dependency of English gentility upon the colonial plantation economy; re-writings of *Heart of Darkness* which expose the deep-seated cultural and geographical assumptions of Western exploration: all present themselves as fundamentally *resistant* texts. Yet theirs is a resistance which is explicitly transformative. For they do not simply respond to the canonical texts but attempt to re-write them in such a way that their overweening cultural assumptions become exposed and subverted. In this way they 'establish an oppositional, disidentificatory voice within the sovereign domain of the discourse of colonialism' (Slemon 1988: 13). Because of its function within the dominant discourse, canonical counter-discourse is a very clear demonstration of the link between resistance and transformation. For although the intertextuality of the canonical texts is crucial, it is no longer their centrality or 'greatness' which dominates, no longer their revelation of the 'universal human condition', but the newly revealed cultural horizons of their hybrid and transformative 'counters'.

The importance of counter-discourse to post-colonial literatures can be seen from the contemporary beginnings of the African novel in English when, in 1958, Chinua Achebe 'wrote back' to Conrad's *Heart of Darkness* in his *Things Fall Apart*. This is a classic to which critics keep returning, and for good reason. The temptation for Achebe simply to reverse Conrad's view of the incomprehensible frenzy of prehistoric man (1902: 68) must have been almost overwhelming. The colonialist's view of Africans as a dehumanized otherness, 'a whirl of black limbs, a mass of hands clapping, of feet stamping, of bodies swaying, of eyes rolling, under the droop of heavy and motionless foliage' (68) seems to have been designed to provoke the African writer into a reversal of the imperial binary, to reinstall the 'good' African culture in opposition to the 'evil' colonizer. But it is the very subtlety of Achebe's description, his presentation of Okonkwo as a deeply flawed and complex man, his exposure of Umuofian society as one which had its own share of ethical dilemmas, which underlies the transformative power of *Things Fall Apart*. It rejects Marlow's stereotyping by confirming the complexity, humanity and even ambivalence of African culture. Achebe's novel cannot be said to be 'resistance literature' in the accepted sense of the term. But its success in entering the discourse of English literature, appropriating a foreign language, taking a dominant tool of imperial representation – the novel form – and providing a creative ethnography of such immediacy that English-speaking readers could feel as though they were standing inside the village, became a model for post-colonial writings ever after.

The crucial feature of counter-discourse is, despite its name, an avoidance of the simple reversal of the imperial binary of civilized and savage. In his brilliant *Season of Migration to the North* (1969), a re-writing of *Heart of Darkness*, Tayeb Salih insists upon problematizing racial and cultural binaries. The narrator recalls that, when he was asked by his fellow villagers, upon his return from Europe, what Europeans were like, they were surprised 'when I told them that Europeans were, with minor differences, exactly like them, marrying and bringing up their children in accordance with principles and traditions, that they had good morals and were in general good people' (1969: 3). As with Achebe's work, the local society is revealed as one with its own moral and ethical dilemmas, its treatment of women symbolizing, in at least one horrific instance, the obsession of colonial desire. It is this refusal to be drawn into the imperial binary which acts as the most effective form of transformative energy in these texts. The *resistance* of counter-discursivity, as it returns the 'gaze' of the imperial text, is fully effective only when it transforms our view of cultural possibilities, even though its exposure of the 'darkness' of colonial power may be trenchant and relentless.

## Resistance and subjectivity

Despite the evidence of such transformative engagements, the dominant note of resistance rhetoric is one of rejection and separation. The intervention of writers such as Amilcar Cabral and Selwyn Cudjoe seems to base itself in the assumption that imperial power is a top-down imposition, a contamination of cultural purity and authentic identity which can be resisted only by cultural and political rejection, by avoidance, by 'returning to the source' as Cabral suggests (1973). It says nothing about the myriad ways of responding to colonial power, ways of engaging colonial discourse which may more subtly resist its hegemonic control. It says nothing about the effect those responses themselves may have on the colonizing culture.

The implication of such a view of resistance is that colonial discourse is so all-powerful in its effect on the colonial subject that it must be avoided at all costs. Such a view might find support in postmodern definitions of subjectivity which see the subject 'interpellated' by ideology, constructed by discourse or language, a site for the operation of power, in other words, a subject for whom acts of 'free' will are already determined to some degree by the context of the action. But the discovery of what colonized people actually do in their encounter with colonial discourse leads us to a very different theory of subjectivity than we find in post-structuralism. We do not need to claim that colonial subjects are entirely autonomous to show that in the material aspects of their lives they make choices, employ strategies of self-formation and production, sometimes of remarkable subtlety, which characterize them as agents who are capable of 'resisting' cultural power even when that resistance is not channelled into any organized political programme.

The question of subjectivity lies at the heart of any exploration of political and cultural resistance, and the postmodern rejection of Enlightenment notions of selfhood is a particularly significant issue for colonial subjects. The development of influential theories of subject construction by ideology, discourse and language in the work of Althusser, Foucault and Lacan seems to provide very effective models for the construction of colonial subjects by a dominant imperial culture. But their practical weaknesses, which stem from a difficulty in accounting for the subject's ability to act as an agent, to contravene the subject-forming power, become exposed by the experience of colonized people. This remains the continuing tension surrounding all discussion of human subjectivity, for while theories of the ways in which human subjectivity is 'constructed' are formidable and persuasive, they have difficulty accounting for the apparent recalcitrance of such subjects in taking action which seems to confirm their liberatory power, their capacity to act as agents.

When we examine the major theories of subject formation we see why they appear to offer such attractive models for the operation of colonial power. For Althusser, ideology is not just a case of the powerful imposing their ideas on the weak, as Marxian ideas of 'false consciousness' would suggest; subjects are 'born into' ideology, they find subjectivity within the expectations of their parents and their society, and they endorse it because it provides a sense of identity and social meaning through structures such as language, social codes and conventions. Ideology is perpetuated, according to Althusser, by ideological state apparatuses such as church, education, police, which interpellate subjects, providing the conditions by which, and the contexts in which, they obtain subjectivity. This process of interpellation has seemed particularly useful for analysing the operation of imperial power upon individual colonised subjects. Imperialism has been supremely effective in disseminating cultural technologies which 'call forth' subjects in a particular way. Phillip Holden (1998) gives a good example of this in the example of the Cambridge Certificate English Composition exam undertaken by Singaporean students early in the twentieth century:

> Correct the following sentences, giving reasons for the alterations which you make:
> Japan has one of the best armies and natives in the world.
> Neither team on the cup, and probably did not do themselves justice.
> Hannibal devoted himself to the ruin of Rome, and it is well within the bounds of possibility that he would have done so, if he had received proper reinforcements.
> The Maoris are of copper-brown colour, and not black like the ordinary negro is.
> (English Composition, 12 Dec. 1906)

What appears to be a simple test of English expression is also a searching test of the student's possession of a cultural grammar, one that forms little part of the formal syllabus but which interpellates 'an imperial subject', one 'who is concerned about the projection of imperial power and historical precedents, and who subscribes both to a hierarchy of races and to a code of late-Victorian manliness encouraged by team games' (Holden 1998: 13).

This capacity to interpellate imperial subjects, to inculcate a particular view of the world, a particular morality, a range of aesthetic, ethical, political and social values in the colonized, is a very good demonstration of hegemony. The explicit interpellation of the student in the English Composition test is magnified many times over when such students study English literature. The range of cultural allusions and references, the assumptions and knowledge invoked in the putatively 'universal' study of literature interpellates students, very deeply and subtly, into a colonial subjectivity. In Gauri Viswanathan's explanation of the invention of English literature for the civilizing mission in India, she points out:

> The strategy of locating authority in these texts all but effaced the sordid history of colonialist expropriation, material exploitation, and class and race oppression behind European world dominance . . . the English literary text functioned as a surrogate Englishman in his highest and most perfect state.
>
> (1987: 23)

This Englishman was at the same time the embodiment of universal human values. This strategy proved a particularly effective one because the discourse of English literature was disseminated with its attendant spiritual values, cultural assumptions, social discriminations, racial prejudices and humanistic values more or less intact.

Although Viswanathan talks later in *Masks of Conquest* about how individual Indians resisted such cultural dominance, her exploration of the hegemonic power of English literature has seemed, to many, to reveal a fundamental problem in all studies of colonial discourse. The analysis of its capacity to form imperial subjects generally leaves little room for discussion of the ways in which such discourse was engaged. Because of its influential nature Viswanathan's thesis has become a pivotal point of contention over the implied passivity of colonial subjects. Since its publication, 'a greater stress on the material practices of colonial communities' (Holden 1998: 4) has led to a closer questioning of colonial discourse theory. As Leela Gandhi puts it, while 'accounts of colonial pedagogy are consistently sensitive to the intentions of colonial administrators, they remain oblivious to the complex and complicating reception of the English text in the colonial world' (1998:

155). Much more attention needs to be paid to the *consumption* of colonial discourse, consumption which very often contradicted the intentions of administrators. 'Rather than being the passive objects of an authoritarian and alien pedagogy,' says Gandhi, 'Indian readers remained obdurately selective in their response to the English syllabus' (155). Cultural consumption reveals itself to be much more than the ingestion of a programme of indoctrination: it invariably emerged as a particular kind of *use*. Acts of consumption and redirection have represented some of the most subtle forms of 'resistance' in colonial life.

Perhaps the best example of the use of colonial discourse theory is Said's theory of Orientalism. According to Said, the knowledge and reality created by the various Orientalist disciplines produce a discourse, 'whose material presence or weight, not the originality of a given author, is really responsible for the texts produced out of it' (1978: 94). By means of this discourse, Said argues, Western cultural institutions are responsible for the creation of those 'others', the Orientals, whose very difference from the Occident helps establish that binary opposition by which Europe's own identity and cultural dominance can be shaped. The underpinning of such a demarcation is a line between the Orient and the Occident which is 'less a fact of nature than it is a fact of human production' (Said 1985: 2). Although Said's use of Foucault was determinedly partial and opportunistic, the criticisms levelled at his formulation are similar to those that might be directed at an Althusserian theory of the interpellation: the analysis all seems to be directed in one way. There is no analysis of the self-perception of the 'Oriental', no analysis of the fragmentary and contradictory nature nor of the 'resistibility' of imperial ideology, and little perception of how the subject might engage its dominance.

When we consider the Lacanian theory of the subject formed within language, we discover a powerful model for the operation of an imperial language. Lacan's view that the unconscious is structured like a language, and that the subject itself is produced through language in the same way that language produces meaning, has proved extremely attractive to those pondering the formation of the *colonial* subject. Though the subject may speak, he or she does so only in terms which the laws of language allow. In particular, the final phase through which the subject is developed, the Symbolic phase, in which the subject enters the Symbolic order, learns language, discovers that the locus of power is now located in the 'phallus', discovers the Law of the Father and obtains an understanding of gender, is most useful as a metaphor of the subject's 'entry' into imperial language.

If we were to follow Lacan's model strictly we might say that on entering the symbolic order of imperial language the colonial subject is both *produced* in language and *subjected* to the laws of the symbolic which pre-exist it. The laws of language are themselves metonymic of the cultural complex of laws and rules and conventions into which the subject moves and obtains identity. Of course, this model is only metaphoric, because the colonized subject has usually already learned a language when he or she enters the 'symbolic order' of imperial language. But when we consider the pedagogic formation of the colonized child in attending colonial schools and learning the colonial language, we see a process in which hegemony, ideology, interpellation and language all come together in a powerful instance of subject formation. Ngugi's famous experience of colonial language policy stands as a representative case:

> one of the most humiliating experiences was to be caught speaking Gikuyu in the vicinity of the school. The culprit was given corporal punishment – three to five strokes of the cane on bare buttocks – or was made to carry a metal plate around the neck with inscriptions such as I AM STUPID or I AM A DONKEY . . .
> The attitude to English was the exact opposite: any achievement in spoken or written English was highly rewarded; prizes, prestige, applause; the ticket to higher realms. English became the measure of intelligence and ability in the arts, the sciences, and all the other branches of learning. English became the main determinant of a child's progress up the ladder of formal education.
>
> (Ngugi 1981: 11–12)

Ngugi's purpose is to draw attention to the political ramifications of using a colonial language. However there is a constant slippage between this political position, which confirms the ability of the individual speaker to make choices, and a position which sees the speaker as unable to avoid the view of the world the language seems to present. To assume that the colonial language inculcates the subject, incontrovertibly, into a way of seeing the world, is to accept, by implication, a theory of the construction of the subject as passive. This occurs when Ngugi claims of colonized African societies that 'it was language which held captive their cultures, their values and hence their minds' (32). To assume that the speaker of a colonial language has a 'colonized mind' is to accept a theory of the subject as agentless.

Indisputably, language is grounded in a particular cultural reality. It provides the terms by which reality may be constituted, it provides the names by which the world may be 'known'. Its system of values, representations and discriminations becomes the system upon which social, economic and political discourse is grounded. But whether these are incontestable acquisitions made by, or forced on, the colonial language learner, whether the language learner can make cultural distinctions between languages, is the real question at the heart of the considerable dispute over the efficacy of writing in English. To claim that language can hold the minds of the colonized captive, as Ngugi does when he exhorts the 'decolonisation of the mind' (1981a), is to deny the very capacity for resistance that his own writing invokes. Yet, when we see the considerable cultural ethnography that a writer in English can produce, we see that the writing subject can be used as an ideal model for the subject's engagement with a dominant discourse.

The importance of language in identity construction occurs at both the personal and cultural levels, and its prominence in post-colonial writing gives us a particular insight into the dialectical nature of subjectivity. For if the subject is produced by ideology, discourse or language, is it trapped in this subjectivity beyond the power of choice, recognition or resistance? Fanon refers to the interpellating power of colonialism in its fight 'to maintain the identity of the image it has of the Algerian and the depreciated image that the Algerian has of himself' (Fanon 1961: 30). But in the conclusion to *Black Skin, White Masks* he rhetorically proclaims an almost Cartesian agency for the colonized subject: 'I am my own foundation. And it is by going beyond the historical, instrumental hypothesis that I will initiate the cycle of my freedom' (1952: 231). Yet how this declaration of independence is to be effected forms the basis of the most intransigent argument in post-colonial politics. The 'historical, instrumental hypothesis' is the representation of the dominated by the dominant. How does the colonized subject 'go beyond' that representation? Is it by rejecting the dominant discourse or by appropriating it that the 'cycle of freedom' may be initiated?

## Cultural capital: the consumption of colonial discourse

The alternative to a passive subject unable to escape the formative pressures of imperial ideology is a subject who consumes the dominant culture in a strategy of self-fashioning and self-representation. The active engagement of the subject with a powerful ideology such as imperialism, which 'calls forth' imperial subjects, can be seen in the subject's use of the imperial language, which, in different situations all over the world, provides the means for the organization of resistance.

Far from operating as the agent of oppression as it does for Ngugi, the colonial language has invariably made collective action possible. But such activity occurs also in the colonial subject's *consumption* of colonial discourse. The very ground of the transformative work of cultural representation is the appropriation (or 'consumption') of the colonial discourse of literature, historical narrative, a global system of book publishing and distribution and, in a sense, a global readership.

The term 'cultural capital' may prove useful in understanding the subtleties and the resistance function of such consumption. In their analysis of pedagogic communication, *Reproduction in Education, Society and Culture* (1977), Bourdieu and Passeron made the discovery that students' achievement was a simple result neither of pedagogic communication nor of academic ability but depended very much upon the possession of linguistic and cultural capital that they obtained, principally, from their families and their social class.

> An educational system based on a traditional type of pedagogy can fulfil its function of inculcation only so long as it addresses itself to students equipped with the linguistic and cultural capital – and the capacity to invest it profitably – which the system presupposes and consecrates without ever expressly demanding it and without methodologically transmitting it.
>
> (99)

This capital is conceived by Bourdieu and Passeron as a product of the 'habitus' of the student: the manner in which each lives out his or her life through a series of repetitive actions and choices which operate according to certain inherent or recursive rules. This idea of the 'habitus' becomes useful in defining the ways in which notions of place are constructed. In terms of educational achievement, which may be conceived as a process of socialization and the acquisition of professional status, the cultural capital associated with one's habitus is crucial, and is something that the teaching process 'presupposes'. But more importantly, perhaps, cultural capital is a negotiable commodity which may be acquired, just as linguistic capital – the increasing emulation of the teacher's language – is acquired through education. Significantly, the acquisition of cultural capital is not necessarily a formal component of the education process, but rather a social by-product. Its function in the socialization process (that is, the ability of the student to play a game with unwritten rules, and consequently to use the game to his or her advantage) is crucial.

From this it becomes clear why the concept of cultural capital is so useful for theorizing individual agency in a 'hegemonic' situation such as colonial occupation. For whereas many theories of (or at least assumptions about) imperial power tend to see the position of the 'powerless' colonial subject as one of almost passive victimage, it is clear that individuals are almost always able to operate within the framework of the dominant discourse to their own advantage. They do this by acquiring the cultural capital the colonizing power presents to them as dominant. We see numerous examples of this acquisition of imperial culture by colonial élites – study in Oxbridge, academic distinction, a knowledge of and familiarity with high culture, often including a propensity to quote Shakespeare – a capital which is then transmuted into anti-colonial struggles (most of the founding fathers of independent post-colonial states were educated at metropolitan centres). Significantly, this is an operation of sometimes quite selective consumption, in which the cultural product (such as various prominent authors in the canon of English literature) may become transformed in the process. For instance, not only do Indian readers respond selectively to the English syllabus, as Leela Gandhi suggests (1998: 155), but canonical authors may also be appropriated to Indian cultural mores, whether for enjoyment or training, in the selective ways in which Indian readers responded to the English syllabus. Crucially, the cultural capital is not acquired formally, but is acquired during the socialization associated with, but not limited to, formal education. This occurs, for instance, in the cultural assumptions underlying the Cambridge Certificate English Composition exam cited above. Students acquire a habitus by internalizing the cultural principles learned during teaching so that they may be perpetuated and reproduced.

Although the acquisition, by colonial élites, of the capital invested in high culture is the most obvious and also the most politically ambivalent example of this process – since it may suggest that cultural capital has no other function than creating élites who follow in the footsteps of the masters – the acquisition of cultural capital occurs at all social levels. We can see it, for instance, in popular consumer culture in the acquisition of signifiers of status such as Nike running shoes, Cartier watches etc. by a range of subjects. Cultural 'resistance' in a global context becomes more complicated when we consider the prevalence of 'pirating' in Third World countries, and the circulation of imitations of these objects of high cultural value. This is itself the circulation of cultural capital even though the capital has, in a sense, been 'forged'. The purchase of these imitations by tourists from the West demonstrates how very subversive the acquisition and reproduction of cultural capital can be: they in turn purchase cheaply that cultural capital invested in the sign value of high status brands. While Third World countries are clearly dominated by the exigencies of world markets and the requirements of loan agencies such as the IMF and the World Bank (whose oppressive effects on poor economies should not be underestimated), the power to resist complete domination that is available to such societies through the acquisition of cultural capital is considerable.

The acquisition of cultural capital is a politically ambiguous process: on one hand the colonized cultural consumer is 'subjected' to a particular situation in which one culture, one form of cultural capital, has prominence; on the other, that cultural capital is available to the individual consumer for a great variety of purposes, a variety of ways in which that cultural dominance may be engaged, and, indeed, resisted. This is the tension between hegemony and individual action.

However, the acquisition of cultural capital is not a one-way process from dominant societies to the dominated. Cultural capital is that capital presented to an individual as most negotiable in a particular circumstance. Thus Europeans who 'go native' acquire the capital necessary to enter a different lifestyle, and the threat this offers to the universal dominance of imperial culture explains the hysteria with which such instances are often regarded by imperial society. A case in point is the 'trekboers', white nomadic pastoralists in South Africa, who have come under criticism from historians such as Hannah Arendt for their failure to influence the culture of their Khoikhoi workers. In fact, trekboers soon adopted aspects of the Khoikhoi culture, living in mat huts which made them more mobile and able to follow their herds, and developing an 'aesthetics of cattle' similar to that of the Khoikhoi (Presbey 1997: 168), a phenomenon which greatly disturbed Cape Town residents who were aghast at what they feared to be 'contamination'. Despite its unusual nature, this case is a clear demonstration that the acquisition of cultural capital can, and often does, flow both ways. Indeed the capacity of the acquirer to influence the dominant culture by a process of consumption shows that the process can be mutually influential.

While the availability of a dominant imperial or global culture as 'capital' appears to marginalize traditional culture, it may enable that traditional culture to take sometimes radical and exploratory forms. We see this particularly in the application of various technologies to cultural ceremony and ritual. Just as cultural capital operates powerfully in terms of class, according to Bourdieu and Passeron's investigation, allowing mobility between classes despite its function to articulate class distinction, so it may also operate in a post-colonial context to facilitate the acquisition of the means of personal empowerment. Rather than being limited to a comprador class of middlemen, the concept of cultural capital exposes a process whereby colonized subjects of all races and classes appropriate, or 'consume', the dominant, 'hegemonic', culture, discourses, technologies, for purposes which may be very different from those of the disseminators of that culture. For instance, the introduction of leading Singaporeans to English literature at the turn of the twentieth century, a discipline which constructed the history of the English nation as a narrative stretching back to archaic traditions, gave them a basis from which to negotiate a place to speak in colonial Singapore, a place from which to articulate their own narrative of Singaporean nationalism (Holden 1998: 9).

Cultural capital lifts the colonized subject out of a simplistic binary of opposition or a myth of passive subjection. Despite the power of colonial representation, a power which Said examines in *Orientalism*, despite the ubiquity and influence of the tropes by which colonized subjects are marginalized, the colonial subject is never simply a *tabula rasa* on which colonial discourse can inscribe its representations: his or her engagement of the culture presented as capital may be extremely subtle. This is, in a sense, a key to post-colonial discourse: post-colonial societies cannot avoid the effects of colonization, but those effects need not necessarily be seen as the tragic consequences of cultural subjugation, nor a cultural contamination to be rejected at all costs. The effects of imperial culture are a form of capital – neutral in itself but politically potent in its possibilities – acquired and utilized in the negotiation of post-colonial cultural transformation. Ultimately, it is this transformation, rather than a simple opposition, which fulfils many of the goals of resistance.

# 2   Interpolation

The colonial subject may engage imperial culture by *using* it as a communicative medium or *consuming* it as cultural capital. But this engagement becomes one in which consumption and production are deeply implicated, and the force of these processes may also lead to changes in that dominant culture itself. The most contentious problems in post-colonial theory continue to be those hinging on the capacity of the colonized subject to intervene in colonial discourse to contest it, change it, or generally make the voice of the colonized heard. The issue is a crucial one because this capacity is the key to the transformative energy of post-colonial discourse. The acquisition of cultural capital provides comprehensive avenues to self-empowerment in the engagement with dominant culture, but the most important aspect of this engagement is not simply the use of cultural capital but the changes made to the system which provides that capital. Gayatri Spivak's now notorious question – Can the subaltern speak? – remains as problematic as ever. Can 'colonized subjects' be effective and, indeed, 'meaningful' only if they speak in the 'voice of their own experience', the language of their own culture? If they 'translate' that experience into the discourse of the dominant power in order to be heard, are they somehow reshaped or co-opted by that discourse, able to speak only in the terms of the dominant culture?

This question is a recalcitrant one in Western metaphysics and has been expressed acutely in Derrida's ground-breaking essay on Levinas, 'Violence and Metaphysics' (1978: 79–153). Indeed in this essay we can find one of the sources of the sentiment behind Spivak's assertion that 'the subaltern cannot speak'. Derrida takes to task Levinas's contention that 'there was a fundamental contradiction between Athens and Jerusalem' and argues against Levinas's attempted contestation of Greek philosophy by Judaic tradition, simply because, claims Derrida, Levinas must contest Greek philosophy with the voice of reason. By pointing out that the interpellation of the Greek by the non-Greek must always be said in Greek, Derrida aims to demonstrate that Levinas's contestation of Greek philosophy could not be designated as arising simply from the non-Greek. '[T]here seems nothing', says Bernasconi, 'to stop this assertion of the Greek logos as the conceptual framework of any encounter between Greece (the West generally) and its Others from serving as a reassertion of the hegemony of Greek reason' (1997: 186). However, we must ask ourselves very carefully whether the hegemony of Greek reason prevents the 'other' from being spoken. For one does not need to speak *out of* otherness, in the voice of the other, in order to speak *of* otherness, nor, for that matter, *as* the other. The proof of this is nowhere clearer than in post-colonial writing. As we saw in the last chapter, hegemony is not impervious to resistance, it does not prevent individual action, nor does its confinement of individual choice negate the individual expression of resistance. The subaltern does need to speak *out of* otherness to speak *as* the other.

As we saw in the previous chapter, the danger implicit in colonial discourse theory, as with postmodern theories of subject formation, is its frequent insistence on the totality and absolute efficacy of the 'silencing' effects of colonialist representation, which, it is sometimes argued, envelops and predetermines even the conscious acts of resistance which seek to oppose and dismantle it. According to this thesis, post-colonial literatures, or the use of dominant literary forms to disseminate a non-Western world view to a wide audience, would have been impossible. In practice, the cultures apparently 'silenced' by this process nevertheless continue to exist, and not only develop their own operations and revisions but develop coherent strategies of self-determination with the new discursive tools at their disposal. The phrase: 'the subaltern cannot speak' need not imply that the subaltern is silenced and has no voice whatsoever. Rather it suggests that the voice of the subaltern does not exist in some pure space outside the dominant discourse. The subaltern can never speak outside the discourse of power. But *all language is like that*. All speakers are constrained in this way: the 'otherness' of each subject's private experience is mediated in a language which situates it, which makes it comprehensible.

The question of language points to the larger questions of decolonization, self-determination and the control of consciousness itself. Does the subject have any agency if subjects exist only within the discourse framed by ideological systems which control them? In Fanon's terms, does a language 'take on' its speaker? (1952: 38). If the cultures referred to as 'colonized' and 'colonizing' are separate oppositional entities, are their members doomed to mutual incomprehension and the maintenance of differentials of brute force, economic control and superior technology? Given the scale of hegemony involved does the subaltern have any access to power at all? We have seen that, while ideology, discourse or language constrain subjects, they do not imprison them, nor are subjects immobilized by power. Their agency emerges in the space where consumption and production meet. Yet still the dilemma keeps re-emerging, on the one hand because the promise of intervention in language and discourse offered by post-structuralism is countered by its theoretical crippling of the subject's agency (or at the very least the perception that this is the case), and on the other because political action usually implies a binary separation of the 'colonized' and 'colonizing' which locks resistance into an imperialist paradigm.

Despite the stubbornness and apparent intractability of this argument, we may nevertheless arrive at a principle of post-colonial agency which concedes, on the one hand, the central function of language in 'forming' subjectivity, but which confirms the capacity of the colonized subject to intervene in the material conditions of suppression in order to 'transform' them. We will see in the next chapter how the agency of the subject and the structure of the system are balanced in language, because language is a social practice. This includes (critically, for post-colonial societies) the balance of agency and structure which can be achieved in a colonizing language. Resistance, as we have seen, need not *necessarily* mean rejection of dominant culture, the utter refusal to countenance any engagement with its forms and discourses. Indeed, not only is such isolation impossible but the most effective post-colonial resistance has always been the wresting, from imperial hands, of some measure of political control over such things as language, writing and various kinds of cultural discourse, the entry into the 'scene' of colonization to reveal frictions of cultural difference, to actually make use of aspects of the colonizing culture so as to generate transformative cultural production. In this way the colonized subject 'interpolates' the dominant discourse, and this word *interpolate* describes a wide range of resistant practices.

Interpolation counters Althusser's proposition of the *interpellation* of the subject, by naming the process by which colonized subjects may resist the forces designed to shape them as 'other'. Interpolation describes the access such 'interpellated' subjects have to a counter-discursive agency. This strategy involves the capacity to interpose, to intervene, to interject a wide range of counter-discursive tactics into the dominant discourse without asserting a unified anti-imperial intention, or a separate oppositional purity. Post-colonial subjects, in their ordinary dialogic engagement with the world, are not passive ciphers of discursive practices. When we view the ways in which a dominant discourse may operate to keep oppositional discourses located, defined and marginal, we see the strategic importance of a form of intervention which operates within the dominant system but refuses to leave it intact. Fundamentally the process of insertion, interruption, interjection, which is suggested by the act of interpolation, is the initial (and essential) movement in the process of post-colonial transformation.

Edward Said has an evocative term for this process, which he calls 'the voyage in'. It is particularly useful because it takes the huge diasporic movement of peoples from colonized countries to the metropolitan centres as a geographical and historical metonym of the essentially political engagement we can call 'interpolation'. In *Culture and Imperialism* he talks about the *voyage in* as the conscious effort to 'enter into the discourse of Europe and the West, to mix with it, transform it, to make it acknowledge marginalized or suppressed or forgotten histories' (1993: 261). Said's 'voyage in' begins by searching for possible sites of resistance. Despite the pervasiveness and hegemonic nature of dominant discourse, there is capacity to resist because 'no matter how apparently complete the dominance of an ideology or social system, there are always going to be parts of the social experience that it does not cover and control' (289).

The 'voyage in', for those intellectuals who actually and metaphorically travel to the centre of empire, is a process of 'dealing frontally with the metropolitan culture, using the techniques, discourses, weapons of scholarship and criticism once reserved exclusively for the European'. Their appropriations achieve originality and creativity by transforming 'the very terrain of the disciplines' (Said 1993: 293). By operating inside the discourse of Orientalism, for instance, these intellectuals negate the Orientalist constructions that have been ascribed to them. It is through this process of negation that they are able to become selves as opposed to the identity of mere others that they inherit. This is precisely the voyage in that Fanon made when he wrote about the experience of colonization from a French perspective, from 'within a French space hitherto inviolable and now invaded and re-examined critically by a dissenting native' (Said 1993: 295).

Language is the key to this personal and cultural voyage. Despite their ideologically 'contaminating' influence, colonial languages can be, and have been, vigorously adapted, their imperial assumptions abrogated and the language appropriated for the specific needs of post-colonial self-determination. This is itself a very clear demonstration of the kind of agency available to the subaltern subject.[2] However, this

strategy of appropriation is itself part of a broader strategy of interpolation. The post-colonial writer may appropriate the language, but
he or she must insert that text into the Western-dominated systems of
publishing, distribution and readership for the strategy to have any
effect. This entry into the systems of commodity production is a material
instance of the post-colonial subject's intervention into dominant discourses of various kinds, such as history, literature, philosophy –
indeed, into any hegemonic form of cultural production. While it is
most obvious in literary textual production, the process of interpolation
covers the full breadth of the 'cultural text'.

The options available to the colonized or disempowered in their
engagement with imperial discourse are varied. Cornel West, although
talking about 'people of colour', surveys several possible ways of
engaging power that are relevant to post-colonial experience in general.
The first is the 'Booker T. Temptation', namely the individual preoccupation with the mainstream and its legitimizing power. The
second is the 'Talented Tenth Seduction', a move towards arrogant
group insularity. The third is the 'Go-It-Alone-Option'. This is the
extreme rejectionist perspective that shuns the mainstream and group
insularity. But, according to West, the most desirable option for people
who promote the 'new cultural politics of difference' is to be a 'critical
organic catalyst' (1990: 33). This is 'a person who stays attuned to the
best of what the mainstream has to offer – its paradigms, viewpoints
and methods – yet maintains a grounding in affirming and enabling subcultures of criticism'. West astutely points out that openness to others
'including the mainstream – does not entail wholesale co-optation, and
group autonomy is not group insularity' (33). The 'critical organic
catalyst' is, in effect, one who interpolates the mainstream.

What we could add to West's observation is that such engagement
with the mainstream may be the only way in which 'potent traditions
of critique and resistance' can be effective, the only lasting way in
which 'subcultures of criticism' may be affirmed. Even those discourses
which represent themselves as 'revolutionary' have a heavy investment
in the mainstream, are themselves heavily involved in the political
culture they are opposing. Rather than a necessarily conscious and
theorized policy, interpolation describes the range of strategies by
which colonized people have historically empowered themselves through
a calculated appropriation of aspects of the dominant discourse. The
accusation that strategies which engage the dominant culture are
reserved for cultural élites, a comprador class which will never speak
for the majority, disregards the widespread effects of such intervention.

## The post-colonial rhizome

The theory of a *transformative* interpolating process begins in a different model of imperial hegemony from the conventional view of it as a vertical and hierarchical structure. The problem with Said's term 'the voyage in' is that it does imply a simple hierarchical or geometrical structure of power relations. The journey to the metropolitan centre becomes the metaphor for a journey towards the centre of power. A better way of conceiving the ambivalent, fluid, chaotic relationships within the colonial exchanges and indeed of social reality itself can be found in the concept of the *rhizome*, first coined by Deleuze and Guattari (1972). This is an alternative to the 'tap root' of experience by which the imperial holds the marginal in place. The rhizome describes a root system which spreads out laterally rather than vertically, as in bamboo, which has no central root but which propagates itself in a fragmented, discontinuous, multidirectional way. The metaphor is useful firstly because the concept of a root system, of a trunk spreading out and colonizing areas of space in a clearly hierarchical way, is, both as an *idea* and a *policy* (or lack of a coherent policy), fundamental to the project of imperialism. But this notion is just as constructed as that of centre and margin, just as much in the interests of perpetuating power as the Manichaean binaries of self and other, colonizer and colonized.

The operation of power, like the operation of social relations themselves, is both perpetual and discontinuous and propagates laterally and spatially like the rhizome. The reason we don't normally think of power operating this way is that structures of power characterize *themselves* in terms of unities, hierarchies, binaries and centres. But it is clear that power doesn't operate in a simple vertical way from the institutions in which it appears to be constituted; it operates dynamically, laterally and intermittently. There is no 'master-plan' of imperialism: the greatest advancement of cultural hegemony occurs when it operates through an invisible network of filiative connections, psychological internalizations and unconsciously complicit associations. If the social generative process is rhizomic, then we must concede that imperialism itself operates rhizomically, producing its effects by a complex, diffracted, discontinuous layering rather than necessarily by acts of brute force.

Gayatri Spivak demonstrates the subtlety of this rhizomic process by pointing to the example of the solitary British soldier walking across the countryside of India in the early nineteenth century. She proffers this as an example of how the colonized space is 'worlded' by the mundane activity of ordinary colonizers: 'He is actually engaged in consolidating the self of Europe by obliging the native to cathect the space of the Other on his home ground . . . he is effectively and violently sliding one discourse under another' (1985: 133). The point Spivak is making here is that the imperial project itself is heterogeneous. This 'cartographic transformation' was achieved not only by the policy-makers but also, and more importantly, by the little people like the solitary soldier – and the thousands of colonists who follow people like him to places which are colonized by an imperial power like Britain. The discourse of mapping, even though it may proceed in a fragmentary and intermittent way, is a formal strategy for bringing colonized terri-tory under control by *knowing it in language.*

A brilliant demonstration of the rhizomic operation of power occurs in David Malouf's *An Imaginary Life* (1978) in which the exiled Roman poet Ovid discovers a child in the wilderness whom he attempts to teach his own language 'so that he might discover what he is' (Malouf 1978: 77). In this way, Ovid, himself exiled from the monolithic centre of Rome, *reproduces* the very imperial power which has exiled him. Not only does he want to teach the child language but he wants to thus give him access to an understanding of being itself. Examples of this occasion in the civilizing mission of colonialism are too familiar to enumerate; the colonized subject always needs to be *brought into* human existence by learning the language, but this is not the result of a simple 'mono-lithic project' of imperialism. Rather the myth of centrality funda-mental to imperialism reproduces itself in a rhizomic way through ordinary individuals to 'territorialize' or 'reterritorialize' the 'abnor-mal' colonized subject.

The rhizome metaphor provides a complicated and less easily repre-sentable model of colonial relations than 'centre and margin' but it does accommodate the various subject positions an individual may occupy within colonial discourse. The colonized subject may also be the colonizing subject depending on his or her location in the rhizome. The complex operations of imperialism themselves problematize the existence of simple political categories of response or identification such as 'resistance' or 'minority'. These positions are constantly dif-fracted and intersected within the rhizome of imperial contact. This intermittent and rhizomic nature is the most difficult thing to combat because it operates alongside a mythology which asserts the presence of the tap root, the canon, the standard, the patented. It is this *myth* of power which the categories of marginality are addressing, not the intermittent, overlapping and intertwining nature of its actual opera-tion. In this way the categories which we see reproduced in critical reading – such as women, native, migrant – evolve as reproductions rather than subversions of imperial discourse.

Once we accept the rhizome as a model of social relations, the inevitable question arises: What is the agency of the subject in this acutely ambivalent rhizomic structure? Clearly, Manichaean binarisms become irrelevant in such a model, but we still seem to be left with a picture of discursive relations in which the colonized subject cannot be extricated as an entity. The question is the same for any discourse. The rhizomic structure of imperialist discourse leaves many spaces or discursive fractures in which ambivalence and intention meet. These fractures are the spaces opened up for counter-discourse. No system of control, no discourse, can ever operate with absolute consistency. 'In modern societies the loci of individual discourses are simply too diffuse . . . the social interests in play are too divergent, for any policy of discursive policing ever fully to expunge the subversive' (Terdiman 1985: 56). Because *both* discourse and counter-discourse are rhizomic, interpolation is already partly a function of our complex subject position within this diffuse structure of social and power relations. The ambivalence of this position is nicely encapsulated in Bhabha's description of mimicry.

> Mimicry marks those moments of civil disobedience within the discipline of civility: signs of spectacular resistance. When the words of the master become the site of hybridity . . . then we may not only read between the lines but even seek to change the often coercive reality they so lucidly contain.
>
> (1985: 162)

But mimicry is not unidirectional, neither is it situated on a unified field of colonial discourse. Interpolation obtains its insurgent effectiveness from the capacity to intervene in the dominant discourse at any number of scattered points on the rhizome of social and political interaction.

If, as Bhabha claims, the ambivalence of colonialist discourse itself causes fractures and slippages which implicate the post-colonial subject in resistance, we must go further to say that it is only by occupying these fractures, by interpolating the discursive field, that the subject can realize the potential of its discursive ambivalence, its mimicry. If imperial power is constituted rhizomically, the acts of interpolation which characterize post-colonial discourse may be seen to be diverse, unsystematic, unpredictable, scattered and quotidian rather than programmatic and organized. Although Said's concept of the 'voyage in' bases itself on a very useful metaphor of diasporic movement from the colonies to the metropolitan centres, the actual 'voyage in' engaged by subjects occurs locally and discursively in a thousand different forms of engagement. Interpolation redefines the nature of 'resistance' by revealing the diversity of subjective agency within the dominant territory. The successful disruption of the territory of the dominant occurs, not by rejecting or vacating that territory but by inhabiting it differently. When we understand the rhizomic nature of power, we may better understand the potential for its transformation by the dominated.

## 'Tactics' and 'strategies'

The rhizomic structure of power means that the interpolation of the dominant discourse is 'tactical' rather than 'strategic'. Michel de Certeau (1984) points out that the practices of daily life are largely tactical transgressions of the rules and structures by which such life is ordinarily held to be ordered. And he distinguishes 'tactics' from 'strategy' in this way: strategy is 'the calculation . . . of power relationships that becomes possible as soon as a subject with will and power (a business, an army, a city, a scientific institution) can be isolated' (36). A 'tactic', on the other hand, is 'a calculated action determined by the absence of a proper locus' (37). 'The space of the tactic is the space of the other.' Thus it must play on and with a terrain imposed on it and organized by the law of a foreign power.

As we saw in the discussion of subjectivity in the last chapter, although ideology serves the interests of the ruling classes, it is not static or unchangeable, and its materiality means that it is also contradictory, fragmentary and inconsistent and does not necessarily or inevitably blindfold the 'interpellated' subject to a perception of its operations. Ideology itself is rhizomic. The rhizome explains the very complex system of opposition and complicity which characterizes the relationship between post-colonial subjects and imperial discourse. This field is already fractured, heterogeneous, ubiquitous. This is why a binary model of resistance can contend with no more than the myth of power, the myth of the tap root of cultural identity and the 'trunk' of cultural control.

Any structure, system or institution can be used in such a way as to constitute a form of tactical resistance. There are innumerable ways of 'playing and foiling the other's game' and the way colonized groups occupy imperial space, 'the space instituted by others', demonstrates the 'subtle, stubborn, resistant activity' by which they operate in 'a network of already established forces and representations' (18). Indigenous Amerindian cultures, for example, diverted the dominant Spanish colonial culture. 'They metaphorized the dominant order: they made it function in another register. They remained other within the system which they assimilated and which assimilated them externally. They diverted it without leaving it' (32). What de Certeau is talking about here, of course, is a process which characterizes post-colonial cultural engagements all over the world. Colonial culture changed, it became a dialogic, hybridized space in which the indigenous could operate. By 'not leaving' the dominant culture they interpolated its processes; by interpolating it they were able to transform it.

For de Certeau, everyday practice is a form of production called 'consumption'. But while for de Certeau it is not *what* is used but the *ways* of using that are important, we can say that there is a point at which *ways of using* become manifest in cultural *products*, be they practices, responses, techniques or artefacts. Everyday practice is not unrelated to the concept of cultural capital introduced by Bourdieu. Both operate relatively unsystematically, sometimes intuitively, but become crucially linked in writing. Post-colonial literatures, in which the 'consumption' of the language, as cultural capital, becomes the production of writing, demonstrates a powerfully effective interpolation of the dominant culture. The tactical procedure of language appropriation is not simply a case of people 'making do' with what they have, as de Certeau puts it (18), but of so proceeding in their articulations within the 'message event' that the language itself, as a range of conceptual and enunciative possibilities, is transformed.

A criticism levelled at de Certeau's view of consumption as production is that the practice of the tactics of daily life negotiates a path round the edges of the formal structures of institutional power, *thus leaving them intact*. But it is possible to see also how the 'indeterminate trajectories' of ordinary practice which weave around the sanctioned and formal networks of discourse begin to enter them, to irrupt through their fortified textures. Discursive interpolation at this point begins to have material effect, it *never* leaves the dominant space intact. In post-colonial discourse, therefore, we discover a space in which the concepts of strategy and tactic overlap – an ambivalent space; a space that is neither the autonomous position of a 'proprietary power' nor the completely mobile and temporary space of the weak. This is, indeed, the space of cultural capital. For, although the appropriation of habitus which cultural capital involves does not itself disrupt the dominant discourse, it provides the means by which such disruption and transformation may take place.

This transformation occurs in many ways and across the whole expanse of discursive activity. It operates in the appropriation of language; the entry into discursive fields such as literature; intervention into fields of representation of all kinds – advertising, television, dance, music; into fields of exchange such as economic relations, marketing; the interpolation into history and the historical process, into anthropological and sociological discourse, even into the analysis of the tropological structures by which many of these discursive activities are impelled. This agency is sometimes only oppositional by effect rather than design, for more often its transformative power is dialogic and regenerative.

Disciplines such as history, anthropology, geography, cultural studies, which have a profound importance, not only in the representation of the post-colonial subject but in the construction of world reality itself, are primary sites for the intervention of transformative perspectives. But it is still, perhaps, in creative writing that the fullest and most energetic interpolation takes place. For such writing engages directly and vigorously with both the semiotic field of textuality and state apparatuses and professional fields of knowledge. Writing appropriates the language, commands the tools of representation; takes over the genre; claims a voice in capitalist institutions such as publishing, and in state institutions such as education, and by these means discursively constructs its audience as participant in its practices.

The effect which seems so difficult to successfully achieve at the level of formal factional politics, the transformation of the structures of power, is the very mode of operation of post-colonial subjectivity at the discursive level, particularly where it engages dominant modes of textual production. The rise of national independence movements has been the most common post-colonial interpolation of world political structures, but they have had far less success in changing those structures than the practices of consumption by ordinary subjects. The post-colonial subject is not simply a kind of 'flaw in discourse' through which the ambivalence of colonialist administration elicits a contrary reaction; nor, on the other hand, can its agency be limited to a questionable intention to resist. The subject actively engages the dominant discourse within those fractures through which its tactics, operating at the level of everyday usage, may transform the discursive field. This capacity to interpolate is the subject's constant, ubiquitous, dialogic and transformative agency in its engagement with imperial power.

# 3 Language

The interpolation of imperial culture, and the appropriation and transformation of dominant forms of representation for the purposes of self
determination, focus with greatest intensity in the function of language.
Those writers who do write in English have used it as a cultural vehicle,
a medium through which a world audience could be introduced to
features of culturally diverse post-colonial societies. But, as we have
seen, the use of colonial languages has opened up a long-running and
unresolved argument. According to the Indian linguist Braj Kachru,
English has been widely accepted as a *lingua franca* in India because of
its relatively 'neutral' nature, since its effects in everyday use are far
less inflammatory than those stemming from the contention between
one or another minority language (1986). On the other hand, the
Kenyan novelist Ngugi wa Thiongo has argued that writing in an
African language 'is part and parcel of the anti-imperialist struggles of
Kenyan and African peoples' (1981a: 28).

We have touched on this dispute in the previous two chapters since it
is so crucial to the struggle over post-colonial representation. But now
we will look more closely at what occurs when post-colonial writers
actually use the English language. Underlying the dispute over the
most effective form of discursive resistance is the question: Can one use
the language of imperialism without being inescapably contaminated
by an imperial world view? It is a question which continues to provoke
argument, because it is ineluctably rooted in real political conflict.
Martinican Edouard Glissant, for instance, says:

> There are . . . no languages or language spoken in Martinique,
> neither Creole nor French, that have been 'naturally' developed
> by and for us Martinicans because of our experience of collective,
> proclaimed, denied, or seized responsibility at all levels. The official
> language, French, is not the people's language. This is why we, the

élite, speak it so correctly. The language of the people, Creole, is not the language of the nation.

(1989: 166)

Although framed in terms of class, Glissant's observation alerts us to the frequency with which a particular *use* of language can be conflated with the language itself. What makes a language a 'people's language'? Does it lie in the facts of its origin, its 'invention', or in the particular conditions of its use? The extent to which either French or Creole will be the language of the people depends largely on *how* it is used as much as upon *how widely* it is used and by whom. An alien language, by Glissant's definition, appears to be one that has not been 'naturally' developed as a function of the experience of the colonized. But when we look at the ways in which colonial languages are often developed and used as a vehicle of local experience, it is often hard to imagine any language more 'naturalized'.

A similar confusion is suggested in Fanon's assertion in *Black Skin, White Masks* that 'To speak a language is to take on a world, a culture. The Antilles negro who wants to be white will be the whiter as he gains greater mastery of the cultural tool that language is' (1952: 38). The key to this astute perception is the term 'take on'. For there can be no doubt that a colonial language gives access to authority and a perception of a certain form of social being. But this access is not gained as a feature of the language itself, through a process by which the speaker absorbs, unavoidably, the culture from which the language emerges. This new, comprador identity comes about through the act of speaking itself, the act of self-assertion involved in using the language of the colonizer. The speaker 'takes on' the language rather than vice versa. This seems a small point but it is crucial because the speaking *need not necessarily* make the speaker 'more white' (itself an appropriated metaphor). The language is a tool which has meaning according to the way in which it is used.

This is, of course, a key to the importance of language as cultural capital. Proficiency in the language does not exclude the capacity to use in a way that 'localizes' it. In his discussion of Eric Williams's speeches, Selwyn Cudjoe gives a very clear account of the appropriation of the master's language as an acquisition of cultural capital:

The ability to 'speak properly' and to manipulate language has always been of enormous importance to Trinidadians and Tobagonians. Apart from the oral, storytelling tradition that allowed self-expression in any manner that one chose and with a great deal of flexibility, skill and diversity, the concern for the 'proper' use of classically based English language always seemed a preoccupation of the society. As a result, in the early part of the twentieth century there arose a number of literary and debating clubs whose main concern was to master the master's language . . . Williams grew up in a social environment in which the proper use of language was of utmost importance.

(Cudjoe 1993: 43)

The concern for 'proper' speech seems a classic demonstration of cultural hegemony. Yet this case also reconfirms the deeply ambivalent nature of hegemony itself: the hegemonic culture is available to specific acts of acquisition. Mastering the master's language has been a key strategy of self-empowerment in all post-colonial societies, and acquiring English fits the cultural pattern of the Trinidadian flair for language. In Williams's case such mastery became the key to his own rise to prominence as a leader of Trinidadian independence. Cultural capital always presents itself as dominant: the 'proper', 'correct', 'civilized', way to behave. But this very dominance means that its appropriation by the colonial subject can be empowering. In Williams's case the ambition of his parents and the emphases of the colonial education system were significant factors, but possibly the most significant factor was his own love of language. Clearly, the acquisition of cultural capital which all these factors promoted became a key political factor in Williams's career. Not only did he rise to prominence in an independent Trinidad, but his exposé of the nature of imperial history in its treatment of the West Indies is a key interpolation of global knowledge.

One of the most ironic aspects of Williams's linguistic virtuosity was his use of language to promote action. In 1955 he declared that the 'age of polemics was coming to a close': 'We want to eradicate from our ranks all satisfied sectarianism, in the place of dead doctrinarianism, we want the spirit of live positivism. WE WANT TO END the scholastic tinkering with WORDS, WORDS, WORDS' (Rogers n.d.: 29). Williams's language itself reveals his fondness for words, and his ability to use the cultural capital invested in language. In the argument between the pen and the sword, language has always proved indispensable to action, effective post-colonial resistance has always used the cultural capital of that imperial system it is dismantling. Even Selwyn Cudjoe acknowledges that 'the reliance on and love for linguistic skills still remained an integral part of the political culture. Even as they moved from a polemical to an action-oriented emphasis, the very presentation was articulated in a peculiarly Trinidadian "styling" of discourse' (1993: 46).

We see, time and again, the practical examples of the cultural capital strategically employed in the colonizing language. But in this chapter we will go to the heart of the intractable philosophical problem that seems to prevent acceptance of this evidence: that to have a language is to have a particular kind of world, a world that is simply not communicable in any other language. At base this problem rests on the question of meaning itself: of how meaning is communicated in texts. This issue lies at the heart of the transformative capacity of post-colonial discourse, because, if the 'colonized' and 'colonizing' are not to be doomed to mutual incomprehension, we must understand the constitutive and dialogic way in which the meaning of texts is accomplished. Transformation, when we examine it in the context of literary and other forms of creative discourse, focuses in the question of meaning. If, for instance, we accept a simple sender–receiver theory of communication we quickly become locked into a binary as tight as the binary between colonizer and colonized. This binary expresses itself in the assertion that the colonizing language colonizes the mind of the colonial subject. The binary between the 'sender' of meaning and the 'receiver' of meaning tends towards a view of meaning itself as fixed by the sender, and invokes an ostensive and static view of the meaning process. Without a view of language as transformable, we can have no proper theory of transformation.

The key to this problem of communicability between colonizer and colonized, and, indeed, to the whole question of transformation, lies in the fact that the written text is a social situation. That is to say, it has its being in something more than the marks on the page, for it exists in the participations of social beings whom we call writers and readers, and who *constitute* the writing as communication of a particular kind, as 'saying' a certain thing. When these participants exist in different cultures, as they do in post-colonial writing (since by 'culture' we mean something quite specific), two issues quickly come to the forefront. Can writing in one language convey the reality of a different culture? And can a reader fully understand a different cultural reality being communicated in the text? One of the most persistent misconceptions about this activity is that the meaning of writing is a kind of static *a priori* to be uncovered: existing either as a function of the language itself, or the inscription of something in the mind of the writer, or the reconstruction of the reader's experience. Indeed, the very term 'meaning' tends to imply some objective content which is the end point of reading.

The contention of this chapter is that our understanding of the capacity of post-colonial literatures to transform imperial discourse itself must begin by seeing that meaning is achieved constitutively as a product of the dialogic situation of reading. The 'objective' meanings of writing come about by a process of 'social' accomplishment between the writing and reading participants. This is because meaning is a social fact which comes to being within the discourse of a culture, and social facts as well as social structures are themselves social accomplishments. If we focus the meaning event within the usage of social actors who present themselves to each other as functions in the text, and see that cultural 'distance' is privileged at the site of this usage, it resolves the conflict between language, reader and writer over the 'ownership' of meaning. The social accomplishment of textual meaning occurs despite the cultural distance between writer and reader. This contention engages, head on, the fact that people in different cultures may well live in totally different, and even incommensurable, worlds: different worlds of experience, expectation, habit, understanding, tradition. The constitutive theory of meaning does not underestimate this. Rather it assesses how meaning can nevertheless be accomplished between writing and reading participants.

Clearly, the somewhat startling notion of the text as a dialectical, even dialogic, accomplishment requires some clarification since our assumption of the 'givenness' of texts (and hence, very often, the fixity of their meaning) is supported at the very least by the evidence of their physical tangibility. To the question, How do you mean? we could say that the *meaning* of a word is *meant* by the person who utters it and is *taken to mean* something by the person who hears it. As a radical oversimplification of the history of European literary theory we could say that it has been an arena in which all of these participants – the language, the utterer or writer, and the hearer or reader – have been locked in a gladiatorial contest over the ownership of meaning. But on closer examination it can be seen that all three 'functions' of this exchange participate in the 'social' situation of the written text. Admittedly, the political impetus of post-colonial analysis has often been to focus meaning at the site of production. But such analysis is in a unique position to resolve some of the lingering questions of critical theory.

Meaning is a social accomplishment characterized by the participation of the writer and reader 'functions' within the 'event' of the particular discourse. To take into account the necessary presence of these functions and the situation in which the meaning occurs, we can call the meaning a 'situated accomplishment'. It is easy to see the understanding reached in conversation as a 'situated accomplishment', for the face-to-face interaction makes possible a virtually limitless adjustment to the flow of talk. The central feature of such activity is *presence*, the presence of the speaker and the hearer to each other constituting language as communication. Yet if we think about it, even in the most empathetic exchange the speaker and hearer are never fully present to one another. The experience of one conversant can never *become* the experience of the other, and in this sense what we call the 'mind' is a retrospective and largely hypothetical construct which we infer from what is 'revealed' in language. So the psychological 'distance' which might seem to characterize interlocutors from different cultures can be seen to be a feature of all communication. The experience aroused by a word, the associations it evokes, may be very different in people *within* a culture – the experiences aroused in men and women by particular words, for instance – but this does not prevent meaning occurring. Meaning and understanding of meaning can occur because the language encodes the reciprocity of the experiences of each conversant. It is the situation, the '*event*' of this reciprocal happening which 'tells', which 'refers', which 'informs'.

The example of conversation alerts us to the extent and the limitation of the capacity of individuals in any social situation to structure and direct their communication. Speakers are not totally free agents, for that would be to deny the effects of society, culture and history upon them and the situation in which they are acting. But neither are they purely ciphers for broader social forces. The situation, with all its attendant antecedents, operates in conjunction with, rather than *upon*, the participating individuals. And though these individuals can direct or unleash the potentialities of the antecedents affecting the situation, they cannot change them. The apparently simple example of a casual conversation clearly demonstrates the extensive array of structuring participations in the social event. But it is the 'event', the *situation* of its structure and participations, rather than the contingent intentions or psychological states of speakers, which imparts a direction and a meaning to the conversation. The *intentionality* of the participants and the *directionality* of the discourse operate in conjunction to produce meaning. In this way the agency of the participants and the structure of the discourse co-operate.

The discursive 'event', the site of the 'communication', therefore becomes of paramount importance in post-colonial literatures because the 'participants' are potentially so very 'absent'. Indeed, unlike spoken discourse, the central problematic of studies of writing is *absence*. It is not so easy to see the meaning of a written text as the situated accomplishment of participants because the message 'event' occupies what seems to be a very tangible object, a piece of writing, an unarguably tangible production of the act of writing, an object which itself seems located in the discursive space in which writer and reader as social actors never meet. But whether the writing is a newspaper article, instructions for the assembly of a model aeroplane or a philosophical treatise, the writer and reader have access to each other only through the mutual construction of the text within certain linguistic and genraic parameters. That distance between minds which seems to be compensated for in the spoken conversation by the situation of the dialogue would appear to elude writing. The written text stands apart in its own material integrity, apparently unrelated to persons, to language or to social systems in any purely mechanical or isomorphic way, but grounded in the semiotic systems by which such persons and systems are imputed.

How meaning is constructed in the writing by its absentee users becomes a central question in any analysis of cultural understanding, and is made much more salient by post-colonial writing systems in which writer and reader might have (particularly if they come from very different cultural backgrounds) ranges of experience and presuppositions which may not be expected to overlap greatly, if at all. The additional perspective which the consideration of post-colonial literatures brings to this discussion is obviously their accentuation of this phenomenon of *distance*. They present us with writers and readers far more 'absent' from each other than they would be if located in the same culture; they present a situation which in some cases (because the genre of written prose is so removed from some cultures) provides a totally original, negotiated and ambivalent site for communication. One qualification to this may be that the sharing of an imperial system of education and cultural patronage, issuing forth in the widespread uniformity of curriculae, readers and other cultural 'guides' used throughout Britain's empire, considerably ameliorates this distancing within the post-colonial world. But even in the 'monoglossic' settler cultures the subcultural distancing which generates the evolution of variant language shows that the linguistic cultures encompassed by the term 'English' are vastly heterogeneous. As we will see, in the process of transforming the language and the genres of literature, post-colonial writing often *installs* distance and absence metonymically in the interstices of the text.

The face-to-face situation of spoken discourse is replaced by the distancing effect of the writing system, freeing the meaning from the constraints of speech and creating a vehicle which at once confirms and bridges the absence of writers and readers. As writing, the message event is not merely a different physical mode but a different ontological event.

> Inscription alone . . . has the power to arouse speech from its slumber as sign. By enregistering speech, inscription has as its essential objective . . . the emancipation of meaning . . . from the natural predicament in which everything refers to the disposition of a contingent situation. This is why writing will never be simple 'voice painting' (Voltaire). It creates meaning by enregistering it, by entrusting it to an engraving, a groove, a relief, to a surface whose essential characteristic is to be infinitely transmissible.
>
> (Derrida 1978: 12)

By freeing language from the contingent situation, writing, paradoxically, gives language its greatest permanence, whilst, at the same time, giving meaning its greatest volatility because it opens up wider horizons of meaning. Writing does not merely inscribe the spoken message or represent the message event, it *becomes* the new event. Nor is it merely the inscription of thought without the medium of speech, for such thought is accessible only as a putative associate of the event. Post-colonial literatures reveal this most clearly when their appropriation of English, far from inscribing either vernacular or 'standard' forms, creates a new discourse at their interface. Post-colonial writing *represents* neither speech nor local reality but constructs a discourse which may intimate them. This distinction ought to be made as clearly as possible. While writing is a new ontological event it does not cut itself off from the voice. The inscription of the vernacular modality of local speech is one of the strategies by which a 'marginal' linguistic culture appropriates the imported language to its own conceptions of society and place. This discourse also questions the Derridian conclusion that writing is infinitely transmissible and hence infinitely interpretable. Infinite transmissibility assumes a totally homogeneous world. It elides the political and cultural limits of interpretation and subsumes all writing into a universalist paradigm which is essentially that of the metropolitan centre.

We find here a perception which concurs with Said's view of the worldliness of texts. The key challenge for Said is to negotiate between two attitudes to the text which in different ways misrepresent how texts have a being in the world. On the one hand the classical realist position sees the text as simply referring to the world 'out there'. Such a view fails to take into account the ways in which language mediates and determines what is seen in the world. On the other hand a structuralist position sees the world as having no absolute existence at all but as being entirely constructed by the text. This view would not allow for any non-textual experience of the world, nor, potentially, for any world outside the text. Said negotiates these extremes by claiming that the text (and by this we can mean speech, pictures and all other forms of text) is important in negotiating our experience of the world, but the worldliness and circumstantiality of the text, 'the text's status as an event having sensuous particularity as well as historical contingency, are considered as being incorporated in the text, an infrangible part of its capacity for conveying and producing meaning' (Said 1983: 39). This means that the text is crucial in the way we 'have' a world, but the world does exist, and that worldliness is constructed within the text. The text has a specific situation which places restraints upon an interpreter, 'not because the situation is hidden within the text as a mystery but because the situation exists at the same level of surface particularity as the textual object itself' (39). The text does not exist outside the world, as is the implication in both the realist and structuralist positions, but is a part of the world of which it speaks, and this worldliness is itself present in the text as a part of its formation.

Texts are in the world, they have various kinds of affiliation with the world, and one of their functions as texts is to solicit the world's attention, which they do in a number of ways. Many texts incorporate the explicit circumstances of their concretely imagined situation. In writers such as Gerard Manley Hopkins, Joseph Conrad and Oscar Wilde, the 'designed interplay between speech and reception, between verbality and textuality, *is* the text's situation, its placing of itself in the world' (40). But it is in the example of post-colonial texts that the worldliness of the text itself becomes most urgent and most explicit. Through metonymic processes which we shall examine below, post-colonial texts insist their worldliness.

However, such worldliness is extremely contentious for much contemporary theory. In fact, this problem begins with structuralist linguistics which tends to reify the linguistic code. In Saussure's distinction between *langue* and *parole*, *langue* is the code or set of codes on the basis of which a speaker produces *parole*, a particular message (Saussure 1916). While *langue*, the description of the synchronic systems of language, is the object of a linguistics, the *parole*, the language in use, the intentional message, focuses a study of language in its actual operation. Now *parole* is precisely what Saussure's *Course in General Linguistics* (1916) is *not* about, and ever since its publication linguistics, the handmaiden of structuralism, has bracketed the message in order to concentrate on the code, in which it is primarily interested.

A post-colonial approach to linguistics, however, redresses this imbalance by focusing on the message, reinstating the *parole* as the realization of the code in social life. *Parole* confirms the importance of the link between individual agency and discursive structure, not only in language but in all discourse, including the discourse of cultural life. But in linguistic terms *parole* establishes the 'margins' of language as the substance of theory. This reassertion of the margins of language use over the dominance of a standard code, a centre, is the most exciting conclusion of the theory of the 'creole continuum' (Bickerton 1973). But it is also instrumental in conceiving the discourse of the post-colonial as rooted in conflict and struggle, as 'counter-discourse' (Terdiman 1985), since the perpetual confrontation with a 'standard code' is that which constructs the language. This does not mean the replacement of one canon for another, or the reconstruction of the centre which is being subverted. Such a reorientation emphasizes the fact that the code is theoretically abstracted from the activity, and it reinstalls the priority of the practical or constitutive semiology of the message. This observation reveals that language has its only practical existence in the *parole* within which the usage of members, rather than a supervenient system or *a priori* referentiality, determines meanings. This becomes particularly true of English in which the notion of a standard 'code' is dismantled by the continuum of practices by which the language is constituted.

This constitutive semiology radically modifies the most fundamental tenets of Saussurian theory, namely, that signs mean by their difference from other signs, and that the link between the signifier and signified, although arbitrary, is stable binary structure. While it is certainly true that meaning is not necessarily determined by the external relation of a sign and a thing, meaning *is* determined within the relations actualized within the *message* rather than those purely abstracted in the system. The message is the very point at which the agency of the subject and the structure of the discourse in which the subject operates come together. In short, language is a social medium for individuals rather than a self-sufficient system of inner relationships. Though it does not determine meaning ostensively, it is a social act within which reality is determined. Consequently, the message event marks the terrain of meaning for the written work, for only the message event gives currency to language within the relations of social beings. Neither the mental lives of speakers and writers nor the objects of their talk can usurp this fundamental concern.

The recognition of the importance of the message event reassesses traditional approaches to meaning such as those in speech act theory

(Austin 1962). While we can inscribe the propositional content of a speech act we cannot, for instance, inscribe its illocutionary force (its capacity to assert, warn, promise, direct etc.), or its perlocutionary force (its achievement of particular results). Such force is carried in the situation of the message. The illocutionary and perlocutionary forces of the sign THIS WAY → are embodied entirely in its character as sign and the social conventions surrounding its role. It is the situation of the sign both physically and within social convention which gives it the power to direct people and to achieve results. Similar conventions surround and determine the forms of different kinds of writing, particularly those given the designation 'literary'. The illocutionary force of these texts similarly cannot be *conveyed* by means of grammar, italics, punctuation, but rather actualized constitutively in the conventional practice – the situation – of the reading. The writing 'event' thus becomes the centre of the accomplishment of meaning, for it is here that the system, the social world of its users and the absent 'participants' themselves intersect.

We can see that post-colonial texts of various kinds affirm the orientation of writing to the message event. The immense 'distance' between author and reader in the cross-cultural or subcultural text undermines the privilege of both subject and object and opens meaning to a relational dialectic which 'emancipates' it (Derrida 1978: 12). Nothing better describes to us the distance traversed in the social engagement which occurs when authors write and readers read. But it is clear that the distances *are* traversed. Writing comes into being at the intersection of the sites of production and consumption. Although the 'social relationship' of the two absent subjects is actually a function of their access to the 'situation' of the writing, it is in this threefold interaction of situation, author function and reader function that meaning is accomplished. We begin to see why this is crucial to a theory of transformation: for, if meaning is locked into any one of these factors, if it is controlled by either the sender, the receiver or the medium itself, then language becomes untransformable.

## Language

Let us examine more closely the contending claims in the struggle for the dominance of meaning. The first of these is language which is commonly held to embody or contain meaning either by direct representation or in a more subtle way by determining the perception of the world. Language which is negotiated in the complex, hybrid and constantly changing environment of post-colonial interchange inevitably contradicts the assumption of a linguistic structure or code which can be characterized by the colonial distinction of 'standard' and 'variant'. All language is 'marginal', all language emerges out of conflict and struggle. The post-colonial text brings language and meaning to a discursive site in which they are mutually constituted, and at this site the importance of usage is inescapable.

Although the view is rarely expressed by anyone conversant with languages in different cultures that language 'represents' or 'reflects' an autonomous reality, it is probably the most ubiquitous Western assumption about the operation of language because our sense of how words mean operates within a discourse in which the world (the object) is irremediably separated from the speaker (the subject). The Cartesian separation of subject and object, the separation of the consciousness from the world of which it is conscious, is the schema which still underlies the modern Western episteme with its passion for 'scientific' objectivity and its tendency to see the world as a continuum of technological data. Such a view is possibly the most crucial factor separating Western society from those societies in which much (though not all) post-colonial literature is generated. The view of language which this schema installs is best represented by the theories of 'reference' which dominated Anglo-empiricism in the earlier part of the twentieth century but which still hold sway in most empirical philosophies. According to this view words have referents in the real world, and what a word refers to is, for all intents and purposes, what it means.

But words are never so simply referential in the actual dynamic habits of a speaking community. Even the most simple words like 'hot', 'big', 'man', 'got', 'ball', 'bat', have a number of meanings, depending on how they are used. Indeed, these uses are the ways (and therefore what) the word means in certain circumstances. A word such as 'bat' can operate as a noun with several referents, a verb describing several kinds of actions and probably several other ways as well. Many other words, such as 'bush' (which has found hundreds of uses in post-colonial societies), reveal that the meaning of words is also inextricably tied to the discourse of place. Post-colonial literature has continually shown both the importance of this discourse and the inescapable linking of meaning to the usage within the event. In his novel *The Voice* Gabriel Okara (1964) demonstrates the almost limitless prolixity of the words 'inside' and 'insides' to describe the whole range of human volition, experience, emotion and thought. Brought to the site of meaning which stands at the intersection between two separate cultures, the word demonstrates the total dependence of that meaning upon its 'situated-ness'.

Language cannot, therefore, be said to perform its meaning function by reflecting or referring to the world in any essential or immutable way, and thus meanings cannot remain exclusively accessible to those speakers who 'experience their referents', so to speak. The central feature of the ways in which words mean things in spoken or written discourse is the situation of the word. In general, one may see how the word is meant by the way it functions in the sentence, but the meaning of a word may require considerably more than a sentence for it to be adequately situated. The question remains whether it is the responsibility of the author in the cross-cultural text to employ techniques which more promptly 'situate' the word or phrase for the reader. While post-colonial writing has led to a profusion of technical innovation which exists to span the purported gap between writer and prospective reader, the process of reading itself is a continual process of contextualization and adjustment directly linked to the constitutive relations within the discursive event.

An alternative, determinist view which proposes that language actually constructs that which is perceived and experienced by speakers is less problematic for post-colonial theory, but it is problematic none the less. Edward Sapir proposed the exciting and revolutionary view that what we call the 'real' world is built up by the language habits of a group, and that the worlds in which different societies live are quite distinct, not merely the same world with different labels attached (Mandelbaum 1949: 162). The central idea of Whorf and Sapir's thesis is well known. It proposes that language functions not simply as a device for reporting experience but also, and more significantly, as a way of defining experience for its speakers.

> the linguistic system (in other words, the grammar) of each language is not merely a reproducing instrument for voicing ideas but rather is itself the shaper of ideas, the program and guide for the individual's mental activity, for his analysis of impressions, for his synthesis of his mental stock in trade . . . We dissect nature along the line laid down for us by our native languages. The categories and types that we isolate from the world of phenomena we do not find there because they stare every observer in the face; on the contrary, the world is presented in a kaleidoscopic flux of impressions which has to be organised in our minds – and this means by the linguistic system in our minds.

> (Whorf 1952: 5)

But even this more attractive view of the link between language and the world may give rise to a number of objections from constitutive theory. Clearly, language offers one set of categories and not another for speakers to organize and describe experience, but to assume that language *creates* meanings in the minds of speakers misconceives the way in which meaning is constituted in discourse. While it is quite clear that language is more than a 'reproducing instrument for voicing ideas' (for what do thoughts or ideas look like apart from their expression in language?), the same objections can be applied to the idea of language as the 'shaper' or 'programmer' of ideas. Such ideas are still inaccessible apart from language.

To possess a language is to possess a technique, not necessarily a quantum of knowledge about the world, as we might suppose if we were to assume that a particular language was more 'natural' for a particular speaker. One speaker 'sees' the world in the same way as another because they share a language, that is, share a technique for putting certain rules into practice; the 'seeing' is embedded in the practice. To speak of language as 'shaping' ideas also logically leads to the identification of one particular 'shaping' with a particular language, or, more commonly, with the use of language in a particular place. In other words, Whorf and Sapir's thesis is haunted by the spectre of cultural incommensurability: that people speaking different languages cannot understand each other's worlds. This sort of identification leaves itself no conceptual room to cope with the phenomenon of second language use or vernacular linguistic variance, for it is only in the most metaphorical sense that we can talk about a speaker 'seeing' a different world when he or she speaks in a second language. The key to this problem is the habitual way in which we tend to conflate experience and meaning. We think that because one person cannot have the same *experience* as another they cannot understand each other's *meaning*. But, as we saw, even speakers in the same culture can never have exactly the same experience of language, yet this does not stop them communicating.

Rather than the linguistic system in the speaker's mind, it is the situation of discourse in which the 'obligatory terms' of language are structured. For instance, Whorf's discovery that Inuit languages have a variety of words for 'snow', thus suggesting they see the world differently from non-Inuits, overlooks the fact that skiers of all languages have a similar variety of words for snow, but could hardly be said to see the world differently in the way Whorf means. The meaning and nature of perceived reality are not determined within the minds of the users, nor even within the language itself, but within the use, within the multiplicity of relationships which operate in the system. Margaret Atwood once made an interesting reference to a North American Indian language which has no noun-forms, only verb-forms. In such a linguistic culture the experience of the world remains in continual process. Such a language cannot exist if language is either anterior or posterior to the world but reinforces the notion that language inhabits the world, *in practice*. The semantic component of the sentence is contained in the syntax: the meaning of a word or phrase is its use in the language, a use which has nothing to do with the kind of world a user 'has in mind'.

What the speaker 'has in mind', like a linguistic system or culture, or intentions or meanings, is accessible only in the 'retrospective' performance of speaking. The categories which language offers to describe the world are easily mistaken to shape something in the mind because we naturally assume that, like the rules of chess, we hold the linguistic system 'in our minds', in advance of the world. But language is coextensive with social reality, not because it causes a certain perception of the world but because it is inextricable from that perception.

Languages exist, therefore, neither before the fact not after the fact but *in the fact*. Languages constitute reality in an obvious way: they provide some terms and not others with which to talk about the world. Because they provide a limited lexicon they may also be said (metaphorically) to 'use' the speaker, rather than vice versa. But the worlds constituted in this way do not become fixed composites in the speaker's mind, a set of images which differs, by definition, from the set in the mind of the speaker of a different language. Worlds exist by means of languages, their horizons extending as far as the processes of neologism, innovation, tropes and imagination will allow the horizons of the language itself to be extended.

## The reader function in the writing

If the written text is a social situation post-colonial texts emphasize the central problem of this situation, the 'absence' of those 'functions' in the text which operate to constitute the discursive event as communication: the 'writer' and 'reader'. The author, the source of vision and intention, the possessor of 'gifted creative insight', has historically exerted the strongest claim upon the meaning of writing. But the concept of the author is quite alien to many post-colonial cultures and is really a quite recent phenomenon in European culture, as Foucault has pointed out (1969). The need to ground discourse in an originating subject was the need to accord it the status of a possession. Speeches and books were assigned real authors only when someone had to be made responsible for them as possessions and subject to punishment first as transgressing religious rules and later as transgressing or affirming the rules of property ownership (Foucault 1977: 124–5). To attain this social and legal status the *meaning* had to be a product attributable to a subject. Consequently, the powerful and densely interwoven forces producing the text could be conveniently located in an originating mind.

This should assist us to find some balance in assessing the author's place in the 'production' of the text. We have made an important start by rejecting the notion that meaning is a mental act, a sort of picture which the author translates into words or vice versa. But how *does* the non-English speaker, for instance, mean anything in English? For after all, this is the ignition point, so to speak, for the transformation process. Firstly, the writer, like the language, is subject to the *situation*, in that he or she must say something *meanable*. This does not mean the language cannot be altered, used neologistically and creatively, but the non-English writer becomes limited *as any speaker or writer is limited*, to a situation in which words have meaning. Take the example of a verse from the poem by the Caribbean poet Linton Kwesi Johnson:

> di lan is like a rack
> slowly shattahrin to san
> sinkin in a sea of calamity
> where fear breeds shadows daak
> where people fraid fi waak
> fraid fi tink fraid fi taak
> where di present is haunted by di paas
> (Donnell and Welsh 1996: 375)

While the poem transcribes the sound of the local dialect, its orthography still 'constructs' a reader for whom its variations pose no serious obstacle. Rather the code variations become a part of the enjoyment of the poem. When we say that the writer is limited to a situation in which words have meaning, the word 'situation' refers to something of extremely wide range. It is, at its simplest, the place of the word within a meanable context, the grammar or rules which make the context meanable, but it is also a continuously unfolding horizon which ever more finely articulates the meaning. This is not to say that some post-colonial writing is not much more inaccessible to the reader, but this inaccessibility is part of a strategy of difference. Literature, and particularly narrative, has the capacity to domesticate even the most alien experience. It does not need to *reproduce* the experience to construct the meaning. This principle applies to even the most recondite culturally specific terms. Athough there is no word in English, for instance, which has the associations of *mana* (oneness with the world) in Polynesian or *Tjukurrpa* (the 'Dreaming') in Pintjantjatjara, there is no insurmountable conceptual difficulty in articulating their associations.

One could go further than this to say that the author is subject not only to the situation of discourse but to the reader as well. The reader is present, as a *function*, in the writing of the text. Thus the relationship between these social forces and the text is the same as that between the linguistic system and the 'text' of a particular world view: neither causal nor representative, but co-extensive. Within the framework of these social antecedents, the writer and reader functions are as 'present' to each other in the acts of writing and reading as conversants are in conversation. The reader may be present in the writing at a conscious level, in the author's sense of an audience, of a purpose for writing, but it is not necessarily so specific. To detect the presence of the reader function in the writing, let us first think clearly whether the act of writing can ever exclude the simultaneous act of reading. That moment of writing in which the self is objectivized is also the moment of a reading in which the other is constituted. It is the other, even when the other is oneself, which confers objectivity on the writing, constitutes it as written. The requirement of meanability itself implicates the reader function. The space within which the writer meets the reading other is neither one culture nor another, neither one language nor another, but the *parole*, the situation of discourse.

## The writer function in the reading

Just as readers 'write' the text because they take it to mean something, and just as the reader function is present in the writing as the focus of its meanability, so the author is present in the reading. This is the specific and practical way in which consumption and production are linked. Again, this is firstly true at a conscious level, where the reader accepts the convention that the author is telling him or her something through the text. Readers respond to the text as 'telling' them something because such ways of using language as this literary text represents come within the rules for the activity of 'telling'. But one cannot 'tell' others anything that they do not incorporate or 'tell themselves'. The mind is active in knowing. Whether a child learning a language or a scientist 'observing' an 'objective' universe, knowing is conducted within the *situation* of horizons of expectations and other knowledge. In reading, a horizon of expectations is partly established by the unfolding text, while the horizon of other knowledge (available by means of other texts), a *relevant* horizon of other knowledge, is established by exploration. The reader constructs the other dialogic pole of discourse because speaking is a social act. But readers do not simply respond to the convention of the authoring other, they respond to the 'intentionality' of the work itself, quite apart from any imputation of an author. The work is a way of seeing and responding, a way of directing attention to that which is 'given to consciousness'. It is more accurate to say that the reader sees according to, or 'with', the text rather than 'sees it'. This orientation to the intentionality of the text occurs whenever we assign an author to a text.[3] We can deduce from this that the intentionality of the text can be *put for* the direction of the author's consciousness. Thus interpretation is never univocal but the reader is subject to the situation, to the rules of discourse and to the directing other as the author is subject to them.

As with language, our natural assumption about understanding is that it must be a discrete experience, that there must be characteristic experiences of understanding when we 'understand' which have corresponding identifiable mental correlates. Consequently how could we 'understand' a writer, even writing in a common language, who has a profoundly different experience of the world? But we can test this assumption that understanding is an identifiable experience. Take the example of a bricklayer who uses the term 'Brick!' to his helper as an elliptical form of the phrase 'Pass me the brick'. Neither he nor the helper needs to translate the word 'Brick!' into the phrase every time it is used, in order to understand it. The word operates perfectly well as a communication within the exchange and it is its use and the continuation of the job which locates the understanding of the word 'Brick' as an order. The same process applies when English variants, neologisms and borrowings are situated in the written English text. As with most words there may be many possible uses but it is the use in this situation which locates the meaning.

The processes of understanding are not limited to the minds of speakers of one mother tongue and denied the speakers of another. Meaning and the understanding of meaning exist *outside* the mind, within the engagement of speakers using the language. Understanding, then, is not a function of what goes on in the 'mind' at all, but a location of the hermeneutic object in its linguistic situation. When I understand a language, I know I understand it when I can converse in it. When I understand what another person says, I am not required to have their mental images nor when they communicate meaning are they obliged to transfer to the listener the 'contents' of their mind, nor any of the mental images and associations which may be aroused by that language. Wittgenstein makes the point in a discussion of Frazer's *The Golden Bough* that cultural misunderstandings usually occur because our explanations contest the reality of the phenomenon we are explaining. He strongly criticizes Frazer's (familiarly Eurocentric) assumption that non-European magic, rituals and beliefs were a function of 'wrong thinking', or 'false science'. 'Every explanation is an hypothesis' (1979: 3e), says Wittgenstein, 'And Frazer's explanations would be no explanations at all if finally they did not appeal to an inclination in ourselves' (6e). For instance, 'If the adoption of a child is carried out by the mother pulling the child from beneath her clothes, then it is crazy to think there is an *error* in this and that she believes she has borne the child' (4e). The symbolic or ritual nature of such an action is perfectly accessible, no matter how strange. Far from understanding between cultures being impossible, the distance created by such an explanation misconstrues the object of understanding, creates a gap which forces 'understanding' to be a mere reflection of ourselves.

The particular facility of writing which uses English as a second language, and invites the reader into the mental and emotional horizon of the 'other' culture, is to bridge this gap, to reveal that understanding is a function of the linguistic situation. The dialectic of writer and reader functions within this situation is particularly significant. Such writing re-emphasizes the constitutive nature of the meaning event and the varied nature of the usage in which meaning is accomplished. Yet, curiously, there is an element in such literature which introduces a gap of a different kind. By stressing the distance between the participating writers and readers, the text prevents itself from being so transparent that it is absorbed into the dominant milieu of the reader of English. Such writing, while it provides a path for cultural understanding that overcomes the exclusionary effect of anthropological explanation, also questions easy assumptions about meaning and its transmissibility, and actively reinstalls the reality of its own cultural difference in quite explicit ways.

## Strategies of transformation

This brings us to the question: If meaning is a social accomplishment, how do we explain the undeniable sense of cultural difference which often emerges in post-colonial texts? How do we explain the 'worldliness' of an alien post-colonial culture which appears to insist itself so importunately in the writing? This, in fact, is one of the most fascinating links between the *constitutive* nature of meaning and the *transformative* use of language. For while meaning in texts is 'socially' constituted, difference and alterity may be similarly constituted within the transformed discourse. The constitutive construction of meaning, and the distinction between meaning and experience, does not therefore mean that we live in a perfectly transparent universe. Cultural experiences *can be* vastly different, and this difference, as well as the communication of cultural experience, is itself a feature of post-colonial texts. It is not that reader and writer have incommensurable mental frameworks but that such difference is actually *installed* in the text in various ways. Not only does this installation of difference occur regularly, but it is a crucial feature of the transformative function of post-colonial writing. The most subtle form of distancing occurs in the installation of what we might call a 'metonymic gap', a sense of distance that comes about through the use of certain linguistic strategies. Language variance has a metonymic function in the post-colonial text.

The metonymic gap is that cultural gap formed when appropriations of a colonial language insert unglossed words, phrases or passages from a first language, or concepts, allusions or references which may be unknown to the reader. Such words become synecdochic of the writer's culture – the part that stands for the whole – rather than representations of the world, as the colonial language might. Thus the inserted language 'stands for' the colonized culture in a metonymic way, and its very resistance to interpretation constructs a 'gap' between the writer's culture and the colonial culture. The local writer is thus able to represent his or her world to the colonizer (and others) in the metropolitan language, and at the same time, to signal and emphasize a difference from it. In effect, the writer is saying, 'I am using your language so that you will understand my world, but you will also know by the differences in the way I use it that you cannot share my experience.'

While the tropes of the post-colonial text may be fruitfully read as metonymy, language variance *itself* in such a text is far more directly metonymic of cultural difference. This is profoundly significant in the ideology of language use, for in the European tradition the contiguous and accidental, those characteristics which seem to accrue to the metonymic, will never have the power of truth. Truth itself is inextricable from power and power is the province of the metropolitan. But what is the 'use of language *as* metonymy'? The intersection of language which occurs when texture, sound, rhythm and words are carried over from the mother tongue to the adopted literary form is one which many writers propose as *the* distinguishing feature of post-colonial literature. This use of language is often regarded as the sign of an individual author's creative capability, or the sign of an ethnographic function by which the 'truth' of culture is inserted into the text by a process of metaphoric embodiment. But quite simply, language variance is a synecdochic index of cultural difference which affirms the distance of cultures at the very moment in which it proposes to bring them together. In this way the inscription of difference becomes a central feature of the transformation of language and literature. The writer concedes the importance of *meanability*, the importance of a situation in which meaning can occur, and at the same time signifies areas of difference which may lie beyond meaning, so to speak, in a realm of cultural experience. The distinctive act of the cross-cultural text is to inscribe *difference* and *absence* as a corollary of cultural identity. Consequently, whenever a strategy of appropriation is used, that is, a strategy which appropriates the dominant language and inflects it in a way which transforms it into a cultural vehicle for the writer, there is an installation of difference at the very site of the meaning event.

The installation of difference occurs perhaps most strategically in the use of code-switching which specifically illuminates the political and cultural gap installed through language. One humorous example in Naipaul's *The Mystic Masseur* finds Ganesh and Beharry deciding to talk in 'proper English', but lasting only a few sentences since the attempt is so artificial and absurd:

> 'All right then,' Beharry said resignedly. 'Let we go.'
> 'It is hot today.'
> 'I see what you mean. It is *very* hot today.'
> 'Look Beharry. This go do, but it won't pay, you hear. You got to give a man some help, man. All right now, we going off again. You ready? The sky is very blue and I cannot see any clouds in it. Eh, why you laughing now?
> 'Ganesh, you know you look damn funny.'
> 'Well you look damn funny yourself, come to that.'
> 'No, what I mean is that it funny seeing you so, and hearing you talk so.'
>
> (1986: 77)

In this case it is the tone and the strangeness of the 'standard' language which create the cultural gap, even though the two converse in Caribbean English. This exchange is a clear demonstration of the cultural specificity of an appropriated English and the artificiality, and even practical non-existence, of some putative standard. Even more striking is the presence of two linguistic codes which are mutually comprehensible, despite their differences. In the story 'Betel-nut is Bad Magic for Aeroplanes', by the Papua New Guinean writer John Kasaipwalova, code-switching is utilized to demonstrate the different registers of social and cultural power signified by the different codes.

> Straightaway my face blooded because many black, white and yellow people, they was watching us too and this white papa dog, he was talking bad like that way to me. Plenty times I hear white people calling black men 'bois' so this time I hear it and my mind was already fire. I wanted to give him some. Maybe good English or maybe little Strine [Australian]. So I says loudly to him, 'All right white man, on what moral grounds is it unlawful for me to chew betel-nut here? This is a free country of which we black people are citizens and unless you can show me the moral basis for your "so called laws" I cannot recognize and therefore comply to that law!'
>
> (1987: 71)

The two codes, one propagandized as 'correct' and the other as 'idiomatic', articulate divisions of power in the colonial system, and the metonymic gap between them. The ability of the writer to move between the codes indicates his subtle awareness of the power relationships involved. Transformation here is not just a matter of inscribing a locally inflected English code alongside the powerful 'standard' but also the ability to move with ease between them.

The location of difference stems beyond the linguistic structure itself. This, indeed, is a basic function of language appropriation: to convey the attitudes and beliefs of a non-Western culture in the dominant language. In the story 'Taboo' by the Fijian Akanisi Sobusobu, the protagonist, an eleven-year-old boy, is beaten unjustly for breaking a fishing taboo instituted at the death of a chief. But when the village finds a turtle stranded nearby, the taboo is forgotten, the turtle cooked, but the boy is denied the feast and sent to cut bamboo. On his return he finds the whole village either dead or dying. The final question he asks at the end of the story, as the people from the next village bury the victims, precariously straddles the cultural gulf without attempting resolution.

'Was the turtle poisonous or had our ancestors got angry?' Manasa wondered to himself.

'Never should we break a taboo', one of the men digging muttered as if he had read Manasa's thoughts.

'Those who try to disobey a taboo always suffer', another added.

(1980: 28)

The most interesting feature of this story is not so much the affirmation of traditional cultural values implied in the exchange as the insertion of a cultural gap between the 'rational' and the 'traditional' explanations. This gap becomes the sign of a fracture between different worlds, worlds which may be sharable in language, but whose apartness, the difference of lifetimes of associations, traditions, simple experiences, learned responses and conventional allusions, is explicitly confirmed. It is not that the reader cannot *understand* the importance of taboo, nor understand Manasa's responses, but that the text confirms the difference of cultural *experience*. In this way the integrity of the traditional interpretation of the world is articulated by difference and located firmly within its own 'world' of experience.

The strategies by which a colonial language is transformed are extremely varied. Apart from direct glossing in the text, either by explanation or parenthetic insertions, such devices include syntactic fusion, in which the English prose is structured according to the syntactic principles of a first language; neologisms, new lexical forms in English which are informed by the semantic and morphological exigencies of a mother tongue; the direct inclusion of untranslated lexical items in the text; ethno-rhythmic prose which constructs an English discourse according to the rhythm and texture of a first language; and the transcription of dialect and language variants of many different kinds, whether they come from diglossic, polydialectical or monolingual speaking communities (Ashcroft et al. 1989: 61–77).

If we look closely at these intercultural linguistic devices and the commentary which surrounds them, we can see that the role they propose for themselves is often that of 'power words', power syntax and power rhythms which *reproduce* the culture by some process of metaphoric embodiment. Evidently many writers believe that by such means they are keeping faith with their own culture and *transporting* it into the new medium (Wendt 1980: 28). Thus the untranslated words, the sounds and textures of the language, are vaguely held to have the power of the culture they signify by a process of ontological union. The historical privileging of metaphor in identity is manifested yet again by this propensity to see truth predicated on a process of cultural incorporation.

Such uses of language are *metonymic*. They are *put for* a certain cultural experience which they cannot hope to reproduce but whose difference is at least validated in the new situation. To be precise the language bears a synecdochic relationship with the original culture, the part of the culture which stands for the whole.

This metonymic function overturns an attractive but decidedly Eurocentric theory of language development which we first find in Vico. According to Vico there are three ages in a cycle of history which correspond with three distinct stages in human language systems which he calls the 'hieroglyphic' (the symbolic, emblematic and hidden), the 'hieratic' (in which language belongs principally to the priestly class) and the 'demotic' (where language belongs 'to the people') (see Vico 1968; Frye 1982). Northrop Frye, perhaps using Jakobson's terminology, calls these stages the *metaphoric* phase, in which subject and object are linked by a common energy, the *metonymic* phase in which words are 'put for' thoughts, and the *demotic* phase in which subject and object are firmly separated and language functions to describe an objective universe (Frye 1982: 5). The movement through these stages took thousands of years in European culture, but clearly such a theory proclaims the idea that European modernity is the fulfilment of an ascending progress of human literacy. The 'metaphoric' phase can be seen to describe those non-Western cultures which have not reached the developmental stage of writing. But it is clear that in preliterate cultures the processes of reading the signs of the land in tracking, hunting and gathering are already well advanced. Such 'preliterate' societies offer a curious confirmation of Derrida's assumption that writing takes precedence over language since they have highly developed reading practices. Clearly reading had existed for millennia before the development of writing, but such reading could not exist without the presence of various forms of inscription.

This situation becomes emphasized in some post-colonial writing from oral cultures, in which the text negotiates a leap from a mother tongue still situated at the 'metaphoric' phase to the demotic medium of the post-colonial text in English. Clearly all three stages of Vico's and Frye's developmental cycle may exist at one time, whatever mode may have cultural ascendancy at a particular historical moment. Rather than a teleological movement from 'primitivism' to 'modernity' we can see a rhizomic interconnection of language use. One of these uses, the demotic European, because it has power, can constitute itself as the most recent, the modern. When writers from an oral culture write in English this rhizomic interchange becomes exposed. In the language of oral cultures, words are *sacred*. They have the *power* of the things they signify because they *are* the things they signify. Rather than representation, language is closer to *presentation*. Language embodies the oneness between speakers and their environment. However, to say that such societies have no concept of representation is false because, whatever the status of writing in the society, all people must be skilled semioticians, reading the signs by which their everyday lives must proceed. One might say that these cultures are skilled at reading linguistic and other signs as *both* presentation and representation, a skill which deteriorates with writing.

Frye puts particular store by the saying in biology that 'ontogeny replicates phylogeny' (that is, that the evolution of a species is replicated in the gestation and growth of its young) to suggest that the evolution of writing in human society mirrors the trajectory of a child's language learning. This perpetuates a centuries-old prejudice in European thinking that equates the 'primitive' with the child, and proposes as a 'natural' process of 'development' that which is simply a variety of equally complicated modes of communication. Indeed, if we consider language at the level of its evocative and presentational power, the 'demotic' phase could just as easily be seen to be a deterioration. However, if we dispense with the idea that the 'metaphoric', the 'metonymic' and the 'demotic' are developmental stages we can see that post-colonial texts may often serve a particular metonymic function, a function which may be said to negotiate the meeting of the metaphoric and demotic. It is not only literature which does this. Melanesian Pidgin, or *tok pisin*, is a language which demonstrates a pervasively metonymic lexicon. The Pidgin word 'Susu', for instance, means 'milk', 'breast', 'breast-feeding' and also a species of milk-white fish. The signifiers within this metonymic space become dense and protean.

There are many cases in literary texts where this process becomes explicit, as in the following passage from Chinua Achebe which demonstrates the device of ethno-rhythmic prose.

> Edogo's mind was in pain over the child. Some people were already saying that perhaps he was none other than the first one. But Edogo and Amoge never talked about it; the woman especially was afraid. Since utterance has the power to change fear into living truth they dared not speak before they had to.
>
> (1964: 112)

This passage is particularly interesting because it demonstrates the text in the process of negotiating the conceptual gulf between the 'metaphoric' Igbo and 'demotic' English. We are told that the words in the original language have a sacred embodying power – 'utterance has the power to change fear into living truth'. But we are informed of this metaphoric power in language through the medium of a demotic language which cannot achieve such embodiment. The language of this text therefore assumes the transformative function of metonymy by adapting the rhythms of the demotic language to the those of the oral and metaphoric. The language itself, with its adapted African rhythms, bears another kind of synecdochic relation with the culture it is describing. It stands for the possibility of discourse in the interstices of language and becomes the signifier of experiences which are ultimately incommunicable.

Language operating in this way achieves something a simple translation could never achieve: it foregrounds the various forms of language use in the text; the metaphoric phase as subject, the demotic as the medium, and the metonymic as the mode. The texture, the sound rhythm and syntax of the original language determine the 'shape' and mode of the English variant. By being 'put for' the cultural experience, they bring the culture into the adopted medium without overwhelming that gap of silence which the text constructs as the signifier of difference. What we find here is a meeting of languages, and it is a meeting which continually offers dimensions of expression by which English will continue to be transformed.

Constitutive theory emphasizes the agency of both writer and reader in the meaning event. Without that agency, and the capacity, for instance, of post-colonial writers to install a metonymic gap, whether in their language or in their cultural descriptions, the transformation of the dominant discourse could not occur. Such theory takes into account the interaction of all functions in the text: the language, the reader and the writer. But perhaps the most fascinating and subtle aspect of the transformative function of post-colonial writing is its ability to signify difference, and even incommensurability between cultures, at the very point at which the communication occurs.

# 4 History

There is a moment early in Peter Carey's novel *Oscar and Lucinda* when Theophilus Hopkins, unable to deter his son Oscar from leaving home, warns him, 'You are travelling down the tide of time.' You have chosen, says Theophilus, 'to throw away the chart our Lord has revealed to you' (Carey 1988: 65). What Theophilus does not know, and the novel comes to reveal, is that he is talking about 'History'. History moves forward to gather in the future as well as looking backwards to gather up the past. History is as inevitable to Theophilus as time itself: history is time's narrative, a story from which Oscar will not be able to escape. In this scene Theophilus sums up the ideology of imperial history: sequentiality, inevitability, purpose, authority; a teleology that is divinely ordained. The father's warning alerts us to what is at stake in Oscar's rebellion, and what underlies the novel's depiction of a journey of discovery: the problematizing of European History. But it also alerts us to the function of history in Theophilus's way of seeing the world. For history is grounded on an authority as transparent as time itself.

'History' is derived from the Greek *historia* meaning 'to investigate', and on the face of it historical investigation asks the most natural, the most innocent of questions – 'What happened?' Isn't this the very essence of the historical? Don't all human societies ask this question? No! In fact, many societies, perhaps most non-Western societies, do not ask this question, simply because 'What happened' is inseparable from what is still happening and will happen. But when we investigate history itself we find that, particularly in its nineteenth-century imperial forms, it stands less for investigation than for perpetuation. Even contemporary Western theories of history contend that the past is essentially unknowable, that the scientific orderliness of historical accounts are the imposition of a particular story. History, indeed temporality itself, is a construction of language and of culture, and, ultimately, the site of a struggle for control which post-colonial writing is in a particularly strategic position to engage. Representations of human time and human space have been the most powerful and hegemonic purveyors of Eurocentrism in modern times. History, and its associated teleology, have been the means by which European concepts of time have been naturalized for post-colonial societies. How they might resist it, why they might want to resist it and what kind of story they might replace it with are crucial to the self-representation of colonized peoples. Ultimately, the transformation of history stands as one of the most strategic and powerfully effective modes of cultural resistance.

The significance of history for post-colonial discourse lies in the modern origins of historical study itself, and the circumstances by which 'History' took upon itself the mantle of a discipline. The emergence of history in European thought is coterminous with the rise of modern colonialism, which, in its radical othering and violent annexation of the non-European world, found in history a prominent, if not *the* prominent, instrument for the control of subject peoples. At base, the myth of a value-free, 'scientific' view of the past, the myth of the beauty of order, the myth of the story of history as a simple representation of the continuity of events, authorized nothing less than the construction of world reality. This was a time in which the European nations, represented by three or four 'world' cities, 'absorbed into themselves the whole of world history' as Oswald Spengler puts it (1926: 32), which is to say that they became the focus of its invention.

The question the human sciences had to face in the nineteenth century was: What does it mean to have a history? This question, Foucault maintains, 'signals a great mutation in the consciousness of Western society, a mutation which has to do ultimately with "our modernity", which in turn is the sense we have of being utterly different from all other forms of humanity known to history' (1970: 219–20). The question we ask at this point is, of course, who is this 'we' if not the West, the initiator and possessor of modernity? Clearly, what it means to have a history is the same as what it means to have a legitimate existence: history and legitimation go hand in hand, history legitimates 'us' and not others.

Hayden White persuasively argues that history, seeking the title of 'scientific discipline' in the nineteenth-century mould, needed to suppress the element of interpretation which had always given it its form, but which came to appear unstable and subjective. The appeal to a moral or political authority underlying historical interpretation had to be sublimated by dissolving the authority to interpret into the interpretation itself. This, and the desire for the 'scientific', generated a particular historiographic ideology: the demand for a single narrative truth which was purely and 'simply' the closest possible representation of events. The discipline of history emerged at a strategic moment of choice between possible discursive options, the apparently neutral narrative form succeeding by virtue of its resemblance of the purity of scientific disciplines. White asks the crucial question: What do we rule out when we constitute history in this rigorous scientific way, and insist that any other procedure would reveal a want of discipline? (1982: 120). His answer is *rhetoric*, which can be described as an awareness of the variety of ways of configuring a past which itself exists only as a chaos of forms.

It is a curious fact that such was the confidence of English constitutional and imperial historians in the rightness and moral justification of imperial rule that the apparent 'scientific narrative' of the past in their histories was never really free of rhetoric, nor was this deemed necessary. At the beginning of his *The Expansion of England* J. R. Seeley typically suggests that

> history, while it should be scientific in its method, should pursue a practical object. That is, it should not merely gratify the reader's curiosity about the past, but modify his view of the present and his forecast of the future. Now if this maxim be sound, the history of England ought to end with something that might be called a moral. Some large conclusion ought to arise out of it; it ought to exhibit the general tendency of English affairs in such a way as to set us thinking about the future and divining the destiny which is reserved for us. The more so because the part played by our country in the world certainly does not grow less prominent as history advances.
>
> (1890: 1)

We do not need to ask who this 'we' might be, nor whose destiny is reserved. Nor can we be in any doubt about the link between history and power, nor of the peculiar moral outworking of such power in the civilizing mission of English culture. The maxim Seeley propounds is already something of a cliché, but the ease with which he links the scientific method of history with its moral function is a classic demonstration of the imperial consciousness at work. The truth of history is not in question, it is the message of history on which England's destiny hinges. For Seeley that message can be understood only if we see that in the eighteenth century 'the history of England is not in England but in America and Asia' (1890: 9). Nothing could better demonstrate the way in which the framework of imperial history is placed over, and becomes the means of understanding, the history of colonized peoples. History has become the site of a peculiarly recalcitrant epistemological argument: does the past have a truth that can be recovered, or is such 'recovery' always merely an invention? Is human experience a kind of chaos out of which the narrative of history tries to create some order, or do people actually experience events in temporal sequence? The status of post-colonial experience puts a particular slant on these questions, because there appears to be an incontrovertible 'truth' in the experience of colonization, yet the discourse by which the continuity of such experience can be ordered has been deeply grounded in assumptions about time and space which arose with the emergence of modernity in Europe. The situation is similar to the one prompted by Spivak's statement that 'the subaltern cannot speak'. The subaltern cannot speak outside the dominant discourse (and this, as we have seen, is by no means disempowering, nor does it render the subaltern 'voiceless'). How does the subaltern construct a story of the past that is 'naturalized', free of the assumptions of the master narrative of European history?

## Narrativity

Truth and reality, says Hans Kellner, are the primary authoritarian weapons of our time, an era characterized by nothing less than a debate about what is true of reality (1987: 6). For this reason, if for no other, they are difficult to ignore. Foucault, for instance, confirms the constructedness of these concepts time and again, yet 'he will not dispense with them, but rather examines the way in which discourse creates reality as reality creates discourse. His own fictions, therefore, are true because they are based upon a certain reality; this reality is real, in part, because it has been figured by his fictions' (Kellner 1987: 6). What strikes us in this is the fascinating intransigence of the dialectic of truth and fiction. The very act of piercing this dialectic to isolate the 'thesis' – reality – is one which invokes the fictive, because constructive, strategies of our discourse. Aristotle's dictum that poetry is truer than history becomes ever more attractive the closer we examine historiographic texts.

Foucault's famous identification of knowledge with power does not dispense with truth claims. We might be immersed in an age dominated by 'the will to truth' and be quite aware of the heavy political investment in such truth claims, but truth and reality seem to remain the foundation (at least implicitly) of our discourse. What Said says about representation is useful here. His *Orientalism* was widely criticized by Foucauldians for the apparent assumption that there was a 'real' Orient inaccessible to the discourse of Orientalism. But, says Said, all representation is in some respects a misrepresentation. Since Islam *has* been misrepresented in the West,

> the real issue is whether indeed there can be a true representation of anything, or whether any and all representations, because they *are* representations, are embedded first in the language and then in the culture, institutions and political ambience of the representer. If the latter alternative is the correct one (as I believe it is), then we must be prepared to accept the fact that a representation is *eo ipso* implicated, intertwined, embedded, interwoven with a great many other things besides the 'truth,' which is itself a representation.
>
> (1978: 272)

Representations, or misrepresentations, inhabit a common discursive field defined for individual representers by a common history, tradition. Each scholar or historian redisposes material within this field in such a way as to co-operate with its internal discursive consistency.

The link between representation and misrepresentation alerts us to the illusoriness of historical veracity. The idea that history itself is a 'fiction' is a cliché which mimics the reversal of the binary truth/untruth. History is neither the opposite of fiction nor is it simply fictional. History is a method rather than a truth (as the histories of nineteenth-century British historians amply reveal), an institutional formalization of the stories we tell ourselves to make sense of our lives. The question of the truth or fiction of history may be best resolved in the concept of narrativity. It is the narrativity of contemporary history which is its most salient and powerful discursive feature. One of the great illusions of narrativity is the assumption that the narrative doesn't simply tell a story but reflects the continuity of events. So great is the influence of narrativity that we assume that life itself is shaped like a story. It was this conflation of temporality and narrative sequence which underlay the nineteenth-century ideology of scientific method in historiography. The continuity of the stories written about history came to reflect the continuity of something transcendent called Human History.

Narrativity is itself much deeper than the story. Hans Kellner, in his account of narrativity in history (1987), analyses the work of Paul Ricoeur, F. R. Ankersmit and Hayden White, who all recognize in various ways that narrativity is a world view, of which story telling is a genre. The range of their positions reveals what a protean concept narrativity can be if separated from the story genre. For Ricoeur, narrativity authorizes the historical enterprise in all its forms; regardless of the *forms* of representation, history rejects any disassociation of cause from effect (Kellner 1987: 14). For Ankersmit the narrative substance of history can never be simple translations of reality, while for White narrative was an option chosen in the nineteenth century at the birth of the discipline of history but which has restricted it ever since by excluding its rhetorical dimension.

In *Time and Narrative* Ricoeur accepts the proposition that the 'story' is elevated in historical writing, and that history is the comprehension of *plots* (1984: 31 passim). But this fails to explain how narrative remains the essence of history when history ceases to be about *events*. This is the key problem for all 'narrativist' understandings of history. For an answer Ricoeur turns to Augustine's treatise on time in the *Confessions* which suggests that whereas time is experienced primarily as an absence, memory and expectation are also two key modalities of time so that one may speak of human time as a threefold present: a present of things past (memory), a present of present things, and a present of future things (expectation). For Ricoeur, Augustine solves the problem of the inevitable slippage of the present of the future into the present of the present and of the past, by linking it to the *distensio animi*, the stretching of the mind in different directions by the structure of temporal experience itself.

Ricoeur's central point about history and narrative is that *'all change enters the field of human history as a quasi-event'* (1984: 109, 224). In effect he reverses the hierarchy in Western historiography which privileges the long span of time over the particular event, by showing how 'any understanding of long time-spans must be saturated with forms of human understanding based upon human time as understood in particular by Augustine as a threefold present' (Kellner 1987: 16). Particular events – and we must remember that 'historical events' are those selected from a vast range of possibilities – are not the isolated occurrences of human experience, but they are themselves what Ricoeur calls 'variables of the plot', the plot which literally *comprehends*, 'grasps together' as an intelligible whole, circumstances, goals, interactions and unintended results. The analogical character of historical categories arises from the extension of the 'threefold present' of human temporal understanding. It is the emplotment of the whole narrative, with its investment in human time, which gives the narrative its legitimacy, rather than any explicit referential function. 'To follow a story', says Ricoeur, is to move forward in the midst of contingencies and peripeteia under the guidance of an expectation that finds its fulfilment in the 'conclusion' of the story . . . To understand the story is to understand how and why the successive episodes led to this conclusion, which, far from being foreseeable, must finally be acceptable, as congruent with the episodes brought together by the story.

(1984: 66–7)

This is nowhere clearer than in the 'story' of empire, in which the conclusion, the *telos*, is that which drives the story itself – the spread of civilization to all humankind. History confirms, as much as any elaboration of the discourse of modernity, the supremacy of the modern, advanced, civilized West over the premodern, primitive, colonized societies. The narrative of events is one which cloaks, with the fiction of empiricism, the teleological and centripetal narrative of empire. But more importantly for strategies of decolonization, the resistance to the narrative of events is bound to be little more than a nibbling at the edges of history. It is the idea of the dominance of the event which must be resisted, for the event is the example *par excellence* of the cultural grounding of the empirical narrative. For 'events' are by no means neutral. The absence of those particular kinds of events which European history privileges renders any other history uninteresting, marginal and even non-existent. The post-colonial interpolation of history depends upon an avoidance of the trap of the empirical narrative which privileges certain species of 'facts'.

In *Narrative Logic: A Semantic Analysis of the Historian's Language*, F. R. Ankersmit proposes a very different relation between the historical text and the historical past, one located in the concept of 'narrative logic', which is found not in relation to time but in the *narratio*, the narrative text taken as a whole. 'The narratio is a linguistic entity essentially different from other coherent systems of sentences such as poems, novels, sermons, mathematical proofs and so on. Therefore the historiographical narrative representation of the past has an undeniable right to a name of its own' (1983: 19). The historical discourse, or narratio, exists only because of other discourses, not because of the past which is always absent by definition. 'The past as such has no narrative structure . . . We can compare one clock to another clock; but we cannot compare any clock to time and it makes therefore no sense to ask which of the many clocks we have is *correct*' (1983: 86–7). Historical disputes are caused by the historicist attribution to the 'past' that which is true *only* of narrative substances. Yet it is not 'the past' but the narratio that is unique.

The three theses of narrative logic are (a) that there are no translation rules for reality, (b) that it is the *whole* of the narratio, rather than the sum of its narrative sentences (and, presumably the nature of the events recorded), which gives an interpretation of the past, and (c) that there is a similarity between historical and metaphoric statements (Kellner 1987: 19). Conflicting histories of post-colonial independence movements such as the Mau Mau in Kenya, for instance, have nothing to do with each other from the point of view of narrative logic, since they refer only to the narrative substances in which they appear. While narrative *statements* may be true or false, narrative *substances* should not be spoken of in these terms. The incompatibility of narratios does not mean that one is true and the other is false because the past itself has no narrative structure. There is *no* absolute view of the past because only a multiple play of perspectives provided by a variety of narratios can enable us to 'see' the contours and specificities of each view of the past.

The question of resistance in post-colonial history becomes explicable as a contest of narratios, which may or may not differ about events, encapsulated in narrative statements, but may offer an incompatible and contesting narratio to official histories. The concept of narratio opens the way for an interpretation of history which may be described as 'appropriating the past'. This model values the past but does so in a way that incorporates it into the narrative project of the present. What the past 'is' becomes what the past 'is for us'. An example of such appropriation is the 'other side of the frontier' thesis of Henry Reynolds's history of Aboriginal resistance in Australia (1981). Conventional accounts see the depredations on the Aboriginal population as a matter of expropriation, killing and a general 'clearing' of Aboriginal tribes from the land desired for grazing and agriculture. Reynolds's thesis is that a protracted guerrilla war was conducted by the Aborigines against the encroaching white settlement. What is most important here is not that a history of Aboriginal guerrilla resistance represents a contestatory narratio, one story in a relativist aggregation of stories, but that it has the potential to become the way in which the past is understood – to transform history. Narratios are not neutral alternatives, but are themselves a feature of the power struggle continually waged in post-colonial societies. Contesting narratios struggle for authority over the explanation of the past.

Hayden White is perhaps the best-known contemporary theorist of history, and in his theory we find a distrust of narrativity itself which emerges from its potentiality as a repressive force, a potentiality which was increased when the emerging discipline rejected rhetoric and presented itself as a 'scientific discipline' in the nineteenth century.

Interpretation was hidden or purified in the interests of this scientism and 'Among the most important and permanent consequences of this sublimation of authority in the constitution of professional historical studies', says Kellner,

> was the deep and lasting distinction between philosophy of history, with its metaphysical goal of articulating the modes of authority and centres of power in historical discourses, and 'proper' history, with its disciplinary mandate to ignore the analysis of the deep, implicit choices in presentation and configuration, and the relative merits of these choices in opposition to other choices.
>
> (1987: 22)

According to White, the suppression of the sublime view of history as a chaos has underpinned the major ideologies of the last two centuries, both capitalist and communist, and narrativity has played an important role in this suppression. White calls into question the unfailing ability of narrative to make sense out of things and to present them in a form that *seems* natural (1982: 71). Narrative turns the chaos of history into an illusion of the immediacy and order of nature. One problem with this view is that it tends to take for granted some kind of uniformity in the discourse of history, despite its many manifestations. (This is something which also appears in White's addition of the phrase 'in itself' to history.) It fails to account for the validity of contesting narratives. The position that sees human dignity obtained in reaction to history's meaninglessness does not provide any strategy for those who are fixed, located, 'interpellated' in a dominant history. If the possibility of historical being itself emerged gradually in Western history, it was a far more cataclysmic event for colonized peoples. For the possibility of being in history was a sudden invasive incorporation into the Western discourse of history which imposed a concept not only of temporality, with its vision of both a 'civilizing' future and a degraded, premodern past, but of an encompassing ontology defined in a binary relation to European reality.

European history itself reveals the way in which a different conception of historicity is predicated upon a different conception of what it means to be human. White notes that the annals of St Gall record a span of some thirty years, listed in a vertical sequence, in which *only some of the years* have an 'event' recorded against them. We might want to dismiss this as the work of a sloppy annalist. But what kind of perception of the annalist's task would motivate such a record? What understanding of the location of human experience within time could justify a list of unembellished dates? Obviously some human experiences and not others are considered worthy of being recorded, and that very process of selection identifies what it is to be human for those people. The significance of this example to the historical consciousness of 'premodern', 'primitive' cultures awaiting the luminous benefits of the civilizing mission of European colonialism is obvious. Not only the narrative of history but time itself, a 'filled' time which is located in place, has a profoundly significant importance to cultural reality. When we see the Aboriginal conception of 'history' we begin to understand how culturally alien the white incursion must have been. Aboriginal culture does not require the record of history as an explanation of life, because time itself as an abstract concept is alien to Aboriginal society. All things stem from and return to the Dreaming, the source and object of the fabric of Aboriginal living, not fixed in time but accessible only as a complex of meanings. It includes an account of customs and laws, but, most importantly, it includes the tales of the Dreaming ancestors, whose travels mark the present site of a clan's property and whose experiences define their understanding of themselves and order their rituals. Apart from these ancestral tales, the Dreaming is a person's most sacred possession – his or her *name* – for this is the key which establishes a relationship with all humans, animals and places.

If we compare this with the threefold present of Augustine – remembered past, present and anticipated future – we see that the privilege of memory within historical narrativity is replaced in Aboriginal cosmology with a luminous present to which the past and future do not appear through the *distensio animi*, the stretching of the mind in different directions, but are *embedded materially in the present*. The past is not so much an unknowable chaos as a constantly and wholly experienced present. This immense difference between the Dreaming and the Western narrative of history is embedded in the language itself. The Dreaming, for the Aborigine, *is* the array of cosmogonic tales learnt as a child; it is the justification these tales provide for daily action; it is a name, totem, birth site, kin relationship, clan's land. It is a person's dance, song, skin painting. In short it is the prolific and infinitely interpretable text of the Aborigine's world. That the Dreaming is all these things testifies to the pervasiveness of this incorporating ontology. It is clear how the Western strategy of narrative potentially confines and limits a non-Western cosmology in the name of the 'superior' discourse of modernity.

Indeed one can see from this example how potentially traumatic the incorporation into the narrative of imperial history might be. In the particular case of Aboriginal cosmology the 'historical' luminosity of the present becomes fractured by the narrativity of history. But for all post-colonial peoples, to be incorporated into Western history is, by definition, to be located at its edges, to be the site of uninteresting 'events', of a marginal reality which has little to contribute to general understanding of the world. The problem of history, with its culturally disruptive and discursively imprisoning severance of time and space, becomes a problem in different ways for different colonized societies, and it becomes particularly crucial for the post-colonial writer. For not only are the questions of truth and fiction, of narrativity and indeterminacy, time and space, of pressing importance because the material ground, the political dimension of post-colonial life, impresses itself so urgently, but the historical narrativity is that which structures the forms of reality itself. In other words, the myth of historical objectivity is embedded in a particular view of the sequential nature of narrative, and its capacity to reflect, isomorphically, the pattern of events it records. The post-colonial task, therefore, is not simply to contest the message of history, which has so often relegated the post-colonial world to a footnote to the march of progress, but also to engage the medium of narrativity itself, to re-inscribe the 'rhetoric', the heterogeneity of historical representation as White describes it. It is in engaging the strategy of narrativity that post-colonial discourse can interpolate history, turning its status as a record to the task of self-determination and cultural empowerment. This, of course, is easier said than done for post-colonial societies which so often have failed to gain access to the very institution of 'History' itself with its powerful rules of inclusion and exclusion. The key function of the post-colonial interpolation of history is to subvert the unquestioned status of the 'scientific record' by re-inscribing the 'rhetoric' of events.

**Empire and history**

The story that decides 'what happened' is a story that determines 'what is'. For this reason history is of crucial importance in constructing a sense of identity. In his *Lectures on Early English History* Bishop Stubbs says:

> The history of our country is in one way of looking at it the history of ourselves; it is the history of our mind and body – of our soul and spirit also . . .
>
>   The knowledge of our own history is our memory, and so the recorded history of a nation is the memory of the nation: woe to

the country and people that forget it; an infant people has no history, as a child has a short and transient memory: the strong man and the strong nation feel the pulsation of the past in the life of the present: their memory is vital, long and strong.

(1900: 1)

Not only is history a narrative of who we are but it is the thing which makes us 'adult'; indeed, history has had a major role in producing a sense of being itself on a national level: 'the national character has been formed by the national history quite as certainly as the national history has been developed by the working of the national character' (Stubbs 1878: 1). The history of empire is itself a narrative of a nation providing a memory – its own history – for those 'infant' people, the colonized under its control. The historical record, even of critical histories, of the political and economic features of imperial control of India, for instance, misses entirely the ramifications of this transportation, the 'expansion of nationality' as Hobson describes the imperial project (1902: 6).

Imperial/empirical history is a story of development towards an imperial end. This is one meaning of the term 'historicism'. But its teleological impetus is one which is centripetal and establishes an order which is the essential aspect of the imperial – it orders reality. For the major British historians of the nineteenth century the writing of history was coterminous with an unshakeable conviction of imperial order. Considering such historians as Gibbon, the shaper of the Roman Empire, Macaulay, the apologist for British imperial greatness, or Trevelyan, the advocate of an English organic wholeness, we are struck by their compelling magisterial quality, an expansiveness of vision which rests on the absolute conviction that the order and the progression of empire had a certain inherent validity and inevitability which could not be countermanded. What was at stake in their histories was a conception of the progress of human civilization itself. J. R. Seeley, the Regius Professor of History at Cambridge at the end of the century, puts it unequivocally when he says, in *The Expansion of England* :

England has grown steadily greater and greater . . . It is far greater now than it was in the eighteenth century; it was greater in the eighteenth century than in the seventeenth, far greater in the seventeenth than in the sixteenth. The prodigious greatness to which it has attained makes the question of its future infinitely important and at the same time most anxious, because it is evident that the

great colonial extension of our state exposes it to new dangers, from
which in its ancient insular insignificance it was free.

(1890: 1–2)

The language of this passage takes for granted that which it proposes:
progress, expansion, the inevitable increase of imperial greatness.
Although, to his credit, he questions the vagueness of the term 'civilization' (4–5), Seeley nevertheless claims that 'No one can long study
history without being haunted by the idea of development, progress.
We move onward, both each of us and all of us together . . . and in
these last centuries at least there is much to favour the view that the
movement is progressive, that it is toward something better' (1890: 3).
This assumption is indisputable to the nineteenth-century historian.
What intrigues Seeley is the 'indifference which we show towards this
mighty phenomenon of the diffusion of our race and the expansion of
our state' (1890: 8). Hobson makes the interesting point that, apart
from the settler colonies, our other colonies 'are plainly representative
of the spirit of Imperialism rather than of colonialism' (1902: 7) because
no large proportion of British settlers living with their families inhabited
them. And yet conceptually, the expansion of England involved more
than the physical occupation of colonies, for it was above all the expansion of the imperial idea, carried in its language and cemented in its
political, administrative and cultural institutions.

The teleological view of history which emphasized the constancy of
progress is, not surprisingly, a strong feature of the school of British
historians who wrote during the emergence and growth of Britain's
empire. In some respects the view, held by some constitutional historians, that British institutions evolved as an organic development,
rather than as the consequence of abstract theory, invokes a particularly
resilient teleology. E. A. Freeman's *The Growth of the English Constitution
from the Earliest Times* celebrates the peculiarly British penchant for
precedent in its constitutional evolution.

There never was any moment when Englishmen drew out their
political system in the shape of a formal document, whether as
the carrying out of any abstract political theories or as the imitation
of the past or present system of any other nation . . . , the Great
Charter, the Petition of Right, the Bill of Rights . . . all claimed to
set forth, with new strength, it might be, and with new clearness,
those rights of Englishmen which were already old.

(1898: 56–7)

The evolution of the English constitution led to, or at least leads to in Freeman's thinking, a paradoxical link between progress and conservatism.

> We have made changes from time to time; but they have been changes which have been at once conservative and progressive – conservative because progressive, progressive because conservative. They have been the application of ancient principles to new circumstances; they have been the careful repairs of an old building, not the pulling down of an old building and the rearing up of a new. The life and soul of English law has ever been precedent.
>
> (57–8)

Here is a view of the 'cement' of history which allows the narrativity of historical writing (and, consequently, the inexorable movement of its imperial destiny) to take precedence over the particular 'event'. This weddedness to precedent distinguishes English institutions from the French, for instance, where 'institutions have been the work of abstract theory; they have been the creations, for good or for evil, of the minds of individual men. The English Parliament is immemorial; it grew step by step out of the older order of things' (66). This meant that the abstract ideas of French law, however magnificent, were fragile and could be overturned by the despotism of the Crown. In France 'no form either of the legislative or of the executive power, has been able to keep up a continuous being for over twenty years' (67). Consequently, according to Freeman, the study of English constitutional history is 'not merely an inquiry, however interesting and instructive, into something which has passed away. It is an inquiry into something which still lives' (91). It is not hard to extend the evolution of the English constitution into an almost natural expansion of English sovereignty. 'The code of our unwritten Constitution has, like all other English things, grown up bit by bit, and, for the most part, silently and without any acknowledged author' (122). This understanding of the benign process of constitutional development by precedent, and the 'rightness' of English law, has an uncanny similarity to English assumptions about the growth of its empire before the New Imperialism and the 'scramble' for Africa. One can see how an organic sense of the 'conservative progress' of constitutional development, and a celebration of precedent in political life, could generate a sense of the inevitability of history, the inevitability of imperial expansion.

Indeed, most English historians in the nineteenth century share a strong conviction of the special calling of the nation to the civilizing mission, even the comparatively sceptical such as Seeley. Perhaps the best-known expression of this belief is Macualay's view in his 1835 Minute that 'whoever knows [the English language] has ready access to all the vast intellectual wealth, which all the wisest nations of the earth have created and hoarded in the course of ninety generations' (1835: 350). The idea of an obligation to disseminate the wealth of the language has deep roots in a heroic view of history itself; of the special calling of 'civilized' nations and their special relevance to the task of history. Bishop Stubbs, in his lecture on the purposes and methods of historical study in Oxford on May 1877, says

> I will say that the true field of Historic Study is the history of those nations and institutions in which the real growth of humanity is to be traced: in which we can follow the developments, the retardations and perturbations, the ebb and flow of human progress, the education of the world.
>
> (cited in Williams 1972: 42)

Though it has the special flavour of British imperial history, such a concept is strongly reminiscent of Hegel's notorious statement that 'Africa has remained – for all purposes of connection with the rest of the World – shut up; it is the Gold-land compressed within itself' (1899: 91). It must be disregarded because 'Africa forms no historical part of the World' (99).

Indeed the consequences of a view of history as teleology are firstly that it paradoxically ignores time since the qualities of the 'civilizing' peoples are held to be timeless, and secondly that the notion of history as progress rests upon a fundamental cultural distinction between the European and colonized populations. It is this distinction which justifies the civilizing mission even in Seeley's ambivalent endorsement of the British rule in India:

> Much may be plausibly alleged against the system under which we govern India. It may be doubted whether it is altogether suited to the people, whether it is not needlessly expensive, and so forth . . . But I think it would be an extreme view to deny that our Government is better than any other which has existed in India since the Mussulman conquest.
>
> (1890: 194)

History (whether strident, thoughtful or cautious) thus becomes the disseminator of an ideology of racial superiority which masks the quite obvious economic imperative of a need for markets. Says Seeley, 'The British ideals have been made manifest – to rescue the races of Africa from the servile status that had become ingrained in their blood, and to create that sense of individual self-respect by which alone the traditions of slavery can be eradicated' (cited in Williams 1972: 171). Here, then, is a quite explicit demonstration of the function of the discursive practice of history in the control of discourse. The control of discourse is the control of representation itself and the representation of the colonized subject underpins some quite explicit material effects in the colonized world. Although not all history is as racist as it is when voiced by many of these historians of the Empire, the preference for absolutism and the reckless *denial* of time and space (or at least other representations of them) is a feature of any unreflective view of history as a record of the movement of the past into the present. In the post-colonial view, time is simply a different time when experienced in a different place.

The idea of the ordered progression of History towards a higher good found a particular foundation for nineteenth-century historians in the idea of a divine plan. In a lecture on the Puritan Revolution Lord Acton stated: 'But we have no thread through the enormous intricacy and complexity of modern politics except the idea of progress towards more perfect and assured freedom, and the divine right of free men' (1906: 202). The divine right of free men seems to derive from the divine ordering of the affairs of men. What this means to historians such as Acton amounts to the very essence of historical teleology. In an essay on the beginning of the modern state he says:

> Taking long periods, we perceive the advance of moral over material influence, the triumph of general ideas, the gradual amendment. The line of march will prove, on the whole, to have been from force and cruelty to consent and association, to humanity, rational persuasion, and the persistent appeal to common, simple, and evident maxims. We have dethroned necessity, in the shape of both hunger and of fear, by extending the scene from Western Europe to the whole world, so that all shall contribute to the treasure of civilization, and by taking into partnership in the enjoyment of its rewards those who are far off as well as those who are below.
>
> (Acton 1906: 33)

This is a supreme demonstration of the unshakeable confidence of the imperial historian in the movement of civilization towards the betterment of humankind, the 'amendment' of both the lower classes and the 'far off' races, and encapsulates the moral dimension of the assumptions of imperial history. Thus the teleological view of human progress seems inevitably allied, in such a history, to the dogma that the civilized nations are its chief subject. As Stubbs confirms in his lecture on the purposes and methods of historical study: 'The most precious Histories are those in which we read the successive stages of God's dispensations with man' (cited in Williams 1972: 42).

From the post-colonial perspective 'History [with a capital H] ends where the histories of those peoples once reputed to be without history come together' (Glissant 1989: 64). But this does not occur auto-matically by post-colonial societies taking command of their own 'memory', so to speak, and simply writing a different history. The presence of European history is manifest in any history of a post-colonial people. As Dipesh Chakrabarty says, 'There is a peculiar way in which all these other histories tend to become variations on a master narrative that could be called "the history of Europe"' (1992: 1). In colonies this tendency becomes even more pronounced: as Glissant points out, Martinican history is simply a reflection of French history. 'The temporary abolition of slavery in 1794, the end of slavery in 1848, adult male suffrage in 1877, and departmentalization in 1946 are the result of events in French history' (1989: xviii). Yet the most profound hindrance to colonial history is not the absorption of colonial reality into Europe in this way. It is the dominance of the assumptions and methodologies of the master narrative of History itself, as a way of conceiving colonial reality.

Responding to this ubiquitous master narrative, the aims of post-colonial writing seem curiously contradictory: the aim is on one hand to insert post-colonial experience into the programme of history, on the other to reject history because of its imperial narrativization of the past. But the problem here is that in history, as in other discursive formations, the post-colonial exists outside representation itself. The remedy is not 're-insertion' but 're-vision'; not the re-insertion of the marginalized into representation but the appropriation of a method, the re-vision of the temporality of events. This is interpolation in its fullest sense, and is crucial to the political interpretation of post-colonial experience because it is an attempt to assume control of the processes of representation. Another possibility therefore offers itself, that is, to change the 'programme' itself, to re-order the teleological construction of history. In Bakhtin's terms this means to re-inscribe the 'hetero-glossia', the hybrid profusion of life, into the linear and teleological movement of imperial history and, by so doing, to change our view of what history is.

## Transforming History

The relationship between post-colonial pasts and the master discourse called History raises many of the same questions as that between the 'subaltern' and a colonizing language. Does the adherence to a particular form of narrativity – a narrativity in which the will to truth predominates, a truth which has systematically excluded the reality of colonized experience – lock the non-European subject into the Western world view, 'colonizing the mind' as Ngugi puts it? As post-colonial discourse liberally demonstrates, the subaltern need not speak *out of* otherness to speak *as* other. Just as the subaltern disrupts the dominant language by interpolating it, so the post-colonial interpolation of history occurs in ways that refuse to leave it intact. But the epistemological assumptions of history nevertheless continue to operate powerfully to order post-colonial reality, and resistance to these takes various forms, a prominent one of which is the problematizing of the boundary between literature and history.

The way in which colonized peoples have been able to enter the narrativity of such patently authoritative and powerful intellectual pursuits as 'theory', 'philosophy' and history is very often through *literary* writing, or writing in the marginal space between literature and history, which may authorize otherwise forbidden entries into the intellectual battlefield of European thought. We may see post-colonial histories giving rise to various counter-narratives which take the view of the colonized, but such narratives may also contest the disciplinary boundaries of history as well. Wilson Harris believes that 'a philosophy of history may well lie buried in the arts of the imagination' (Harris 1970: 24–5). For Harris such imaginative arts extend beyond the 'literary' to include the discourse of the *limbo* dance or of *vodun*, all examples of the creativity of 'stratagems available to Caribbean man in the dilemmas of history which surround him' (25).

Perhaps the reason for this is that the false symmetry of a history conceived as linear progression conceals the many histories, the many narratives which constitute social life. This is not a startlingly new perception, but for colonized peoples it is a crucial, even life-or-death consideration. Edouard Glissant comments on the acute consequences of the totalizing power of the discourse of history for such societies as those in the Caribbean:

> History is a highly functional fantasy of the West, originating at precisely the time when it alone 'made' the history of the World. If Hegel relegated African peoples to the ahistorical, Amerindian

peoples to the prehistorical, in order to reserve History for European peoples exclusively, it appears that it is not because these African or American peoples 'have entered History' that we can conclude today that such a hierarchical conception of 'the march of History' is no longer relevant.

(1989: 64)

In post-colonial societies the term 'literary' may well operate in its traditional canonical way, but more often it has come to operate as a mode by which the objectivity of narrative is contested. This may be a particularly potent tactic, because it simply circumvents specific arguments about the status of the real, and demonstrates the provisionality of those assumptions about the real which underlie historical, and even philosophical, narratives about the world.

In a post-colonial experience there is only a difference of degree between 'History' and 'Imperial history'. As Oswald Spengler compellingly puts it, 'Imperialism is Civilization unadulterated' (1926: 36) and clearly 'History' is the history of 'Civilization'. There are various ways, then, in which the colonized can respond to the imperial function of history: they may acquiesce with its historical narrative; they may reject history outright; they may interject a different perspective into the discipline of history; or they may interpolate history in a way which reveals its assumptions and limitations. The simplest is *acquiescence*, a characteristic of those colonial histories which ask no questions at all about historical method, and which accede to the idea of colony as an outpost of civilization, an 'empirical record' of the movement of civilized values into the wilderness of an 'undiscovered wasteland'. History, like every other discourse in these places, is seen to be a 'branch of the parent tree'. It remains, as Bishop Stubbs says, a record of 'the real growth of humanity . . . the retardations and perturbations, the ebb and flow of human progress' (Williams 1972: 42), the concept of the 'human' as ideally European being an assumption which requires no debate.

The contrary position is *rejection*; one such as that taken by those who dispute any relevance at all to Eurocentric discourse. Writers such as Derek Walcott 'refuse to recognize' history and focus instead on the 'simultaneity of myth' (Slemon 1988: 159). This is a powerful statement of the reality of a different cultural consciousness, a different conception of time, and one we see present in images of history such as Harris's view of *limbo*. The problem is that such exclusivity may function as a kind of group insularity, neglecting the transformative way in which cultures may develop by using appropriated influences, and disregarding the perhaps more insidious ways in which Western 'global culture' affects colonized cultures. The dominant feature of post-colonial experience, indeed the major lesson it teaches, is the efficacy of *engagement*. Divergent and revitalized views of history will only have a power in global terms coincident with their ability to engage, to interpolate the master discourse of History.

A very different form of rejection is made by post-structuralists who reject history as a fabrication of order out of the chaos of human experience. Even when that chaos is seen to be a deferral of signification rather than a complete uncontrollability, any concession to historical discourse is forestalled by its narrative closure. Roland Barthes's essays on 'Historical Discourse' and 'The Reality Effect' spell out in structuralist terms how the illusions of reality are achieved in the realistic texts of both history and fiction. In $S/Z$ history emerges under one of the five codes which give rise to the creation of meaning in the text – the 'referential'. History serves there merely as one of the systems of reference which generate the 'effect of reality' in narrative, just as, in a different way, it is narrative that creates the possibility of historical discourse. By implication and assertion, history becomes another form of fiction since it employs the narrative code of the 'reality effect'. The problem this response presents to a colonized society in its various strategies of engagement with colonialism is obvious: no matter how much we reduce history to a 'reality effect', the need for a contesting narrative of the reality of colonial experience, of the post-colonial story, is urgent. The prospect of an endlessly deferred colonial reality holds no joy, nor any usefulness for a post-colonial historical narrative.

A third, and specifically post-colonial, response to history is *interjection*, in which the basic premises of historical narrative are accepted, but a contrary narrative, which claims to offer a more immediate or 'truer' picture of post-colonial life, a record of those experiences omitted from imperial history, is inserted into the historical record. For instance, nowhere has the claim of history to 'understand the present from the past' seemed more spurious than in British historians' treatment of the West Indies, and particularly the Jamaica rebellion (Williams 1972). By 1870 historians of empire wrote as if the rebellion had never occurred. This is not merely the convenient forgetting of an uncomfortable event. Imperial history could make no place for this scandal without undermining its own premises. Such are the conditions which lend urgency to the tactic of interjection. The tactic is outlined by William Luis when he says that:

The native history of America begins with the struggle to subvert Western man's powers, that is, with the attempt to re-write his writing of history . . .

By subverting writing, the oppressed usurps the power of language and, consequently history, to uncover a different version of the same history.

(Luis 1981: 250)

This insertion of contesting narratives, a 're-writing' of history, is an important strategy in the process of discursive resistance. The astute statement that 'The Slave, Caliban, uses Prospero's imposed language to undermine the master's powers' (Luis 1981: 250) recognizes the powerful strategy of engaging and appropriating the imperial language. But the appropriation of language operates in subtle and sometimes powerfully effective ways. The post-colonial seeks to coin a *method* by which the profusion and hybridity of post-colonial reality can be stated *within* the spaces opened up by History, and in this way redirect it. This method is fundamentally a political contestation of imperial power. But it is one that works through, in the interstices of, in the fringes of, rather than in simple opposition to, history.

Such a method is demonstrated when the post-colonial alternative, the contestation of the dominance of the European narrative, inter-polates history. *Interpolation* is not so much 're-writing' as Luis conceives it, inserting the marginal histories that have been excluded (although this is an important tactic), but 'writing back'. The model for this is 'counter-discourse', which is not a separate oppositional discourse but a tactic which operates from the fractures and contradictions of dis-course itself. When Jean Rhys writes, in *Wide Sargasso Sea*, the 'history' of Rochester's mad wife in *Jane Eyre*, the subsequent interpolation not only fractures the 'completeness' of the classic novel by revealing an invisible narrative but reveals how limited is the unitary perspective of the historical mode. In Coetzee's *Foe* the interpolation is of a different order. Because *Foe* re-writes the entire Crusoe story on the level of both race and gender, he inserts the post-colonial allegory – and thus, in a sense, post-colonial history – into the elaborately erected myth which the *Robinson Crusoe* story has become in Western imagination. These 'canonical counter-discourses' are not 'histories' but they show the process of historical re-visioning at work. This kind of 'writing back' has a far more profound effect than 'setting the story straight', tidying up the margins of European history, or simply adding one more voice to a Eurocentred pluralism of narratives. Ultimately, the object of this strategy is to transform the situation in which History simply means 'variations on a master narrative that could be called "the history of Europe"' (Chakrabarty 1992: 1). A key strategy in the transformation of history is therefore the interpolation of historical discourse. This involves not simply the insertion of a contestatory voice, a different version, or a radical perspective, although it may involve all these, but an entry into the discourse which disrupts its discursive features and reveals the limitations of the discourse itself. This form of interpolation does not occur only in literary texts, of course, but it is in literary texts that some of the most disruptive and evocative potentialities of historical interpolation may occur because it is in literature that the allegorical nature of historical discourse becomes revealed.

# 5  Allegory

The blurring of the disciplinary distinction between History as a scientific record and literature as a creative construction has led many post-colonial intellectuals to a much more emancipatory view of the historical. Apart from anything else, the Eurocentrism of the discourse of History relegates the periphery of empire to the margins of history itself, to a practical historylessness. In talking about the difficult phenomenon of Caribbean history, the history of a people robbed of a prehistory, taken out of their own history, so to speak, and then denied a reality within early accounts of plantation society, Edouard Glissant conceives a history in prophetic terms: a past conflated with the present which the writer must continually strive to capture. For the Caribbean subject:

> The past, to which we were subjected, which has not yet emerged as history for us, is, however, obsessively present. The duty of the writer is to explore this obsession, to show its relevance in a continuous fashion to the immediate present. This exploration is therefore related neither to a schematic chronology nor to a nostalgic lament. It leads to the identification of a painful notion of time and its full projection forward into the future, without the help of those plateaus in time from which the West has benefited, without the help of that collective density that is the primary value of an ancestral cultural heartland. That is what I call *a prophetic vision of the past*.
>
> (Glissant 1989: 64)

Such a prophetic vision of the past radically revises our understanding of the nature of 'unfilled time' (the consequence of modernity) and the teleological progress of European history. Such a prophetic vision confirms that 'a philosophy of history may well lie buried in the arts of the imagination' as Wilson Harris says (1970: 24–5). As we have seen, because post-colonial societies have been marginalized from the disciplinary structures of European discourse, their access to those structures has often occurred by means of *literary* writing. But what makes the textual response to imperialism so efficacious is that 'the actual experience of life in a colonial or post-colonial culture has been, and continues to be, "written" by the texts of colonial discourse' (Slemon 1987: 10). The dominant mode of representation of these colonial texts is allegorical and hence allegory becomes the site of cultural struggle, a prime site of counter-discourse:

> Allegory, that is, becomes an historically produced field of representation upon which certain forms of post-colonial writing engage head-on with the interpellative and tropological strategies of colonialism's most visible figurative technology. Allegory becomes a site upon which post-colonial cultures seek to contest and subvert colonialist appropriation through the production of a literary, and specifically anti-imperialist, figurative opposition or textual *counter-discourse*.
>
> (Slemon 1987: 11)

Allegory is important because the actual experience of life in a colonial culture has been written by the allegories of colonialist discourse (10). The 'great' literary allegories of the English literature canon have been the most influential formulators of what it is to be human and have thus become the particular objects of counter-discourse.

But why should allegory be such a potent site for *historical* revision? The analysis of theories of narrativity in the previous chapter hints at the answer: fundamentally, all historical writing is allegorical. 'One virtue of quantitative history, cliometric history, theory-oriented history and psycho-history', says Hans Kellner, 'is that they are far more openly and self-consciously allegorical than more traditional narrative histories' (1987: 27). This is because narrativity reproduces, metonymically, the teleological progression of the history it 'records'. The virtue of a conscious allegory is that it 'questions its own authority by inescapably drawing attention to the *will* exerted in its creation; this will to represent is revealed as a human need, the product of desire or "Care" and can be understood only within the authoritative confines of . . . another allegory' (Smith 1982: 113). The literary interpolation of history therefore unveils the figural mode on which history is based and which narrativity serves to conceal.

The significance of allegory to post-colonial, and particularly non-Western, accounts of history is firstly this 'questioning of its own authority' as Kellner says, and secondly the capacity it gives for what Glissant calls a 'prophetic vision of the past'. Such a prophetic vision is not unlike the vision of myth, which 'enfolds' the present rather than outlining the past. The kind of history which foregrounds the allegorical propensity of the discourse is one that goes to the heart of those elements which define a particular culture, and, in many cases, define the cultural trajectory of its experience of European colonization. This prophetic vision of the past need not occur in literary texts. Indeed, one of the most striking examples of a historical allegory is Wilson Harris's proposal that the ubiquitous *limbo* dance found in the carnival life of the West Indies is an allegory of the slaves' passage from Africa to the Caribbean. '*Limbo* was born, it is said, on the slave ships of the Middle Passage. There was so little space that the slaves contorted themselves into human spiders' (1970: 25). 'Not only has the journey from the Old World to the new varied with each century and each method of transport,' says Harris, 'but needs to be re-activated in the imagination as a limbo perspective when one dwells on the Middle passage: a *limbo* gateway between Africa and the Caribbean' (26). This is a compelling image of a history which functions in the present, which not so much forms a dialectic between memory, future time and the present as *enacts* the presentness of history.

However, it is in literary texts that we may find the most sustained engagement between the allegorical dimension of history and its narrativity. Indeed, Harris's own novels, particularly *Carnival*, an allegory modelled on Dante's *The Divine Comedy*, demonstrate the densely transformative process of 'infinite rehearsal' through which he enters a tradition of his own making, creating 'gateways' into an imaginative release from the monumental inheritance of history. The historical allegory of the *limbo* dance alerts us to the cultural specificity of allegorical forms. The literary text and the hybrid genre, the South American *testimonio*, discussed below, recast post-colonial history according to very different allegorical modes. The first, Shashi Tharoor's *The Great Indian Novel*, retells the story of the breakdown of empire in India and the emergence of independence through the lens of the *Mahabharata* which forms the counter-discursive allegorical frame through which the scientific pretensions of a colonial history may be dismantled. Tharoor's novel is consciously counter-discursive in its reproduction of history through a Hindu lens, reversing the historical gaze by putting the reader in the place of the Indian consumer of a dominant but culturally alien discourse. The second text, *I, Rigoberta Menchú*, uncovers the allegorical nature of historical narrative in a much more subversive way and provides the site for a vigorous and controversial debate over the truth function of 'literary/historical' representation. Discussing these vastly different texts together shows something of the heterogeneity of the struggle with history in post-colonial discourse.

## Myth and history: *The Great Indian Novel*

The central issue in *The Great Indian Novel* (1989) is the problematizing of history, and particularly the history of India's move to independence. This novel, the title of which satirizes literary pretensions to universal value, is by no means 'canonical' yet it provides a powerful 'prophetic vision of the past' by applying the *Mahabharata* to the events of India's colonial history. The genius of the book is its ability to undermine the seriousness of history by rendering the most complex cultural issues, and the most tragic historical events, in the tone of a sophisticated and ambivalently ironic comedy. In this way the comic tone comes to express that 'menace' which is the constant companion of mimicry. The subversive power of the comic tone is nowhere more in evidence than in its description of the absurdity and bungling of imperial administration, indeed of the obtuseness which led to the creation of India itself.

The story of partition is the narrative in which time and space, history and geography meet. But the truth this novel expresses so well is that every effect of imperial power in South Asia is at the same time a moment of redefinition of empire. The catastrophic construction of India, so contingent a demonstration of imperial power, is nevertheless an engagement in which the effects of change work dialectically. And this dialectical relationship is most potently revealed in the use of the English language itself. The process within which the relationship of the colonizer and colonized operates is one which becomes dialogic when the master-tongue is appropriated. This is the insistent message of post-colonial writing, and of the principle of interpolation in general: that the colonized can enter into dialogue only when they acquire the cultural capital of imperial culture to make themselves heard. The English language is not simply appropriated to describe Indian culture, it is in a subtle way implicated in its construction. And conversely both the language and the range of master discourses in which it is involved are themselves reconstituted by the association.

In *The Great Indian Novel* we find a consummate demonstration of this strategy by which the epistemological categories of history itself are disturbed. Its interpolation of the discourse of history occurs by means of what might be called a 'cultural transparency'. This term alludes to Homi Bhabha's use of the concept of 'negative transparency' to indicate

the ambivalence of post-colonial mimicry. In this novel the broad outlines of the *Mahabharata* are overlaid upon the story of India's post-
colonial history in a way which not only provides a reconceptualization
of events in the context of a dense mythology but also serves to disrupt
the discourse of history itself, projecting it into the future. We can think
of it as the overlaying of an allegorical cultural map upon the narrative
of official history to effectively 'reshape' it. The *Mahabharata*, or at
least its creative co-option in the narrative of modern India, becomes a
'positive transparency'. The process of this overlaying provides a 'timeless' allegorical framework for the events of India's move to independence without necessarily discarding historical narrativity. Indeed the
contingent and dialectical movement of that narrative is emphasized,
and, by interpolating the *Mahabharata*'s sense of the timelessness and
recurrence of historical events, the power of the imperial/empirical
history of India is undermined in a kind of allegorical one-upmanship.

The embracing syncreticity of the process by which the 'positive
transparency' of the *Mahabharata* adds a layer of narrative to those
already in existence is one which provides rich possibilities for the project of a post-colonial history. This writer's India is therefore one
which becomes endlessly redefinable.

> History, Ganapathi – indeed the world, the universe, and all human
> life, and so too, every institution under which we live – is in a
> constant state of evolution. The world and everything in it is being
> created and re-created even as I speak, each hour, each day, each
> week, going through the unending process of birth and rebirth
> which has made us all. India has been born and reborn scores of
> times, and it will be reborn again. India is for ever; and India is
> forever being made.
>
> (Tharoor 1989: 245)

It is in the light of this salutary view of the universe that the writer is
given a free hand in his intervention into historical truth. The 'positive
transparency' by which he appropriates the past captures the dialogism
by which the written text comes into meaning. By extension it is also
the dialogue by which the texts of history and of culture itself emerge.

The process of using the *Mahabharata* as the 'transparency' of history
has a formidable counter-discursive function. For the non-Indian
reader the access to Hindu cosmology occurs in exactly the same way
that the Indian readers of the Great Tradition of English literature
were expected to absorb the values of Western civilization from their

reading. This reversal is a profound reversal of the strategy of reading. *The Great Indian Novel* demonstrates not only the process of the post-colonial interpolation of history but the kind of 'resistance' which can be achieved by an interpolation of the category 'literature' itself. What we find is not a simple reversal of history; at one level the narrative of history is left untouched. But the layering of the transparency of Indian cosmology, values, assumptions, world view upon that history via the *Mahabharata* enacts the civilizing mission *in reverse*.

One brilliant strategy in this reversal lies in the function of naming. By naming those people who played the major parts in contemporary Indian history according to the names of the *Mahabharata*, history itself is 'known' in a different way. The story becomes a 'prophetic vision' because it so manifestly exceeds the linear narrative of history, and the story of India is known in a way which cannot be confined by History. The immense depth and spread of Indian cosmology exists as a kind of ground on which the story of India's move into independence can be read, a story in which irony and parody are all the stronger when read from the perspective of the timeless Indian myth. That this is an inter-polation rather than an imposition is supported by the fact that history allegorizes individuals *as though* they were the characters of myth. Of Gandhi (Gangaji), for instance: 'He might as well have been a character from the *Mahabharata*, Ganapathi, so completely had they consigned him to the mists of myth and historical legend' (47).

The allegorical mode makes visible that which exists as a hidden func-tion of historical narrativity. Nowhere does allegory seem more appro-priate as a mode of history than in the vibrant and irreducible complexity of India. In this novel the transparency of the *Mahabharata* gives way directly to allegory at the moment of historical crisis: the break-up of India itself. This occurs in the birth of Draupadi, the beauti-ful symbolic progeny of the union of empire and decolonizing state. Draupadi, the daughter of Dhritarashatra (Nehru) and the Vicerine (Lady Mountbatten), is India herself; beautiful, hybrid, mysterious, 'Draupadi was like the flame of a brass lamp in a sacred temple of the people' (309). Her marriage is the allegory of India's future: 'Yes of course. Draupadi had to be married one day. But to tie that boundless spirit to any one man – it would be a crime; it would diminish and con-fine her, and all of us' (311). In a dream Ved Vyas sees that it is Arjun the perfect, Arjun the hero of mythology, who succeeds in winning her.

But Arjun has five brothers and all have sworn to obey every injunc-tion that their mother makes, however casual it might be. When they take Draupadi to meet their mother, her impatient response to them when told they have a surprise for her is that they should 'share it among themselves'. This seems a dismaying calamity for Draupadi and Arjun, but this is precisely the kind of arbitrary historical moment by which India enters the ambivalent realm of modernity. Draupadi, post-colonial India, is to be wed to democracy and all it entails, for she must marry all the brothers:

> She stood erect and calm amidst the confusion, unquestioning, untroubled, reading each brother's mind, seeing through Kunti's ambivalence. In her self-possessed silence it was apparent that, though she had given her heart to the god-like youth who had won her hand, she realized that democracy's destiny, and hers embraced his brothers too.
>
> (315)

Although the dream of India's future is the union of Draupadi and Arjun, 'a man of contradictions, [who] perfectly reflected both the diversity and the discordance of the Indian masses' (320), this future must also embrace the stolidly political and bureaucratic (Yudhishtir), the warlike (Bhim the soldier), the glib banalities of diplomacy and the agonizing dilemmas of administration (the twins Nakul and Sahadev) (321).

Draupadi expresses in her own body the post-independence turmoil of India, its symbolic changes in fortune, as she oscillates between sickness and health. But she is also a character in the novel, a character in the history. History itself in a place such as India is both allegorical and 'real': this is, in a sense, the function of 'positive transparency', to represent the 'allegorical real'. The following events, in which Arjun is forced to travel around India, and eventually meets up with Krishna, continue the allegorical transparency by which the novel reads contemporary Indian history. And yet at no stage does the novel abandon its perception of the very immediate, very real fortunes and misfortunes of the country under Priya Duryodhani (Indira Gandhi).

The point of all this is the point that Ved Vyas's Hindu consciousness has already made concerning history: 'there is no end'. In terms of India's post-independence history there is also no real beginning. India's history is not some appendix to the story of empire. The Raj itself is but one phase in a story that is so vast that it has no beginning and no end. This assumption is cataclysmic for the authority of historical discourse. Neither the imperial pretensions nor the national passions of independence nor the cynical politics of post-independence India can lay claim to historical integrity. All these immensely evocative periods are part of a larger story, a story through which history can be read. The historical truth of *The Great Indian Novel* has to do not with chronology or verisimilitude but with its engagement with the vast perspective of the Hindu cosmology.

Nevertheless, and perhaps somewhat curiously, one of the discursive modes of the novel is that of realism. Obviously it is a far more ambivalent realism than that suggested by simple verisimilitude, a political, subversive, yet emotional realism which displays its discursive ambivalence even when allowing the serious reality of colonial oppression to show through. This is particularly so when the novel describes the social action such as the plight of the indigo farmers which began Gandhi's career (50): 'You can't know, you with your ration-cards and your black markets and the cynical materialism of your generation, what it was like in those days, what it felt like to discover a cause, to belong to a crusade, to *believe*' (52). The reality is a political reality, one which bears a particularly contestatory position to the authorized history:

> Do you think the merchants and adventurers and traders of the East India Company would have first sailed to a land of poverty and misery? No, Ganapathi, they came to an India that was fabulously rich and prosperous, they came in search of wealth and profit and they took what they could take, leaving Indians to wallow in their leavings.
>
> (95)

However, this novel displays the full panoply of historical strategies in its narrative. It never slackens its own narrative, satirical and intertextual modes. It is a story within which certain truths may contest the dominant but it is, in Indian fashion, a *story* which must bear the marks of its own invention. Imperial history is like a stage on which the sequential and teleological progress of the civilizing mission is played out:

> We tend, Ganapathi, to look back on history as if it were a stage play, with scene building upon scene, our hero moving from one action to the next in his remorseless stride to the climax. Yet life is never like that. If life were a play the noises offstage, and for that matter the sounds of the audience, would drown out the lines of the principal actors. That, of course, would make for a rather poor tale; and so the recounting of history is only the order we artificially impose upon life to permit its lessons to be more clearly understood.
>
> (109)

History is not a staged play, a theatre played out on the passive stage called 'India', as imperial history might contend, but it is also a story without end. This strikes at the very heart of the teleological perspective of imperial history because the end of such history is the perfection of the civilizing process:

> 'the end' was an idea that I suddenly realized meant nothing to me. I did not begin the story in order to end it; the essence of the tale lay in the telling. 'What happened next?' I could answer. But 'what happened in the end?' I could not even understand . . .
>
> There is, in short, Ganapathi, no end to the story of life. There are merely pauses. The end is the arbitrary invention of the teller.
>
> (163)

But to which story shall we return? (165), he asks later. The story of history is many stories, none of which has an end but all of which continue intersected and overlapping. It is this secret of history that the transparency of the *Mahabharata* can reveal. For India 'History is Krukshetra. The struggle between dharma and adharma is a struggle of our nation, and each of us in it, engages in [*sic*] on every single day of our existence. That struggle, that battle, took place before this election; it will continue after it' (391). In the 'end' there is no end, only the ambivalence of history: the present overlapping the past: 'Something had passed whose shadow would always remain, and something had begun that would not endure' (402).

## Truth, allegory and testimony: *I, Rigoberta Menchú*

The blurring of the distinction between literature and history allows literary representations to figure a truth which may have an inclusive rather than exclusive validity for a society or people. It also allows them to play havoc with the fetishization of historical truth in its disciplinary 'scientific' form. But where writing impinges on the area of historical veracity, even in a genre which operates in the space between literature and history, the tyranny of truth quickly comes to the fore. The ability of literary texts to disrupt the apparently transparent narrativity of history and expose its allegorical nature is almost boundless. But however energetic and subtle the literary dismantling of historical truth, literature is to some extent shielded by its *simulation* of the political struggle over 'the truth of what is real' in colonial experience. The allegorical mode, because it is acceptably 'literary', makes possible a subtle exposure of the allegorical nature of history. But in the genre of testimony, the struggle is much more urgent. Testimony, in Western society, is firmly attached to legal discourse and hence to the legal requirements for veracity. Thus, any sense of the allegorical in its witnessing of a communal experience is, because of the very immediacy of the account, exceptionally confronting to Western notions of the narrative structure of truth.

In *testimonio*, associated almost exclusively with Latin America, we discover that the appropriation of the *means* of representation, such as the colonial language, might also entail a reconfiguration of the very notion of *truth* in representation. *Testimonio* generally involves the recording, transcription and editing of an oral account by an interlocutor who is a journalist, writer or social activist (Beverley 1989: 12–13). It coalesces as a clearly defined genre around the decision in 1970 of Cuba's cultural centre, Casa de las Américas, to begin awarding a prize in this category in its annual literary contest (Beverley and Zimmerman 1990: 173). It is arguable that if this decision had not been made, or some other like it, the genre might not have existed. Paradoxically, *testimonio*, which problematizes the boundaries of genres such as literature and history, demonstrates this problem most acutely by the contingency of its own emergence as a genre.

*Testimonio* transforms the discourses of literature and history by inserting itself between them, coming into being at the margins of both, a 'zone of indeterminacy' from which genraic expectations are disrupted. *Testimonio* has been the subject of an extended debate since the 1980s, and it would be difficult to find any form of writing which so comprehensively focuses the issues surrounding the politics of representation, the reality of history, the corrigibility of genre boundaries, the efficacy of political intervention and, indeed, the endlessly complex and argumentative relationship between colonized speakers and dominant First World forms of language use. The power of *testimonio* to interpolate both literature and history – to insert not only a different account but a different discursive modality, a different array of narrative assumptions – stems from its immediacy, its anonymity and its identification of the personal and the political.

Few literary genres have had such success in providing this degree of immediacy in conveying historical experience. This arguably leads to a greater, or at least a more immediate, more urgent understanding of the problems of Central American nations than can any social science or historical research. The most compelling achievement of *testimonio* is its representation in history of the unhistoricized, the 'voiceless'. By reinforcing what René Jara calls a 'public intimacy' (*intimidad pública*), the *testimonio* narration achieves the metonymic power denied history and literature. The narrator in *testimonio* is a real person who continues living and acting in a real and continuous social history. Thus the text can never be complete in itself in the manner of a literary work: it is both provisional and transitional, but this extra literary dimension gives it an explicit power in transporting the reading subject into an intimacy with historical and political action that neither literature nor history can easily achieve.

The most striking strategy in *testimonio* is the construction of what might be called a communal subject position, which, more than anything else, sets it apart from similar narrative forms. *Testimonio* affirms a self-identity that is inseparable from the collective oppressed group or class. Related to autobiography and at the same time ideologically distant from autobiography, it fulfils a major mandate: to rewrite and retell, to correct Latin American history and reality from the people's perspective (Gugelberger and Kearney 1991: 11). The construction of a communal or collective subject position involves a questioning of the role and thus also of the hermeneutic primacy and textual presence of the author. Consequently there is a disruption of the ideological function of textual authority and of the truth function which history in particular is designed to invoke.

### Control of representation

At the level of its struggle over representation *testimonio* has a problematic relationship with 'truth'. Edward Said suggests that all representations are in some sense misrepresentations (1978: 272) and, at base, Menchú's work of representation (*I, Rigoberta Menchú: An Indian Woman in Guatemala*, 1983) operates no differently from any other: representation is always a process by which concrete form is given to ideological concepts. The problematic identification of representation with 'truth' is an outworking of the power of Western culture in which the concept of objectivity has achieved such prominence. Menchú's representation of Quiché life (mediated so heavily, we must remember, by her interlocutor Burgos-Debray) offers rather an 'experienced truth' of the reality of Guatemalan oppression.

A key function of *testimonio* is the strategic attempt to control representation, to interpose a voice that has been silenced, oppressed or misrepresented, a goal which lies at the core of all interpolating strategies. The task of *testimonio* is 'not to reproduce but to make visible' (Gugelberger 1996: 4) and this gives it a peculiarly powerful purchase on the 'truth' of representation. The very act of telling the story, and getting it 'heard' by being published and widely disseminated, initiates this self-representation, but the *control* of the representing process can occur in more subtle ways. A clear example of this is the recurrent evidence of Menchú's secrets. Not only does she withhold certain 'secrets' which she feels both define her as a Quiché and represent a region of inner knowledge which the communal subject must keep to itself, but she lets the reader know that such secrets are being withheld. The fact that Menchú can keep communal secrets, even in the very process of appropriating a discourse which will reveal her people's plight in a compelling and evocative way, is a clear example of the way in which many post-colonial texts install a metonymic gap in the text (see Chapter 3) – a gap which, by its very articulation, installs cultural difference even while purporting to communicate across that difference. She has no real need even to mention her secrets, so this very public refusal to disclose them heightens the reader's sense of that cultural integrity which political action is designed to protect. Although Menchú underplays any less-than-heroic features of Quiché society (such as sexism and alcoholism), she does so because the form is not so much the representation of a 'scientific' truth as formal history might claim to be, but the urgent representation of the *experience* of oppression. The balance between secrets and revelation conveys a powerful sense of the political struggle in Guatemala as a battle over identity itself.

It seems paradoxical that in the act of representing, these secrets should be announced in a voice that is so present and immediate. Indeed, the scandal of *testimonio* for post-structuralist theory in particular is its shameless construction of presence, through the invocation of the speaking voice, and the syntax of conversation. Although this narrative construction is unreservedly invented and its illusion of presence is perhaps easily deconstructed, it makes an unparalleled claim upon the urgency of the real present. How we approach this theoretically is problematic, as Elzbieta Sklodowska cautions: 'although the *testimonio* uses a series of devices to gain a sense of veracity and authenticity – among them the point of view of the first-person witness narrator – the play between fiction and history appears inexorably as a problem' (1982: 379). The tension between historical truth and fiction which Sklodowska raises as a problem for *testimonio* is in fact not *testimonio*'s problem alone but an inherent problem of historical discourse. By occupying the discursive zone between literature and history *testimonio* brings this problem to prominence. What is at stake, however, is the particular nature of the 'reality effect', as Barthes puts it (see Chapter 4), of the *testimonio*. The most important feature of the *testimonio* is that it produces, if not the real, then certainly a sensation of *experiencing the real*. As Jara points out, *testimonio* is 'a trace of the real, of that history which, as such, is inexpressible' (Vidal and Jara 1986: 2). This question of the 'reality' of the *testimonio* account is curiously persistent in commentary on the form. In his introduction to the collection *The Real Thing* (1996) George Gugelberger explains that the title is:

> a reflection on the dilemma of present critical discourse that is so much engaged with issues of representationality, realism, truth, etcetera. Testimonio, perhaps more than any genre in the past, has foregrounded the issue of what is 'real' and has been defined by Jara as 'una huella de lo real,' a trace of the real . . . The 'real' thing is also the thing with the real, the issue of what is and can be real.
>
> (5)

This concern with the real is no doubt a consequence of the inherited demands of historical discourse. But the balance between veracity and rhetoric problematized by *testimonio* focuses the importance of this issue to post-colonial writing. For *testimonio* is *both* truth and fiction (in a more obvious way than history), for it is constructed in the narrative mode, but the interlocutory character of its narrative enters the problematic space of historical truth with a clear formula for conveying the *rhetoric* of the real. If Hayden White is correct in suggesting that rhetoric was discarded by the scientific discourse of history in the nineteenth century (1982: 120), then *testimonio* represents a radical re-installation of the rhetoric of experience in 'historical' narrative.

Another problematization of historical truth is raised by the question of whether this work of translation, transcription and production by the Western interlocutor is a form of 'contamination' of the subject position of the text. The interlocutor might be accused of manipulating or exploiting the material the informant provides to suit her own cosmopolitan political, intellectual, and aesthetic predilections (Beverley 1989: 20). One response to this question is to see such 'contamination' as material evidence of the reader function, a function which is open-ended in the sense that it is endlessly replicated in individual readings. Rather than assume that the meaning issues from a discrete authoring centre, *testimonio* encourages us to recognize that, even with a discourse that is so very 'present', it is the meaning event, the situation of discourse, which constructs meaning, through the constitutive action of writer and reader functions. The relationship between narrator and interlocutor itself focuses the very function of such a text as an interpolation. In giving voice to a previously voiceless and anonymous collective popular subject, *testimonio* interpellates the intellectual or professional reader as a part of and dependent on this subject.

The contamination of the relationship between the narrator and interlocutor is itself metonymic of the discursive relations between a master discourse such as literature or history, and a colonized subaltern subject whose participation in them appears so dependent. This issue is never clear cut. The long polemic against US imperialism which concludes the original version of *I, Rigoberta Menchú* is omitted from the English language version. But this may in fact be seen to enhance the sympathy of the US audience for the Guatemalan victims. Such a 'contamination' and positioning is a recognition of the hybrid nature of the discourse which history attempts to regulate. By interpolating the communal voice of the oppressed people into these discourses in this urgent and evocative way, the communal subject reorganizes the discourse for its political and historical purpose, it constructs the reader as ambivalent participant.

## Reversing the gaze of history

One of the most compelling justifications for a post-colonial reading of Latin American *testimonios* such as *I, Rigoberta Menchú* is the pervasive and continuing reality of the original colonial invasion to Indian culture. If historicism is the naturalization of time, then Menchú's testimony denaturalizes time by inscribing the practices of denaturalization which are constantly present in communal life. Menchú shows how the Quiché ceremonies conflate history in such a way that the Spanish invasion is made to seem an aspect of present experience. The blurring of these boundaries between the present and the past is one of the most troubling transgressions of the historical mode. While the evidence of political, ethnic and social oppression is manifest in these texts, the reality of colonization underpins these contemporary examples of injustice and the reality of colonial conquest is constantly inscribed and re-inscribed in the life of the Quiché.

Historicism fixes the indigenous subject at a static moment in the past, a prehistory located under the sign of the primitive; a primal innocence or barbarity. This is the static historical moment from which History, the record of civilization, begins. In response to this the Quiché Indians continually re-inscribe the arrival of the white man in their rituals and ceremonies, thus exposing the originary colonial moment as a prominent feature of the present. At every major rite of passage for the Quiché – tenth birthday, marriage, major fiestas and death – a crucial feature of the ritual or celebration is the reiteration of the disaster of colonization. This is an astonishing process of embedding which demonstrates the power of the historical conflation in oral cultures. When a child turns ten it is introduced to various aspects of cultural knowledge, a key one being the reminder that 'our ancestors were dishonoured by the White Man, by colonization' (Menchú 1983: 13). The preparations for marriage and the marriage ceremony itself are a time of intense cultural commitment, a time when the couple is enjoined to 'honour the Indian race' (67). They affirm the importance of the community, referring back 'to the time of Columbus', saying 'Our forefathers were dishonoured by the White Man' (67). They engage in a day of talking to remind themselves that 'this is what the White Man did' (69), and are encouraged to maintain cultural purity and avoid the contamination of *ladino* attractions such as Coca-Cola (71).

This insertion of the historical disaster of colonization into their present-day rituals also extends to an active opposition to the white history which presents the arrival of the white man as a conquest, a victory 'while we knew that in practice it was just the opposite' (170). This opposition takes the form of fiestas such as the fiesta of Tecún Umán, national hero of the Quiché (204). (More specifically, they do not celebrate this since they regard Tecún Umán to be still alive.) But normal saints day fiestas are accompanied by dances called the 'Dance of the Conquest'.

> There are dances in which the Indian represents how he repelled the Spaniards. We call it the 'Dance of the Conquest.' The Indians put on white or red masks to represent the Spaniards. The Spaniards have horses and the Indians fight them with the weapons of the people – machetes, stones. So they have a battle. And they do it as a dance. I liked everything but I like the 'Dance of the Conquest' very much because it gives an exact meaning to what Indians think about the 'Conquest'.
>
> (206)

In such ways time is dismantled so that the location of the indigenous subject by history in a fixed time of primitive innocence is disrupted. By showing the distant historical event of invasion as an aspect of the present of Indian consciousness, the time of the colonized Indian is constituted as the present time, and thus a time amenable to change and alteration in a political sense, while also being the time of a change-less tradition. The fascinating aspect of this disruption of time is that the present oppressors are not 'white' in the sense of being Spanish but are mestizos produced by centuries of intermarriage. By continually re-inscribing the colonizing event as a permanent feature of the continuing present, the 'history' of Latin American independence and hybridization which has, according to many Latin American critics, made the region inaccessible to post-colonial theory is itself disrupted and denaturalized by at least one colonized group. It is interesting to compare the Quiché's 'anachronistic' experience of the present with that 'prophetic vision of the past' which Edouard Glissant proposed at the beginning of this chapter as the key to a liberatory conception of history.

One of the most traumatic features of *I, Rigoberta Menchú* is the pathological way in which the state inscribes its power on the bodies of the Indians, through torture, rape, abuse and killing as a material sign of its cultural and political devastation. Such is the expectation of suffering that one of the ceremonies performed by a woman about to be married includes the statement: 'I will be a mother, I will suffer, my children will suffer, many of my children will die young because of the circumstances created for us by white men' (70). The Guatemalan government, through its army, and indeed through the exploitation of white landowners, perpetrates shocking abuse on the Indians. But perhaps the most appalling occasion occurred at a time when villagers from all over the *altiplano* were commanded by the army to assemble at a central village to witness the power of the government as it has been inscribed on the tortured bodies of the villagers' friends and family members. The trucks arrived with friends and relatives of the people of the surrounding villages, people who were 'monstrously disfigured, unrecognizable', tortured almost to death. They were placed in a line, hardly able to stand, while the officer harangued the assembled people about the evils of communism. 'Every time he paused in his speech, they forced the tortured up with kicks and blows from their weapons' (177). The people were monstrously disfigured, damp from the moisture oozing out of their bodies. Their clothes were cut off them so that the people could see for themselves what their punishment had been. Rigoberta's brother was particularly bad:

> His head was shaved and slashed. He had no nails. He had no soles to his feet. The earlier wounds were suppurating from infection. And the woman *compañera*, of course I recognized her; she was from a village near ours. They had shaved her private parts. The nipple of one of her breasts was missing and her other breast was cut off.

She had the marks of bites on different parts of her body. She was bitten all over, that *compañera*. She had no ears. All of them were missing part of the tongue or had their tongues split apart. I found it impossible to concentrate, seeing that this could be. You could only think that these were human beings and what pain those bodies had felt to arrive at that unrecognizable state . . .

After he'd finished talking the officer ordered the squad to take away those who'd been 'punished', naked and swollen as they were. They dragged them along, they could no longer walk. Dragged them along to this place, where they lined them up all together within sight of everyone. The officer called to the worst of his criminals – the *Kaibiles*, who wear different clothes from other soldiers. They're the ones with the most training, the most power. Well, he called the *Kaibiles* and they poured petrol over each of the tortured. The captain said, 'This isn't the last of their punishments, there's another one yet. This is what we've done with all the subversives we catch, because they have to die by violence. And if this doesn't teach you a lesson, this is what'll happen to you too . . . they lined up the tortured and poured petrol on them; and then the soldiers set fire to each one of them.

(178–9)

The issues raised by this passage seem to exceed the capacity of rational analysis. It is terrifying in its obscenity and pathology. But three aspects of this incident reveal it to be in essence a colonial engagement, extending and completing the trauma of colonization which is so cemented into Quiché ceremony and memory: the inscription of colonial power on the body; the way in which colonial power both literally and metaphorically controls the gaze of the colonized; and the alternative forms of resistance metaphorically suggested by the passage.

Nothing could more forcefully demonstrate the way in which colonial power inscribes itself on the bodies of its subjects. The torture and disfigurement seem more than a brutal inflicting of pain, the depravity rests on an organizing principle: that of the 'ordered' power of the state (the body politic) against which the bodies of its subjects are rendered subhuman. Although Menchú talks about her young brother and the torture victims are both men and women, there is a distinct sense of the communal body as metaphorically female – subject to the literal and violent rapacity of colonial and patriarchal power.

Yet it is not the numbing bestiality of this scene, its subhuman morality, nor the disfigurement of the bodies of the colonized which appears the most profoundly brutal act, rather it is the excessive and violent attempt to control the gaze of the community. The act of forcing the people to watch this appalling spectacle is to interpellate them as the objects of genocidal authority, as powerless voyeurs of their own abjection. Apart from its obvious function of terrorizing the people, it operates discursively as a metonymy of the historical gaze – they are forced to watch their own violation. The gaze in which they are interpellated is the gaze of history. It is this terrorism of the gaze which Rigoberta's interpolation into history is specifically designed to reverse. By revealing the appalling horror of these actions in this book, by constructing an audience of Spanish and hence English speakers, she appropriates the power of the historical gaze, she turns the gaze of the reader and hence of history on to these criminals. By this means of interpolation the gaze of history itself is reversed.

### The Stoll controversy

*I, Rigoberta Menchú* quickly became one of the most celebrated texts of Central American resistance. Winner of the Nobel Peace Prize in 1992, celebrated publicly throughout the world, flooded with demands for lectures in America, Rigoberta Menchú has arguably been one of the most critical figures in the change in US and world consciousness about Central America. In 1999 the problematic status of truth in *testimonio* received its most vigorous confirmation. David Stoll's *Rigoberta Menchú and the Story of All Poor Guatemalans* dropped a bombshell in the academic world when he declared that many of the events in Menchú's *testimonio* had not occurred, or at least had not occurred in the way they had been recorded. Chief among these events was the horrific story of the torture and burning alive of Menchú's brother, which, Stoll found, could not be recalled by any of the inhabitants of the village in which it had ostensibly happened. Although this event probably happened *somewhere*, and most of the events in Menchú's *testimonio* occurred to *someone*, the veracity of her story was to be questioned by the normal methods of anthropological investigation.

Stoll's argument was quite simple: Menchú had structured her story to exaggerate the importance of her father in particular, and the guerrilla movement in general. According to Stoll, the horror of the Guatemalan army's oppression of the Quiché Indians would not have occurred if the resistance movement had not made the area a seat of their ultimately unsuccessful operations. Stoll's condemnation raises questions which lie at the heart of post-colonial representations of political struggle: questions about the nature of resistance, the distinction between representation and truth, the connection between 'truth' and 'reality', as well as the more familiar questions raised by Menchú's *testimonio*: the link between literature and history, the issue of authorial autonomy and the possibility of a 'collective subject' of the discourse. The Menchú controversy reveals the complications which occur in the appropriation of dominant discourse. Stoll's thesis, however painstakingly constructed, simply has no room to consider a narrative located in the interstitial space between literature and history, a narrative that is tangential to, and disruptive of, the narrative forms it employs. Since we have no way of assessing the truth of Stoll's research, nor the 'truthfulness' of his own interlocutors, we may assume that Menchú's text, at the very least, presents radical problems to our expectations about how historical truth should be 'testified'. As post-colonial literature has revealed time and again, appropriating the dominant technologies of representation to communicate the reality of the colonized world can also transform the cultural bases of that representative process. This is possibly the most profound demonstration of 'transculturation' – that mutual alteration which occurs when two cultures come into contact. But it hinges on a process that has exercised Western theory a great deal, that of representation.

At base, the Stoll attack hinges on the centrality of the 'will to truth', a condition which is important to the cultural discourses Menchú appropriated. As Foucault suggests, the 'will to truth' characterized the Western episteme once the subject of enunciation (*énoncé*) came to predominate over the enunciation itself (*énonciation*). 'The day dawned', says Foucault, 'when truth moved over from the ritualised act – potent and just – of enunciation to settle on what was enunciated itself: its meaning, its form, its object and its relation to what it referred to' (Foucault 1971: 10). Given the cultural importance of this shift to Western habits of discourse, we may assume that Menchú incorporates into her text a remarkably non-Western, or premodern, view of the relationship between truth and representation. For her the truth of the discourse is located not so much in the verisimilitude of the *énoncé* as in the veracity of the *énonciation*. This preference for truth function over truth content possibly also underlies the blurring of the distinction between past and present in Quiché life. When this preference is incorporated into her employment of Western cultural capital, a great disturbance of its cultural expectations occurs.

Clearly, this wider and apparently looser veracity is more pertinent to her purposes. At the beginning of her book she makes the famous statement, 'My name is Rigoberta Menchú. I am twenty three years old. This is my testimony. I didn't learn it from a book and I didn't learn it alone. I'd like to stress that it's not only *my* life, it's also the testimony of my people' (Menchú 1983: 1). In Spanish the title is *Me llamo Rigoberta Menchú y así me nació la conciencia*, and clearly the raising of her consciousness was both an awareness of her people's political plight and a model for their own politicization.

The privileging of the *énonciation* in her account, the privileging of the telling over the told, is directly related to the effectiveness of the text in raising the consciousness of the world to the plight of 'all poor Guatemalans'. What makes Menchú's account so confronting is the assumption that testimony has a narrative function, it *should* maintain a supreme focus upon the truth content, the *énoncé*. In her account the predominance of the *énonciation* and the insistence upon a communal narrative both confirm the fundamentally allegorical structure of historical narrative. That which is acceptable in the literary is unacceptable in the historical. Yet we may be reminded of Hayden White's contention (Chapter 4) that the demand that history be a single narrative truth that was purely and simply the closest possible representation of events was a choice made from a number of discursive options at a particular moment in Western history.

In the light of the discussion of *testimonio* we might ask Menchú's readers, indeed, we might ask David Stoll: Which account, the anthropological, the historical or the immediate and urgently allegorical testimony, gives a better account of the horrific truth of Quiché experience? Clearly, truth itself enters a realm beyond simple verisimilitude, beyond the scientific account of the past. In the context of cultural capital discussed in Chapter 1, Menchú's utilization of cultural capital obtains its power through the *énonciation*, the act of discoursing, through using and investing that capital, rather than through the discourse, the statement, around which that capital appears to establish its cultural boundaries. The act of cultural investment rather than the capital itself is the key to cultural and political profit.

*Testimonio* is possibly more disruptive of Western assumptions about representation than any other genre, but its occupation of the space between literature and history achieves an unprecedented power in communicating the truth of oppression, because it reveals the extent to which the allegorical orientations of a 'communal' narrative can scandalize our assumptions about the narrative structure of historical truth. By apparently transgressing the putatively 'scientific' truth claims of history, *testimonio* reveals the extent to which the allegorical is the mode of historical narrative, grounded so firmly, as it is, in the global dominance of Western culture.

# 6    Place

Where is one's 'place'? This question is fundamental to the cultural impact of colonization and affects every aspect of colonized society. The issues surrounding the concept of place – how it is conceived, how it differs from 'space' or 'location', how it enters into and produces cultural consciousness, how it becomes the horizon of identity – are some of the most difficult and debated in post-colonial experience.

The physical occupation and control of space have been crucial to British imperialism. In contrast to the Spanish, for instance, who used ritual to help establish their authority, English colonialism relied on the architectural symbolism of residences to provide the visual confirmation of imperial solidity, stability and even majesty. Even more important than the architectural symbol was the map. It has been said that 'Spanish colonialism produced the census, British colonialism the map' (Seed 1992: 206–7). With architecture and mapping British colonialism held a two-pronged grip on the spatial reality of colonial societies. Yet the domination of place in its various dimensions has been a feature of all colonialism. 'Ideological and political hegemony in any society', says Harvey, 'depends on the ability to control the material context of personal and social experience' (1990: 227). Over the last four hundred years European colonization has demonstrated this principle more comprehensively than any other socio-political phenomenon. So complete has been the reorganization of the 'lived place' of many ethnic groups into the political, economic and cultural boundaries of colonial space that the concept and experience of 'place' could be the one discourse of post-colonial life most resistant to transformation. Yet, as significant as the engagement with history might be, it is in the creative reconstruction of the lived environment, the reassertion of place in language and textuality, that the key to a deep-seated cultural transformation may be found.

Place, and the experience of displacement, emerge out of the inter-action of language, history, visual perception, spatiality and environ-ment in the experience of colonized peoples. The importance of one's 'place' in the business of forming cultural identity, the myriad cultural connections it evokes, its importance as a context for cultural knowl-edge, make it particularly resonant in the experience of colonialism. In many cases a sense of place may be embedded in cultural history, in legend and language, in art and dance, without becoming a concept of contention and struggle, until colonization disrupts a people's *sense* of place. Such intervention may disrupt this sense in several ways, depend-ing on the nature of the colonization: by imposing a feeling of displace-ment in those who have moved to the colonies; by physically alienating large populations of colonized peoples through forced migration, slavery or indenture; or by dispersing peoples throughout the world. In the case of diasporic peoples, 'place' might not refer to a location at all, since the formative link between identity and an actual location might have been irredeemably severed. But all constructions and disruptions of place hinge on the question: 'Where do I belong?' The place of a diasporic person's 'belonging' may have little to do with spatial loca-tion, but be situated in family, community, in those symbolic features which constitute a shared culture, a shared ethnicity or system of belief, including nostalgia for a distant homeland. It is when place is least spatial, perhaps, that it becomes most identifying.

There are many things which disrupt or regulate the colonized society's sense of place. The way in which the West has perceived vision and spatiality since classical times, its 'ocularcentrism', as Martin Jay (1993) puts it, its habit of objectivism, the revolutionary development of modern mapping, the discovery of longitude, the estab-lishment of Greenwich Mean Time, the emergence of the discipline of geography, in short, the whole gamut of European ways of constructing space and place comes into operation, including the separation of space and time and the 'disembedding' of local communities from their sense of lived place (Giddens 1990: 21). To understand the impact of concepts of place in colonization and the ways in which place is recon-structed in post-colonial experience, we need first to understand the ways in which 'space' and 'place' have been constructed in modern European consciousness.

The beginning of the European disruption of colonial space lies in the way in which the West conceives space itself. More specifically, it lies in the prominence given to vision since classical Greek thought privileged sight above all other senses. Aristotle opened his *Metaphysics* by claiming the primacy of sight, which alone among the senses 'makes us know and brings to light many differences between things'. Perhaps the best-known example is the allegory of the cave in Book 6 of Plato's *Republic* – whether its inhabitants come to know the higher truths depends upon whether they see real things in the light of day or as mere shadows. Socrates argues that the creator of the senses has lavished the greatest expenditure on the faculty of seeing because, whereas hearing and the other senses do not need a third factor to operate, seeing needs light and this comes from the Sun. The Sun is the divinity which makes 'our vision see best and visible things to be seen' (508, a). Vision is the most sun-like of all the instruments of the sense, since it receives the power dispensed from the sun. Thus when the soul 'is firmly fixed on the domain where truth and reality shine resplendent it apprehends and knows them and appears to possess reason, but when it inclines to that region which is mingled with darkness, the world of becoming and passing away it opines only and its edge is blunted' (508, d). For Plato, and for Western society ever since, vision, knowledge and reason were inextricably tied to each other by means of this imagery of the truth 'shining resplendent'.

Yet this equation of knowledge and light was by no means inevitable. Hebraic and Islamic cultures reveal a contrary emphasis upon hearing and the word (Jay 1993: 23), and Rorty has pointed out that there was 'no particular reason why this ocular metaphor seized the imagination of the founders of Western thought' (1980: 38–9); it might just as easily have happened in some other way. Indeed the clash between ocular-centrism and other ways of conceiving knowledge becomes immediately obvious in much colonial contact. But the linking of knowledge, reason and sight attended the birth of philosophy and prompted a wide range of social and cultural practices, from the emphasis on optics to the idealization of the nude body. The verb 'I know' in classical Greek is the perfect form of the verb *eido* 'I see' and both are related to the Latin *video* 'I see'. Furthermore, as Hans Jonas has pointed out, this equation conferred habits of thought that remain difficult to dislodge, such as the conviction that one can grasp a range of ideas simultaneously (just as one can survey a wide field in one moment), belief in the existence of abstract being rather than particular becoming (because vision is less temporal than the other senses) and, most significantly, the inevitable sense of detachment from the objects of one's regard (Seifrid 1998: 438; Jay 1993: 24).

The progress of Greek ocularcentrism in Western thought has not been seamless and uncontested, but it has remained a key paradigm in both epistemology and ontology, a dominant trope of knowledge and being which has tended to promote specular cognition as the natural goal of any serious activity. The identification of 'I see' with 'I know' is so deep in European consciousness that it goes completely unremarked.

That one of the defining eras of modernity is called the Enlightenment merely underscores ocularcentrism's persistence since the Greeks, as do a multiplicity of cultural forms belonging to the twentieth century, from our now thoroughly visual everyday vocabulary (including casually deployed words and phrases like *evidence*, *insight, shed light on, obvious, appears, brilliant*) to the rampant videoism of popular culture.

(Seifrid 1998: 438)

We tend to think of poetic *imagery* as being purely visual, and yet the imagery of other senses such as smell, touch and hearing has been more common in Western literature than we generally suspect. Our attention is drawn to visual imagery because visual perception has become the supreme metonym of consciousness itself.

In the European engagement with, and reconstruction of, colonized space the ocularcentrism of Western thought has played a critical role. When we think of what our 'place' might be, how we may best represent it, the paradigm of spatiality and vision, of site and location, does not necessarily automatically come to mind. But the prominence of the visual, and the equation of knowledge and sight, have had a profound impact on the conception, representation and experiencing of place in the colonized world. Other ways of knowing, whether through other senses or other intuitive or imaginary forms of cognition, have been suppressed beneath the passion for the ocular, despite the reassertion of these contrary ways of representing place by post-colonial and diasporic peoples.

The extent to which the dominance of visual or pictorial space may be considered to be a *limitation* of our experience of space may be seen when we consider a striking passage from George Santayana:

Pictorial spaces are pictorial in various degrees: they range from the simplest essence of extensity, through all images of motion, collapse, swiftness or scenic confusion; or they may culminate in a reposeful landscape, and in the essence of empty volume or immensity which, save for the absence of analysis, would fuse with the notion of geometrical space. Perfectly obvious, but not at all geometrical, is the space revealed by internal sensations, when in one's insides something is felt moving, it would be hard to say what, where, or in how many dimensions. In dizziness and dreams there are lapsing pictorial spaces; in semi-consciousness there are unmapped unrelated spaces waxing and vanishing. It is not only the latitude and longitude of visionary places that are unassignable, but their spatial quality that is unearthly: the talk about flatland and four dimensions is but a thin scientific parody of the uncertainty of animal sense. Even in rational human experience, the living intuition of space is endlessly qualified.

(1928: 249–50)

When we consider the extraordinary variety of ways in which space may be experienced we may be struck by the simultaneous limitation and power of the visual in Western discourse (a spatiality which enters even into Santayana's description of the limitation of spatiality), a power which has come to effect its greatest intervention in mental and material life by means of the trope of the boundary. Even in Western society the ways in which space is *experienced* and the ways in which it is habitually *represented* may differ considerably. If spatiality itself so exceeds the visual, how much more the lived place in which people come to locate, define and understand their identity. For Santayana, the talk of a flatland and four dimensions is a 'thin scientific parody' of the human experience of space. That this thin parody has come to exert such influence is all the more noteworthy. It is at least arguable that such influence has come about because spatial metaphors best express the exertion and extension of imperial power in the expansion of European modernity. The European dominance of space is therefore also a matter of the dominance of vision over other ways of experiencing, and the dominance of the imperial language over other languages in the inscription of the colonized environment. Both of these find their profoundest impact in the creation of the map of the world.

## Cartography

Apart from the invention of History, there has been no more profound effect on people's understanding of the nature of the world than in its representation in maps. Geography, maps and mapping have arguably had a greater effect on our ways of imagining the world than any other discourse. The development of world maps during the Renaissance arose from voyages of discovery which produced a wealth of knowledge about a globe that was finite and potentially knowable. Maps emerged as a practical consequence of the monetary and strategic value of geographical knowledge. But, crucially, they represented an ability to *see* the world as a whole, an ability which amounted to an ability to *know* the world. It is a very particular form of knowledge, a special exercise of the power of surveillance (as anyone who compares an elevated view of a city, say, with their street-map can see immediately), but it is metonymic of power none the less. 'Objectivity in spatial representation became a valued attribute because accuracy of navigation, the determination of property rights in land . . . political boundaries, rights of passage or transportation, and the like, became economically as well as politically imperative' (Harvey 1990: 245). Maps not only represented space, they represented the power of the fixed, all-seeing viewpoint: the power to create a universal space.

Ptolemy's map, imported from Alexandria to Florence around 1400, employed a geometrical grid which offered a mathematical unity to the representation of space, and showed how the globe as a whole would appear to the human eye looking at it from outside (Harvey 1990: 246). 'As a result, it seemed as if space, though infinite, was conquerable and containable for purposes of human occupancy and action' (246). Mercator completed Ptolemy's ambition by developing maps of the world from about 1538, and with these world maps we discover that the perspective from which the globe was *seen* had an incalculable effect on how the world was to be *known*. In 'Allegories of *Atlas*' José Rabasa contends that Mercator's *Atlas*, completed about 1595 and published in its final form in 1636, established Europe as the 'privileged site of meaning for the rest of the world' (1993: 181). Our most firmly held, ubiquitous and unquestioned assumptions about the physical shape of the globe and its continents can thus be seen to be a specific evidence of the power of European discourse to naturalize its construction of the world itself. Through the map of the world the 'trace of European expansionism continues to exist in the bodies and minds of the rest of the world, as well as in the fantasies of the former colonizers' (181). There has been perhaps no more powerful discursive elaboration of Eurocentrism than that which permanently established the way in which the physical world was to be conceived.

The key to this expansionism was also the key to the geographical conception of the globe: the substitution of the Ocean for the land mass of Eurasia as the principal medium of world communication. 'This use of the Ocean, first by sailing ships and then by steamships, enabled the West to unify the whole inhabited and habitable world, including the Americas' (Toynbee 1948: 70). Just as the physical globe as it is now understood cannot be divorced from the ideological power of Europe, so it cannot be divorced from the chief practical means of that power –

ocean travel – which 'unified' the world by making it the accessible domain of European travel.

The most significant development in the navigability of the globe by European ships was its mathematical ordering, through the invention of latitude and longitude, which represented the strictest exertion of imperial control over global space. Longitude was a relatively recent invention, defined by the 'Transit Circle' telescope built by Sir George Biddell Airy, the seventh Astronomer Royal, at Greenwich in 1850.[4] The expansion of sea travel by British ships and the consequent increase in wrecks made the discovery of longitude imperative.[5] But even more interesting, perhaps, than the emergence of this grid are the ways in which cartography became validated in rituals such as the 'crossing the line' ceremonies celebrated from the time European ships first crossed the equator. This ceremony, with the prominent place given to Neptune, and the incorporation of a hybrid mixture of mythic figures, seemed to be the example *par excellence* of a mariners' subculture. But the ceremony confirmed and celebrated the existence of what was no more than an imaginary line on the map. The persistent ritual celebration of the 'lines' (not only the equator but on some occasions the 180° meridian) confirmed both the significance of the cartographic construction of the world and the sense of the importance of the grid for signifying imaginary cultural boundaries. The separation of space into North and South, West and East was not simply a division of empty space, but the establishment of a boundary between the civilized world (the northern hemisphere) and its nether regions, a physical boundary which intimated a cultural distinction between Europe and its others.

This characteristic of the world map as a trace of Europe is as difficult for non-European cultures to avoid today as the Gregorian calendar. The sign of this dominance can be seen in the very orientation of the map, with the northern hemisphere on 'top', but it has also been demonstrated in the monsters and unearthly creatures who inhabited the furthest reaches of the world on early maps. It was continued in the period of European imperialism by the sense of 'darkness' and impenetrability which left many regions, though accessible by navigable oceans, as 'blanks', ready for exploration and discovery. Significantly, despite the predominance, in the nineteenth century, of the use of tropes of 'darkness' and mystery to describe the uncolonized, 'primitive' continents such as Africa, oceans were never regarded as dark and forbidding, no matter how untravelled, for they represented an unhindered access to the world, a site for the assertion of European maritime power. In Joseph Conrad's *Heart of Darkness* this is strikingly demonstrated by Marlow's passion for maps:

Now when I was a little chap I had a passion for maps, I would look for hours at South America or Africa, or Australia, and lose myself in all the glories of exploration. At that time there were many blank spaces on the earth, and when I saw one that looked particularly inviting on a map (but they all look that) I would put my finger on it and say, When I grow up I will go there.

(1901: 33)

For whom are these spaces blank? What makes them so inviting? Obviously this is meant to say something about Marlow. Indeed it says something about Conrad himself, who records a similar occasion in his 'Geography and Some Explorers' (1926). But the blank spaces are there because Europe isn't, these places represent the absence of modernity, of 'civilization', an absence which must be 'filled' by exploration, mapping and naming. There is no suggestion that Marlow cannot *go* there. The iconography of light and darkness portrayed the European penetration of the continent of Africa as 'simultaneously a process of domination, Enlightenment, and liberation' (Driver 1992: 31). The fact that such spaces may be richly filled for their occupants, densely inscribed with local cultural reality, is entirely ignored.

The map *itself* in which names, numerous in some places and sparse in others, inscribe a pattern of knowing by metonymizing the act of seeing, establishes the authority of European consciousness and European desire to enter the 'unknown'. We are in the habit of positing Africa as the 'other' of Europe but it was less a binary opposite in common thought than an absence, a blank. 'Europe's exclusion of Africa from history, from religion and from philosophy', says Bernasconi, 'has been so total, so extreme, so hysterical, and marked by such ignorance and prejudice that one cannot even say that Africa was inscribed within Western metaphysics as its opposite. Africa was regarded as non-assimilable' (1997: 185). This non-assimilable blankness justified every excursion, every annexation, every proprietorial occupation of European 'Enlightenment'. The penetration of the darkness to bring 'light' was the self-fulfilling prophecy of imperialism.

'In British literature, from about the 1830s to the 1870s,' says Brantlinger, 'white heroes rarely doubt their ability to tame various geopolitical mistresses – Africa, the sea, the world – and to bring civilized order out of the chaos of savage life' (1988: 44). It was not done in the name of imperialism until later in the century, but it was done with the supreme confidence of those for whom the map of the world seemed to have been drawn. Brantlinger's terminology raises the issue of the gendering of the geographical process itself, since geographical knowledge was inevitably shaped by the heroes of the colonial landscape: 'the explorer, the hunter, the soldier, the missionary, the administrator, the gentleman', who provided 'moral models for a generation of empire builders' (Driver 1992: 27). Cartography and geography seemed to have provided consummate models for the imperial ideal of masculine domination.

Such domination is not a simple matter of drawing outlines and mathematical co-ordinates. Rabasa reveals how Mercator's world map shows geography to be a palimpsest of erasures and re-inscriptions, and, crucially, how it gains power through its alliance with and signification of history. As Mercator says in his 'Preface': 'I have principally endeavoured to describe before every Mapp the order and nature of the most remarkeable places in every Province, the better to profit, the studious, and carefull of Politick matters and states of affairs' (in Rabasa 1984: 2). The map demonstrates that geography, like place itself, 'is a series of erasures and overwritings which have transformed the world' (Rabasa 1993: 181). The map maker had to 'forget' or erase earlier knowledges of the structure of the world, and he overlaid these erased knowledges with different ways of knowing the world in the commentary accompanying the map itself. The importance of palimpsestic inscription cannot be overestimated in the colonial construction of place. As Carter (1987) points out, colonial discourse turns 'empty' space into inhabited 'place' through the discourse of naming and mapping, which must, as a matter of course, either erase previous inscriptions and knowledges or reincorporate them into the privileged discourse of the imperial map.

Not only is naming crucial to the *Atlas*, but written commentary also gives the map its ideological significance. Writing is indispensable to the meaning of the map. The world acquires spatial meaning only after the different regions have been 'inscribed' by Europeans and the meanings of this inscription are elaborated by geographic and historiographic commentary. Through writing itself, the spatial dimensions of the map achieve an ideological, hierarchical and even gendered specificity which establishes Europe as the centrepoint round which the symbolic status and character of the rest of the world revolve. The structural and ideological distinction between a European 'centre' and a variously understood periphery in the map rationalizes and justifies the spread of European civilization through its colonization of the periphery. As Conrad confirms, the darkness of the 'Dark Continent' is justification enough for the intrusion of the 'light' of European civilization.

The *Atlas* is intended to be a mirror of the world. But it is a mirror through which History – 'the eye of the world' – defines the national character of the territories depicted. It is not just the European man but specifically the Christian European man who can hold this mirror up to the world and reveal its universal semblance in the *Atlas* (Rabasa 1993: 193):

> Here [Europe] we have the right of Lawes, the dignity of the Christian Religion, the forces of Armes . . . Moreover, Europe manageth all Arts and Sciences with such dexterity, that for the invention of manie things shee may be truely called a Mother . . . she hath . . . all manner of learning, whereas other Countries are all of them, overspread with Barbarisme.
>
> (Preface, cited Rabasa 1993: 193–4)

This passage makes manifest, says Rabasa, 'how global histories and geographies, despite their "introduction" of other regions into the world scenario, always retain a Eurocentric perspective that defines the position and value of the rest of the world' (1993: 194). The sentiments of Mercator's Preface can be seen repeated time and again throughout the history of European imperialism, reaching the status of revealed truth by the nineteenth century, when the British centre was held to be the repository of all civilized values. Perhaps its most cynical expression came from King Leopold II in justification of the brutal suppression of the Congolese after the division of Africa:

> Our refined society attaches to human life (and with reason) a value unknown to barbarous communities . . . But if, in view of this desirable spread of civilisation, we count upon the means of action which confer upon us dominion and the sanction of right, it is not less true that our ultimate end is a work of peace.
>
> (Kimbrough 1988: 126–8)

Leopold is merely making explicit those contradictions which are implicit in Mercator's commentary.

Maps have continued to be a prime means of 'textualizing' the spatial reality of colonized peoples, by enforcing a Eurocentric view of spatiality, and naming, or renaming, existing places as a demonstration of power. The initial ideological impact of the *Atlas* as an inscription of European dominance is perpetuated in further mappings and namings which exert an almost ontological control as such places are, in a sense, brought into being. In all cases the lands so colonized are literally re-inscribed, written over, following the same process that formed Mercator's map, as the names and languages of the indigenes are replaced by new names, or are corrupted into new and Europeanized forms by the cartographer and explorer. The dynamic of naming becomes a primary colonizing process because it appropriates, defines, captures the place in language. The provision of names to the non-European world through exploration and 'discovery' is thus an elaboration of the dynamic of control which the *Atlas* presupposes. To name place is to announce discursive control over it by the very act of inscription, because through names, location becomes metonymic of those processes of travel, annexation and colonization which effect the dominance of imperial powers over the non-European world.

## Perspective

The most crucial development in the 'modern' dissemination of concepts of space and place was directly related to the development of the grid-maps of Ptolemy and Mercator: the revolution, during the Renaissance, in the very nature of spatiality – the development of perspective. The Renaissance technique for the visual representation of space had an impact on the world, particularly the colonized world, that was at least as far-reaching as that of the world map. This revolutionary development was intimately associated with, and perhaps even arose from, the ability, provided by maps, to see the world from a fixed point of view. The importation of the Ptolemaic map from Alexandria to Florence around 1400 seems to have played a crucial role in the development of perspectivism. As Edgerton says:

> The Ptolemaic system gave the Florentines a perfect, expandable cartographic tool for collecting, collating, and correcting geographical knowledge. Above all, it supplied to geography the same aesthetic principles of geometrical harmony which Florentines demanded of their art.
>
> (1976: 114)

By designing a grid which allowed the viewer to see what the world would look like from the outside Ptolemy's map seemed to render space 'conquerable and containable for purposes of human occupancy and action. It could be appropriated in imagination according to mathematical principles' (Harvey 1990: 246).

The 'discovery' of perspective during the Renaissance, the invention of the perspectival method, was a huge and crucial shift in European spatial perception, and became so embedded and naturalized that visual perspective became the only and 'true' way to see. The fundamental achievement of the Renaissance was that it shaped ways of seeing for the next four centuries. Yet Europeans took a remarkably long time to 'discover' the secrets of perspective in the visual arts because, as Piaget remarks, to do so, individuals had to unlearn all the compensations they naturally learned as children. Perspective comes from the Latin *perspicio*, which means 'to see through, behold', and its development required a philosophical basis in the idea of the separation of the seer from the seen; the separation of subject and object, which becomes most highly developed in the seventeenth and eighteenth centuries with Descartes and Locke.

The polarization of consciousness and the world was the central feature of Renaissance theories of art such as that of the extraordinarily influential Leone Battista Alberti, Italian architect and theorist (1404–72), who believed that art should be realistic and representational, and should strive to approximate the stance of science, particularly mathematics, since individual perception was prone to error. To achieve this, he suggested certain mechanical devices by which perception could be regulated, methodized and generalized – a fixed and immobile perspective (to eliminate the mobility of vision and the multiple perspectives it produced); the use of monocular vision; and the use of a grid or 'veil' interposed between oneself and the scene. The painter's access to the world should be restricted to the channel of visual perception, not to visual perception as it occurred 'naturally' but to visual perception as it is regulated by a precisely defined method (1956: 17). The world confronting the painter is, as a result, compelled to reveal itself only in terms of its strictly visible dimensions. The reality of things was seen to reside solely in their contours or forms, their geometric properties.

For Alberti, and for Descartes, scientific method makes possible, and also guarantees, the universal perception of the true, by *regulating* it. For to both thinkers there is a geometrical foundation to the objective universe which provides its order. According to Descartes, although there may be many different viewpoints on a given subject, 'no more than one of them can ever be right' (1964: 13). It is method, and above all scientific method, which can ensure a uniformity of perspective. In the Sixth Meditation: *The Existence of Material Things* he says:

> It may be that not all bodies are such as my senses apprehend them, for this sensory apprehension is in many ways obscure and confused; but at any rate their nature must comprise whatever I clearly and distinctly understand – that is, whatever, generally considered, falls within the subject-matter of pure mathematics.

(1964: 116)

The mathematical codification of visual perception is a striking demonstration of the effort to reach a universal viewpoint through the regulation and standardization of individual differences, which otherwise might imply the presence of the subject in the perceived world.

This construction of the method of perspectival perception offers an exceptionally clear example of the development of a discourse. That which we take for granted today as the way the world really *is* visually is the result of a highly codified method which grew out of Renaissance theories about the separation of the individual subject from the world. The discourse of space is one which we enter as we enter ideology. So complete is the success of the perpectival method that this is the way we (Westerners, and increasingly all cultures) understand what the world looks like. And, of course, in one respect it is, but it is not the only, or necessarily most important, way in which the world can be viewed. What Alberti declared to be the inferior 'natural' vision is itself a kind of learned method, or more specifically, the learning of compensations for binocular vision, which his perspectival method supplanted. During the Renaissance the political and religious importance of painting ensured that developments in its codification would be influential, and indeed they came to influence and determine Europeans' 'natural' way of seeing the world: an objective universe.

The creation of an objective universe, removing all elements of subjectivity, is really the creation of a world that is outside time, a world viewed *sub specie aeternitas*, truly revealed to a single glance. The development of perspective is therefore intimately connected with the separation of time and space that became characteristic of modernity. The eighteenth-century optical device called the 'Claude-glass', created by the French painter Claude Lorraine for people on tours, is a classic example of this passion to objectify space. In effect, the device made the scenery appear as though it were a painting. When viewed in the Claude-glass, a tinted plano-convex mirror, natural objects appeared 'as if painted, with composition and lowered tone' (Manwaring 1965: 168), thus effectively removing the viewing subject from the scene and providing a metonymy of the perspectival method.

Classical perspective is, as Merleau-Ponty says, more than a secret technique for imitating a reality given as such to all people. It is 'the invention of a world which is dominated and possessed through and through in an instantaneous synthesis' (1960: 50). This world must dispense with the perceiver located in the perceived world, a perceiver who, in the act of perception, compounds the spatial and the temporal. It must dispense with the concept of the perception of space altering through time. It relies on an observer positioned outside it and comprehending it in a single instant of vision.

Renaissance theorists succeeded in creating a space that was homogeneous, uniform and absolute. Removed from the field of vision, artists no longer experienced a space as the setting or horizon in which they lived. It was now constituted as a global entity – completely present to the perceiving mind, absolute in its existence and uniform throughout its extension. In 'natural' perception space is generated by intentional movement – it exists on the horizon of every object. But in Renaissance perspective space is not so much perceived as conceived. Viewed from an external fixed position and through a monocular gaze, the scene solicits no response, no movement towards it on the part of the viewer. In the actual event of spontaneous perception, however, space can be generated by movement because the observer is located in the field of vision.

That perspectivalism need not be the automatic or universal method of the visual arts has been demonstrated by the rift which occurred between the Western and Eastern traditions of religious art. Thomas Seifrid points out that this rift was especially apparent to Russians in the aesthetics of the icon. 'With reverse perspective and a decentred, implicitly mobile vantage point, the icon represents the antithesis of the static, apex-of-the-visual-pyramid optic of Western art, perhaps even to the point of embodying an entirely different ethic and sense of self' (1998: 439). Tolstoy's younger compatriot Pavel Florenskij excoriates perspective in Western painting as an impious 'attempt by individual consciousness to detach itself from reality, even from its own reality – from the body, from the other eye' (Seifrid 1998: 439). Although this does not suggest a simple binary between Western and Eastern orthodox traditions, since perspectivalism had a role in Eastern visual arts, it does reveal a level of resistance to the idea of the perspectival method as the inevitable metonymy of seeing.

A resistance to perspectivalism's absolute and timeless view of space occurred in the West itself in the work of modernist and impressionist artists around the turn of the twentieth century. Significantly, modernist aesthetics were influenced by the belated 'discovery' by artists and writers of those 'primitive' images which had been collected as booty by successive generations of colonialists and stored in museums. The existence of forms of representation which existed outside the canons of European aesthetics stimulated creative artists to grasp new ways of writing and painting. Most crucial, and perhaps most intransigent in the array of traditions questioned by modernism, was the perspectival tradition of European spatial perception itself. Given the influence of the art of the colonized world upon modernist aesthetics, it might not be too much to see the challenge to traditional perspective as a model for post-colonial engagements with Western visuality. Certainly modernism can be seen as a consequence of the transcultural disruptions of European institutions by colonized societies.

One example of the questioning of traditional perspective can be seen in the painting after 1880 of Cézanne, whose early work one critic called 'the painting of a drunken privy cleaner' (Merleau-Ponty 1961: 9). Cézanne's life was a long struggle with the principles of representation, and by not accepting the method of perspective, says Merleau-Ponty, 'Cézanne discovered what recent psychologists have come to formulate: the lived perspective, that which we actually perceive, is not a geometric or photographic one. The objects we see close at hand appear smaller, those far away seem larger than they do in a photograph' (1961: 14). This suggests that we largely accept the fact that the way we experience the world is just like the way that experience is represented in perspectival representation. But trying to escape that method of representation is extremely difficult. 'To say that a circle seen obliquely is seen as an ellipse is to substitute for our actual perception what we would see if we were cameras: in reality we see a form which oscillates around the ellipse without being an ellipse' (14). Similarly, in Cézanne's view the outline of things should be a result of colour if the world is to be given its true density:

> For the world is a mass without gaps, a system of colors across which the receding perspective, the outlines, angles and curves are inscribed like lines of force; the spatial structure vibrates as it is formed. 'The outline and the colors are no longer distinct from each other. To the extent that one paints, one outlines; the more the colors harmonize, the more the outline becomes precise . . . When color is at its richest, the form has reached plenitude.'
> (Merleau-Ponty 1961: 15)

When we think of the extent to which this contradicts four centuries of accepted wisdom about perspective, how it disrupts the idea of a static, timeless point of view, and when we see how different the traditional, accepted view of vision might be to other ways of conceiving the experience of seeing, we begin to understand how disruptive European ideas of spatiality may have been to colonized peoples' ways of perceiving place.

Nevertheless, the perspectival concept of space, the sense of static extension and the isolation of the viewer from the scene, the separation of subject and object, are all characteristic of European painters' views of colonial space. In most cases colonial painters find in the open spaces of many of the colonized places a spatial extension, a horizon of 'uninhabited' land which provides a ready opportunity to impose the priority of perspective, indeed the priority of visual space itself over any other indigenous modes of spatial perception. For instance, in Aboriginal societies place is traditionally not a visual construct at all in the perspectival tradition, neither a measurable space nor even a topographical system but a tangible location of one's own Dreaming, an extension of one's own being. A particular formation, like a stream or hill, for instance, may embody a particular Dreaming figure, whose location on the Dreaming track has a particular significance to a person's own life, 'totem', clan relationship and identity because that person may have been conceived near it.

Aboriginal art is metonymic and symbolic rather than representational in function, and deeply implicated in the performance of religious obligations. Animal and abstract forms are drawn for their sacred significance because, like language, they *embody* rather than represent the power of the things they signify. The Aboriginal paints on things and on the body itself, rather than painting the perception of things, because the individual's art is an activity which expresses the community's participation in this power. Sometimes paintings may seem to follow the principles of a map but the elements are organized in terms of ritual power and inhering relationships rather than in terms of spatial extension. On the other hand, the art of the white settlers in Australia appears to be obsessed with landscape, and especially with the task of inventing the spatial representation of a landscape as a way of 'indigenizing' place. Such passion for the visual space with its Gothic overtones of vastness and hostility is evident in the literature as well, but it is in the landscape that we find the most striking visual metaphor for a sense of cultural uniqueness which the settler society constructs as a sign of its distinctiveness from imperial culture.

The Aborigine has no need to paint the landscape in traditional artistic activity because the land as visual space is nameless. What matter are those *named* features into which the Dreaming ancestors metamorphosed when they completed their travels on the nameless plane of the original universe. By relationship with these beings the land is a function of the Aboriginal's own being, an embodiment which is expressed in art. Says Galarrwuy Yunipingu:

> most great paintings talk about the land and the significance of the land. Aboriginal people use other forms of art to talk about the

land, for example bark paintings and the dance. When I get out and paint myself and go bush, whether I am performing a sacred ceremony, or corroboree, I am performing an art that talks about the land . . . When aboriginal people get together we put the land into action. When I perform, the land is within me, and I am the only one who can move, land doesn't, so I represent the land when I dance. I pretend to be the land, because the land is part of me. So I perform whatever I do on behalf of the land.

(Yunipingu 1980: 13–14)

This art, which includes the very important elements of song and dance, embodies the land. The idea of not owning the land but in some sense being 'owned by it' is a way of seeing the world that is so different from the materiality and commodification of imperial discourse that effective protection of one's place is radically disabled when that new system – perspectival vision – becomes the dominant one as European spatial representations are 'inscribed' upon the palimpsest of place.

The contrast with Western perspectivalism and naturalism is possibly most distinct in Aboriginal art, but it occurs in various ways, and to various degrees, in all colonized societies. Partha Mitter in *Art and Nationalism in Colonial India 1850–1922* (1994) discusses the cultural significance of the adoption of, resistance to and partial transformation of Western painting styles in the development of Indian painting. Here the adoption of the full range of European artistic institutions at the turn of the twentieth century – 'foreshortening, linear perspective, chiaroscuro and other naturalist devices . . . profoundly altered the meaning and function of art in Indian society' (1994: 12–13). Not the least of these influences was the Romantic image of the artist as a unique individual beyond social convention. Such apparently harmless influences reach right to the heart of the function of art in society and indeed to a culture's ways of seeing the world.

Mitter shows how complicated the impact of colonization can be in aesthetic activity. 'Even if India shared [with other colonies] certain global assumptions about colonialism, its own experience was rooted in its history; Indian colonial art, for instance, represented a dialogue between Western ideas and a search for Hindu identity' (8). The first period (1850–1900) was dominated by an active pro-Western art form, the consequence of the immense impact made by Renaissance perspectivism on Mughal art. The counterpoint (1900–1922) was the cultural nationalism of the Bengal movement. 'A new sensibility, expressed by the *swadeshi* (indigenous) doctrine of art, closely linked it to the emergent Hindu identity . . . The perceived opposition between "pure" and "hybrid" colonial art sparked off a debate that affected the choice of a suitable style for artists during the nationalist struggle' (9).

This Bengal Renaissance, striving to celebrate nationalist cultural symbols and indigenous artistic traditions within the medium of Western art, demonstrated how deeply embedded in traditions of representation the experience of place may be. The great controversy this resurgence engendered also demonstrates how difficult it may be to make the shift from colonial opposition, with its tendency to construct essentialist cultural binaries, to post-colonial transformation, with its capacity to re-articulate dominant forms of representation. In the Indian case the parties to the struggle polarized into intransigent positions, sometimes supported by spurious or clichéd aesthetic arguments, until they were overtaken by the West's own questioning of naturalism in the modernist movement.

## Surveillance

In the imperial passion for perspective, space and distance in colonial painters, whether Arcadian or Sublime, we find an allegory of imperial control, because it is the representation of the surveillance by which the surveyed comes into being. One of the most powerful strategies of imperial dominance is that of surveillance, or observation: because it implies a viewer with an elevated vantage point, it suggests the power to process and understand that which is seen, and it objectifies, and interpellates, the colonized subject in a way that fixes its identity in relation to the surveyor. The importance of the gaze was emphasized by Lacan, since the gaze of the mother in the mirror phase is the initial process by which identity is achieved. This gaze corresponds to the 'gaze of the *grande-autre*' within which the identification, objectification and subjection of the subject are simultaneously enacted: the imperial gaze defines the identity of the subject, objectifies it within the identifying system of power relations and confirms its subalterneity and powerlessness.

Jeremy Bentham's eighteenth-century design for a circular prison divided into individual cells, all of which could be observed from a single vantage point, was a form of prison architecture in which guards could maintain constant vigil over the imprisoned. Such surveillance revolutionized the effectiveness of incarceration because its power came from the assumption of the incarcerated that they were always under surveillance and therefore must always act as if they were. For the observer, sight confers power; for the observed, visibility is powerlessness. Clearly, the discipline instilled by the panopticon, and its imposition of 'constant' surveillance, provides a powerful metaphor for the 'disciplinary' operation of dominant discourse of all kinds.

The panopticon remains a powerful metaphor for the surveillance of inmates in all 'total institutions' such as mental asylums, whatever their physical architecture. Whereas imperial power over the colonized subject may not be necessarily as direct and physical as it is in a 'total' institution, power over the subject may be exerted in myriad ways, enforced by the threat of subtle kinds of cultural and moral disapproval and exclusion. The colonized subject may accept the imperial view, including the array of values, assumptions and cultural expectations on which this is based, and order his or her behaviour accordingly. This will produce colonial subjects who are 'more English than the English', those whom V. S. Naipaul called 'The Mimic Men' in the novel of that name. More often, such conversion will be ambivalent, attenuated, intermittent and diffused by feelings of resistance to imperial power, leading to what Homi Bhabha calls 'mimicry', a 'conversion' which always teeters on the edge of menace.

Surveillance of colonial space is a regular feature of exploration and travel writing. The emergence of 'landscape' and the concomitant desire for a commanding view which could provide a sweeping visual mastery of the scene was an important feature of nineteenth-century poetry and fiction. It became a significant method by which European explorers and travellers could obtain a position of panoramic observation, itself a representation of knowledge and power over colonial space. The desire for a literal position of visual command is metaphoric of the 'panoptic' operation of the imperial gaze in which the observed find themselves constituted. When a writer takes this position, as occurs time and again in Orientalist discourse, the invulnerable position of the observer affirms the political order and the binary structure of power which made that position possible. As in the panopticon the writer 'is placed either above or at the centre of things, yet apart from them so that the organization and classification of things takes place according to the writer's own system of value' (Spurr 1994: 16).

Spurr gives a good example of this in Henry Morton Stanley's description of the land known as Unyamwezi:

> if you look west, you will see Unyamwezi recede into the far, blue, mysterious distance in a succession of blue waves of noble forest, rising and subsiding like the blue waves of an ocean . . . Hills of syenite are seen dotting the vast prospect, like islands in a sea, presenting in their external appearance, to an imaginative eye, rude imitations of castellated fortresses and embattled towers. Around

these rocky hills the cultivated fields of the Wanyamwezi – fields of tall maize, of holcus sorghum, of millet, of vetches, etc – among which you may discern the patches devoted to the cultivation of sweet potatoes and manioc, and pasture lands where browse the hump shouldered cattle of Africa, flocks of goats and sheep.

(1994: 17)

'Stanley's eye moves systematically out to the horizon', says Spurr, 'then returns to the ground which can be inspected in its minute particulars. It ranges freely over the scene, providing general outline and points of focus, bringing about spatial order from a fixed point of view' (1994: 17). We can see in Stanley's assumption of panoramic dominance the fixity and universalism of the perspectival method. For the perspectival gaze renders the scene as static spatial extension, allegorical in import, but overwhelmingly visual in its mode. The gaze of European travellers as they secured a prominent vantage point and took in the panorama is a practical demonstration of the establishment of a fixed and all-seeing point of view which underlay the project of Renaissance mapping.

However, surveillance is also a subject for post-colonial deconstruction, since the vision from the locus of a cultural centre may be regarded as limited. Jacobus Coetzee, the central character in *Dusklands*, articulates the importance of surveillance in the control of space when he experiences the primal binary of colonization, the encounter between 'civilized' subject and the wild:

In the wild I lose my sense of boundaries. This is a consequence of space and solitude. The operation of space is thus: the five senses stretch out from the body they inhabit, but four stretch into a vacuum. The ear cannot hear, the nose cannot smell, the tongue cannot taste, the skin cannot feel . . . Only the eyes have power. The eyes are free, they reach out to the horizon all around. Nothing is hidden from the eyes. As the other senses grow numb or dumb my eyes flex and extend themselves. I become a spherical reflecting eye moving through the wilderness and ingesting it. Destroyer of the wilderness, I move through the land cutting a devouring path from horizon to horizon. There is nothing from which my eye turns, I am all that I see. Such loneliness! Not a stone, not a bush, not a wretched provident ant that is not comprehended in this travelling sphere. What is there that is not me? I am a transparent sac with a black core full of images and a gun.

(1974: 79)

In Jacobus Coetzee's vision of colonial space we find the echoes of that ocularcentrism embedded in Western consciousness since Plato's *Republic*. The crucial challenge to this Eurocentric predisposition is the loss of a sense of boundaries, for boundaries, as we shall see, are fundamental to virtually every aspect of Western consciousness. But in this case the eye has the special political task of overcoming the 'vacuum' of the senses which the 'wild' presents to the colonizing subject. The act of seeing not only *knows* what is seen, it occupies space, it *becomes* that which it sees, thus suggesting the incorporating ontological reach of the imperial gaze. Coetzee is explicit about the violent ramifications of this seeing, for the gun is in some ways an extension of his eye, and, like seeing, a way of being: 'The gun stands for the hope that there exists that which is other than oneself.'

> I move through the wilderness with my gun at the shoulder of my eye and slay elephants, hippopotami, rhinoceros, buffalo, lions, leopards, dogs, giraffes, antelope and buck of all descriptions, fowl of all descriptions, hares, and snakes; I leave behind me a mountain of skin, bones, inedible gristle, and excrement. All this is my dispersed pyramid of life. It is my life's work, my incessant proclamation of the otherness of the dead and therefore the otherness of life.
>
> (79)

Whatever overweening and magisterial claims may appear appended to the vision of European travellers, their surveillance is culturally limited, a limitation allegorized in the boundaries of vision. Coetzee surveys the country from the vantage point of his oxwagon: 'Coetzee cut his double swathe (forward journey, return journey) through the partially unknown between the Piquetberg and the Orange River, his keen hunter's eye distinguishing every bush within a hundred yards of his wagon' (116). The oxwagon, the emblematic vehicle of Boer pioneering and a virtually institutionalized symbol of Afrikaner nationalism, is a movable but inadequate locus of vision which allows Jacobus's naming of the wild to extend only a short distance. The vision of European expansion in an explorer such as Stanley claiming a panoramic view over the vastness of Africa is just as limited, perhaps, as the restricted view of Boer nationalism, which can see only to the circumference of its own fixed and self-contained centre. In either case the claims of European spatiality, the privilege of the eye in *knowing* the world, seem to be called radically into question.

## Geography and empire

The capacity to see the whole world, the capacity to survey the entire globe in a single view, which was first provided by Renaissance maps, generated the link between geography and empire, a link which became cemented by what Africa, perhaps more than any other region, represented to European consciousness – a blankness which seemed to resist surveillance and knowledge and so could be controlled only by mythology and demonization. Just as Orientalism served to establish Europe's power over the object of its study, its Oriental others, so Africa played a prominent role in the emergence of geographic scholarship, a discipline closely tied to the European imperial mission in the continent, and one which, rather than discarding the stereotypical mythology of the Dark Continent, simply validated it.

The striking feature of the link between geography and empire is its very transparency. As far back as 1589, Richard Hakluyt's *The Principal Navigations, Voyages and Discoveries of the English Nation* provided an ideological foundation for a descriptive study of the wider world. It encouraged the English to see themselves as separate from the continent and made 'an important contribution to a growing awareness of England's imperial greatness – her autonomous sovereignty and ability to export that power for the control of commerce and, potentially, colonies' (Cormack 1994: 22). Naturally, claims Hakluyt, 'all Princes ar desyrous to Imploye theire study and theire power to advance theire dominions Kingdoms and Terrytories' (Cormack 1994: 23). This explains the perils and labours they endure to such an end. Geography, so linked to the spatial construction of the world, was never a secret ally of empire, because European imperialism (unlike contemporary globalization) was so manifestly based upon the colonization of foreign territory. The link between the geographical knowledge of space and the military control of territory remained so firm that even up to the First World War military defeat in France was blamed upon geographic ignorance – French generals who didn't know whether the Rhine flowed north or south.

By the apogee of Europe's nineteenth-century imperial expansion, geography was indispensable to the interests of imperialism in its various aspects, including territorial acquisition, economic exploitation, militarism and the need for racial domination which prompted such excursions as 'moral climatography' (Smith 1994). These various uses of geography formalized the ideological function of cartography that had been present for several centuries. The Royal Geographic Society of Britain was formed in 1830 as an outgrowth of the Africa

Association. Indeed Britain's overseas expansion in the nineteenth century was largely orchestrated through the Royal Geographic Society, on the explicit grounds that geography's 'advantages are of the first importance to mankind in general, and paramount to the welfare of a maritime nation like Great Britain, with its numerous and extensive foreign possessions' (Livingstone 1994: 134). Similarly, according to Watts, the Franco–Prussian War directly stimulated an increase in French geographical societies. 'At the Second International Congress of Geographical Sciences held in 1875 and attended by the President of the Republic of France, knowledge and conquest of the earth was seen as an obligation, and geography provided its philosophic justification' (Watts 1993a: 174). With the Darwinian revolution in the nineteenth century, geography became a 'sternly practical science' (Livingstone 1992: 216) and in concert with evolutionary theory justified the colouring of the globe with the pink patches of empire. The 'new geography' and the 'new imperialism' became inseparable and 'the iconography of light and darkness, which embodies powerful images of race, science and religion, portrayed the European penetration of . . . Africa as simultaneously a process of domination, enlightenment and liberation' (Driver 1992: 31).

Geographical knowledge was an eagerly promoted feature of late-nineteenth-century imperialism. In 1884, the President of the Paris Geographical Society (Société de Géographie de Paris) wrote in the society's journal:

> Sirs, Providence has dictated to us an obligation to know the earth and to conquer it. This supreme order is one of the great duties prescribed for our intelligence and our efforts. Geography, this science which inspires such fine devotion, and to which so many victims have been sacrificed, has become the philosophy of the planet . . . Abstract science does not suffice in human activity. The great motive of civilised people in their enterprises consists above all in the accumulation of wealth, wealth which can only be produced by an increase in transactions and exchange. It is to this end that commercial and economic geography have recently been created.
>
> (Aldrich 1996: 104–5)

The importance of geography to both the economic and cultural motives of imperialism could not be clearer, and geography paved the way for the enthusiastic colonial lobby in the latter part of the nineteenth century. The secretary of the Sociedad Geográfica de Madrid urged the importance of geographic education in the project of imperial advancement:

> The earth, we repeat, will belong to whoever knows it best. It is not possible to use the wealth that a country contains, nor to govern its inhabitants in a manner in keeping with the innate, historical condition of their race, without a profound knowledge of the people and the land. If we lack this knowledge, we will face economic and political questions with false or incomplete information, we will commit errors, we will persevere with it, and there will come a time when people will protest, the land will be lost and the various national groups divided.
>
> (in Capel 1994: 72)

We could hardly find a clearer statement of the multiple imperatives of Orientalism: the desire to know and by knowing to 'own' the Earth; the desire to rule in a way that is in keeping with 'the innate historical condition' of colonized races; the sense that not to rule through knowledge will lead to rebellion. Knowledge, understanding, pacification, control: all these things were seen to be available through geographical knowledge.

But geography was more than a discipline in the nineteenth century, it was a discourse which found its way deep into Western thinking. According to Edward Said, most historians, and certainly literary scholars, have failed to remark 'the *geographical* notation, the theoretical mapping and charting of territory that underlies Western fiction, historical writing, and philosophical discourse of the time' (1993: 69). There is firstly the authority of the European observer, but, more interesting to him, there is a hierarchy of spaces, accessible by a process of 'contrapuntal' reading 'by which the metropolitan centre and, gradually, the metropolitan economy are seen as dependent upon an overseas system of territorial control' without which prosperity at 'home' would not be possible. This geographical notation may be read from novels such as Jane Austen's *Mansfield Park*. The authority of the observer is buttressed by a (geographical) discourse 'relegating the non-European to a secondary racial, cultural, ontological status' (70). Underlying the construction of social boundaries, of social spaces, with their racial, class and ethnic dimensions, were the geographical domains, the 'actual geographical underpinnings of the imperial, and also the cultural contest' (93). Said's view of the significance of geography as something which gave real substance, real spatial dimension, to imperialism's discourse of power suggests the depth of spatial thinking in imperial consciousness:

> The actual geographical possession of land is what empire in the final analysis is all about. At the moment when a coincidence occurs between real control and power, the idea of what a given place was (could be, might become), and an actual place – at that moment the struggle for empire is launched. This coincidence is the logic both for Westerners taking possession of land and, during decolonization, for resisting natives reclaiming it. Imperialism and the culture associated with it affirm both the primacy of geography and an ideology about control of territory. The geographical sense makes projections – imaginative, cartographic, military, economic, historical or in a general sense cultural. It also makes possible the construction of various kinds of knowledge, all of them in one way or another dependent upon the perceived character and destiny of a particular geography.
>
> (1993: 93)

Geography, then, was a conception of space which had extremely deep cultural purchase as well as very specific material effects in the lives of colonized peoples, as demonstrated in the division of Africa after the 1880 Berlin Congo Conference which marked the beginning of the 'scramble for Africa'. In 1899 the future President of the Royal Geographical Society, Thomas Holdich, declared:

> Truly, this period in our history has been well defined as the boundary-making era. Whether we turn to Europe, Asia, Africa or America, such an endless vista of political geography arises before us, such a vast area of land and sea to be explored and developed; such a vision of great burdens for the white man to take up in far-off regions, dim and indefinite as yet.
>
> (1899: 466)

Boundaries, as we shall elaborate in the next chapter, are more than simply a method of parcelling up the world, they are critical to the Western passion for seeing and the prominence of vision in the ideological control of space. Both geography and imperialism, according to Peet, were held together by a kind of neo-Lamarckian environmental determinism which legitimated the expansionary power of the fittest (1985: 327). In the scramble for Africa this contest of legitimacy revealed itself at its most sordid, but the impulse for the control of space stemmed from the status of the world map since Ptolemy and Mercator as a demonstration of the power and legitimacy of European civilization. The actual division of the globe was preceded by what Said calls 'imaginative geographies' which relied for their force on a narrative development very different from the presumed ideal of scientific discourse (Driver 1992: 31).

The combined importance of imaginative and disciplinary geographies marked the rise to prominence of US global power during and after the Second World War. The future of territories and colonies was a subject of extensive debate and consultation in the US Foreign Office well before the end of the Second World War and demonstrated the curious ambivalence of US policy. 'The ruling American vision of a new global order was the product of an intense colloid of seemingly selfless altruism and extreme self-interest' (Smith 1994: 272). Roosevelt presented an extreme, Wilsonite anti-imperialism while recognizing the American interests in economically recolonizing the decolonized British Empire. A key figure in discussions with the British was Isaiah Bowman, President of Johns Hopkins University and the US's most distinguished geographer. Geography and geographers were actively and widely employed for the war effort – 670 involved in some way in the war effort and the largest group, 129, by the Office for Strategic Services. The First World War 'was not a brief diversion for academic geography,' says Kirby, 'it was a catalyst' (1994: 305). Geographers played various roles in the bureaucratic machines of war and formed a ready pool to be utilized when hostilities broke out again in the 1930s. The strategic importance of geography in the prelude to and construction of the postwar Pax Americana represents the firm belief in the mastery of geographic space as an essential accompaniment to military domination. A striking feature of this geographic mastery has become the increasingly refined technology of surveillance:

> The process of surveillance has passed over to orbiting satellites, so that the panopticon is now truly global in extent. The processing of spatial imagery has become a crucial element in warfare, and the United States Department of Defense has invested heavily in this technology. For instance, the Defense Mapping Agency (DMA) has spent in excess of $2.6 billion since 1982 on a 'Data Integration/Segment' programme. This has involved the creation of an automated system that coordinates the needs of the armed forces in terms of maps and charts, and over 7000 people are employed in this project alone. The DMA recruits actively within 200 US universities, and is a significant employer of students with

automated cartography, remote sensing and Geographic Information Systems training. It is hardly coincidental that these are
the largest specialty groups within the Association of American
Geographers.

(Kirby 1994: 314–15)

This materialization of the metaphor of surveillance is one of the most
fascinating aspects of the new global imperialism. What Said claims for
nineteenth-century imperialism – that 'the moment when a coincidence
occurs between real control and power, the idea of what a given place
was (could be, might become) and an actual place' – is *still* the
moment when the struggle for empire is launched. But now the crucial
feature of a globalized imperialism is that it does not necessarily involve
the occupation of territory. The practical materialization of the link
between surveillance and geographical knowledge coincided with the
declining relevance of territorial occupation and the increasingly
diffused and subtle nature of neo-colonial control. The centrality of
educational and disciplinary structures has become even more obvious.

How one might resist this control of place is a question which invokes
the problem of decolonizing knowledge itself. What might a post-
colonial geography look like? Such a question exposes some of the most
intransigent issues in post-colonial transformation. For do we not fall
into the same dilemma as bedevils the use of imperial language?
Geography is a Western discipline. Will it be, as Chakrabarty says
about history, inevitably a geography of a 'European' world? Will it be
caught within the disciplinary and epistemological assumptions of the
Western 'scientific' mastery of space? Crush suggests that the aims of a
post-colonial geography might be defined as:

> the unveiling of geographical complicity in colonial dominion over
> space; the character of geographical representation in colonial dis-
> course; the de-linking of local geographical enterprise from metro-
> politan theory and its totalizing systems of representation; and the
> recovery of those hidden spaces occupied, and invested with their
> own meaning, by the colonial underclasses.
>
> (Crush 1994: 336–7)

In practice this programme has proved more theoretically problematic than expected. What does a 'de-linking' of local geography from
'totalizing systems of representation' actually entail? How far back do
we go? Do we abandon mapping co-ordinates, forms of measurement,
the shape of the world, as well as forms of description and disciplinary

conventions? Clearly, we live in a world which has a universally agreed cartographic shape and structure, even though that shape is an invention and a confirmation of Eurocentrism. How we live in such a world, how we describe our place in it, is a resonant metonymy of the dilemma of a decolonizing knowledge. Here we see why interpolation has been so strategic to post-colonial discourse. For a decolonizing geography may well interpolate the discipline, employing some conventional practices and technologies and yet injecting them with non-Western ways of conceiving space itself (perhaps even ways that are totally incommensurable with Western conceptions). Indeed such an interpolation is exactly the direction of many radical geographies. One can use the fundamental technologies of the discourse without *necessarily* being bound by them. The achievement of such post-colonial transformations is limited only by the confidence with which disciplinary processes are reconceived in terms of indigenous spatial consciousness. The result has been and will probably continue to be, the re-inscription, the re-embedding of post-colonial *place* in geographic representations.

What remains striking about the link between geography and empire is that the great utility of geographic knowledge was based upon a self-evident assumption of the transparency of space. Just as Stanley had surveyed African space from a vantage point which established his mastery, comprehension and vision, so geography assumed the spectral stance of the *grande-autre* establishing a similar mastery with the aid of 'objective' and 'scientific' disciplinary structures. Indeed geography was affected by the nineteenth-century mania to establish objective 'scientific' premises for all fields of study: philology, ethnology, craniology, anthropology. Geographic space was still simply 'there', and now scientifically proved. The idea that space itself might be subject to the historical vagaries or ideological requirements of geographic method was as unthinkable as questioning the moral authority, and indeed obligation, of European powers to assume geographic control of the world. The link between surveillance and geography has only become more strikingly confirmed in contemporary practice. For space itself had long been reified out of time and locality, those factors of human experience of place in which it had been embedded.

## Language and the transformation of colonial space

The Western construction of global space has become a given for contemporary representations of place, and remains the inevitable context in which those local representations must occur. In effect, the discourse of place operates within the same set of power relations as effect other forms of post-colonial transformation, and indeed, becomes their most contested site. The Mercator *Atlas* was a key instrument in that reorganization of space and time which characterized the great historical and discursive shift of modernity. The most far-reaching impact of this reorganization upon colonized societies was the severance of the traditional links between time, space and place within modern consciousness. This is not only because many pre-colonial societies were (and are) what might be called 'premodern', and have therefore experienced very great social and cultural disruptions through colonization, but because all post-colonial societies, indeed all societies today, are subject to global representations of time and space, which have little reference to locality.

The world map is the first instrument by which a structural connection with people who lived very far away could be made. As we have seen, it was made under the energetic sponsorship of European imperialism. The movement of European society through the world, the 'discovery' and occupation of remote regions, was the necessary basis for a separation of space and place and the creation of what could be called 'empty space'. With the emergence of the Mercator *Atlas*, and other universal maps, 'where perspective played little part in the representation of geographical position and form' (Giddens 1990: 19) and established space as a measurable, abstract concept independent of any particular place or region, the idea of space became disengaged from place. Consequently, while the separation of time and space allows social relations to be lifted out of their locale, a process which leaves virtually no local society untouched today, the concept of 'place', which is in some senses left behind by modernity, becomes a deeply evocative site of the link between language and identity, a possible site of those local realities which the universal separation of time, space and place leaves virtually untouched.

While the separation of space and place appears to be an irreversible consequence of modernity, the suppression of the specificity of place, and the marginalization of place by imperial prejudices about what might be a suitable and 'natural' ecology, have been contested by post-colonial reconstructions of place in language, writing, art and other forms of cultural production. Military and economic strength enabled the colonizing power to establish its legal and economic perceptions of place as dominant, but it was the mode of representation, the language itself, which effected the most far-reaching pressure, which established the concept of place as a particularly complex site of colonial engagement.

In all colonial experience colonialism brings with it a sense of dislocation between the environment and the imported language now used to describe it, a gap between the 'experienced' place and the descriptions the language provides. The nineteenth-century commentator Barron Field (!) suggested the tension between language and the experience of colonized place.

> All the dearest allegories of human life are bound up with the infant and slender green of spring, the dark redundance of summer, and the sere and yellow leaf of autumn. These are as essential to the poet as emblems, as they are to the painter as picturesque objects; and the common consent and immemorial custom of European poetry has made the change of the seasons, and its effect upon vegetation, a part, as it were, of our very nature. I can therefore hold no fellowship with Australian foliage.
>
> (Field 1825: 423–4)

The far-reaching and astonishing implication of Field's remarks is, according to Paul Carter, that 'Australia is, strictly speaking, indescribable' (1987: 44). Its uniformity means, fundamentally, that it cannot be named, because no nameable parts distinguish themselves. Language, as poetry so aptly demonstrates, is much more than a series of descriptive signifiers. The connotations of seasonal movement are a part 'of our very [European] nature'. This tension, this gap, between the experienced place and the language available to describe it, lies at the heart of the experience of the post-colonial subject, the very essence of displacement. Whether it remains permanently disabling or whether it becomes the beginning of a transformation of colonial discourse is a pivotal moment in post-colonial cultures, since it is language which enables colonized peoples to turn displacement into a creative resistance. In many respects the political economy of property is a much less complicated aspect of imperial dominance than the discursive activity of language and writing and its involvement in the concept of place.

A sense of displacement, of the lack of fit between language and place, may be experienced by those who possess English as a mother tongue or by those who speak it as a second language. In both cases there appears to be a lack of fit between the place described in English and the place actually experienced by the colonized subject. This comes about firstly because the words developed to describe place originated in an alien European environment, and secondly because many of the words used by the colonizers described 'empty space' or 'empty time' –

had thrown off any connection to a particular locale. Place can thus be a constant trope of difference in post-colonial writing, a continual reminder of colonial ambivalence, of the separation, yet continual mixing, of the colonizer and colonized. Just as the discourse of naming is a key to the cartographic dominance of the globe by Europe, so the renaming of places becomes a prominent feature of the transformation of place from wasteland, chthonic region, heart of darkness to a fertile and abundantly productive site for the imagination.

The most concerted discussion of place and its location in language has come from settler colony writers for whom the possession of English as a first language has produced a particularly subtle, complex and creatively empowering sense of the lack of fit between the language available and the place experienced. Canadian Robert Kroestch in 'Unhiding the Hidden' suggests that the particular predicament of the Canadian writer, and perhaps all settler colony writers, is that they work in a language that appears to be authentically their own, and yet is not quite. Just as 'there was in the Latin word a concealed Greek experience, so there is in the Canadian word a concealed other experience, sometimes British, sometimes American' (1974: 43), and in recent Canadian fiction, he says, 'writers resolve the paradox – the painful tension between appearance and authenticity – by the radical process of demythologizing the systems that threaten to define them. Or, more comprehensively, they uninvent the world' (43). This leads Canadian writers to the ultimate *contra-diction:* 'they uncreate themselves into existence' (45).

For another Canadian writer, Dennis Lee, this experience has had a profound effect on his writing, even drying up his writing altogether at one stage because he felt he could not find the words to express his experience authentically (1974). For if 'we live in space which is radically in question for us, that makes our barest speaking a problem to itself' (154). Lee's feeling that 'the language was drenched with our non-belonging, and words . . . had become the enemy' dried up his creative energies. Although the first task of a writer is to write about what is known, 'His imagination must come home. But that first necessity is not enough. For if you are Canadian, home is a place that is not home to you – it is even less your home than the imperial centre you used to dream about . . . Try to speak the words of your home and you will discover – if you are colonial – that you do not know them.' Lee's discovery was that perhaps in some sense placelessness, the experience of displacement, *was* home: 'perhaps our job was not to fake a space of our own and write it up, but rather to find words for our space-lessness. Perhaps that *was* home' (1974: 163).

Displacement is not necessarily a feeling. To some extent any 'sense' of placelessness felt by people who are born in a place is just as much constructed as identity itself. More often it displays itself in forms of behaviour which occur as a consequence of colonization: uncertainties about the location of value, ambivalence or argument about certain kinds of cultural or political affiliation, social contestation over the 'proper' use of language, confusion about the use of the word 'home'. Kroestch and Lee articulate, with great specificity, the cultural density of this word *home*, the discursive richness of place, which resides not simply in one's visual experience but in the cultural provenance of the words used to describe it. Whatever the nature of the post-colonial society, language always negotiates a kind of gap between the word and its signification. It is this gap, more than any identifiable emotional or psychological experience, which identifies the sense of displacement. For there is nothing inherent in words which severs them from place, and yet, for writers like Lee, to explore the cadence of one's writing is 'to explore the nature of colonial space' (1974: 154).

What becomes apparent in these writers is that 'place' is much more than the land. The theory of place does not propose a simple separation between the 'place' named and described in language, and some 'real' place inaccessible to it, but rather indicates that in some sense place *is* language, something in constant flux, a discourse in process. These writers become compelled to try to construct a new language that might fit the place they experience because the language does not simply report the visual or proximate experience but is implicated in its presence. Dennis Lee coins the term 'cadence' to describe this: 'a presence, both outside myself and inside my body opening out and trying to get into words' (1974: 397).

One of the most sustained discussions of the linguistic construction of place occurs in Paul Carter's *The Road to Botany Bay*, which proposes a concept he calls 'spatial history'. Such history examines place as a palimpsest on which the traces of successive inscriptions form the complex experience of place, which is itself historical. Language, naming, the inscription of a colonial presence on the map, turn 'space' into 'place'. Thus history is spatial, the land identifying the progress of place unfolding through language. Imperial history, the teleological narrative of civilization and settlement, distinguishes itself by ignoring the place, the environment, as simply the empty stage on which the theatre of history is enacted. But if we see place as not simply a neutral location for the imperial project, we can see how intimately place is involved in the development of identity, how deeply it is involved in history, and how deeply implicated in the systems of representation –

language, writing and the creative arts – which develop in any society but in colonial societies in particular.

The concept of palimpsest begins to undermine the spatiality of place and the priority of the boundary by *re-embedding* time and space, history and location, through the agency of language. Place may be seen as the material and experiential site in which the traces of history exist in the erasures and re-inscriptions of language. This occurs most obviously through the agency of naming, by which the map becomes a metonym of imperial knowledge and hence of imperial control of space and time. But the re-embedding of time and space in this way may also be seen to articulate a strategy of resistance and transformation. For no inscription is indelible, and, although formal maps may remain the province of formal political and cultural power, the palimpsest defines a process by which place may be re-appropriated from the tropes of boundary, map and seeing itself, by means of the appropriation of dominant modes of representation.

Place is never simply location, nor is it static, a cultural memory which colonization buries. For, like culture itself, place is in a continual and dynamic state of formation, a process intimately bound up with the culture and the identity of its inhabitants. Above all place is a *result* of habitation, a consequence of the ways in which people inhabit space, particularly that conception of space as universal and uncontestable that is constructed for them by imperial discourse. The transformation of imperial conceptions of place, and of imperial technologies of spatial representation, has often been carried out successfully in imaginative acts of resistance through the *creative* representations of place. Such place forms itself out of the densely woven web of language, memory and cultural practice and keeps being formed by the process of living. This is the message of Kim Scott's *True Country*, a novel set in a remote Aboriginal community. Not till the death of the protagonist does his spirit see this movement of place:

> See? Now it is done. Now you know. True country. Because just living, just living is going downward lost drifting nowhere, no matter if you be skitter-scatter dancing anykind like mad. We gotta be moving, remembering, singing our place little bit new, little bit special, all the time.
>
> (1993: 255)

Even beyond language and culture, the movement of the spirit, the essence of habitation, 'singing our place, little bit new, little bit special, all the time', transforms place.

# 7  Habitation

In a small town in Uganda called Mbarara there is a BP service station. There are few cars in Mbarara, no electricity, no gas, no sewerage. Yet this service station uses more electric power than the whole town. It provides petrol for travellers and the few public vehicles in the region, but it is the brightest, best-lit and glossiest place in Mbarara. Here is an extravagant image of the intrusion of global capital. What, we might ask, does this absurd symbol of the West's profligate use of energy have to do in this small African town? Yet when we look more closely, when we track the procession of people through this place in a week, we discover that this service station functions very differently from similar outlets in the West. It is the best-lit and main meeting place of the town; it is the place on which bicycle taxis converge; the many bicycle owners in the region come to inflate their tyres here, a task made much easier by pressurized air; groups of people can be seen sitting around talking at all times of the day. This service station has a different *meaning* for the local inhabitants from the meaning it might have in the West; it is possibly less artificial, less soulless, than it might be elsewhere, it is perhaps even less anomalous, because it is incorporated more seamlessly into a broader spectrum of local life. Consider a typical scene: a woman comes with a small Coca-Cola bottle to have it filled with paraffin for her stove. Without demur she inserts the simple round of her life in between two significant forms of global capitalism – Coca-Cola and British Petroleum – to maintain the simplicity of her daily cooking. This place has a different meaning to these inhabitants because they inhabit it differently.

Habitation is a strategy which addresses the problem of the current universality of Western representations of place. It describes a way of being in place, a way of being which itself defines and transforms place. It is so powerful because the coercive pressures of colonialism and globalization have ultimately no answer to it. Whether dominated by imperial discourse or global culture, the local subject has a capacity to incorporate such influences into a sense of place, to appropriate a vast array of resources into the business of establishing and confirming local identity. The question 'Where is my place?' is connected to the more difficult question 'Where do I belong?' When we look at the startling cultural intrusion represented by this service station, the question of 'belonging' seems very remote. Or at the very least such a place seems decidedly *not* to belong here. But what determines belonging? To what extent is inhabiting a place not only a statement of identity but also a means of transforming the conditions of one's life? The conceptual shift from spatiality to 'place-ness' which occurs as a result of colonial experience is a shift from empty space to a human, social space which gains its material and ideological identity through the practice of inhabiting.

This 'practice' of inhabiting is in fact a dense fabric of interwoven acts in which the issues of inheritance, ethnic identity, belonging, history, race, land are all intertwined. Sally Morgan's novel *My Place* recounts her search for roots, her search for some physical and cultural location from which she can trace her identity, and it describes the eventual return to Corunna Downs from whence her family came. But here the search for place reveals itself to be inflected with the core condition of colonial displacement, the search for that static and transcendent object of desire, elusive and ultimately non-existent: the authentic pre-colonial identity. Corunna Downs represents but one stage in the location of Sally's family's 'place'. The very term 'my place' is polyvalent, for clearly, it can, and does, refer to a place in various physical and imaginative environments. For this reason, 'place' is always more than mere location for the subject whose identity is in crisis. Early in the novel we discover, from Sally's grandmother, a way of inhabiting space that can transform it, that can own it, make it an extension of self. Sally is told to sit still on the step and be very quiet.

> Suddenly, the yard filled with a high trilling sound. My eyes searched the trees. I couldn't see that bird, but his call was there. The music stopped as abruptly as it had begun.
>
> Nan smiled at me, 'Did you hear him? Did you hear the bird call?'
>
> 'I heard him Nan,' I whispered in awe.
>
> (1987: 14)

Nan has a way of inhabiting that makes the place her own, that dwells in a space beyond location, an imaginative space deeply imbued with the place-ness of her own carefully nurtured sense of being. This practice of habitation is more than the occupying of a location, it is itself a *way of being* within which, and through which, place comes to be. Bell hooks suggests that for a diasporic or estranged people, in particular for those dislocated in one way or another by the historic disruptions of colonization, 'Home is that place which enables and promotes varied and ever-changing perspectives, a place where one discovers new ways of seeing reality, frontiers of difference' (1991: 148). But this is only part of the story. For Nan, the inherited ways of being in place, of seeing place as a numinous and liberating mystery, determine her Aboriginality more effectively than any location, as indeed it must. This gift of being is the opposite of exile, for it turns location, any location, into home, into owned place.

Habitation is critical to the ability of a colonized or dislocated people to transform that external cultural pressure which constricts them because it extends through the widening horizons of the experience of place, from the intensely personal (often regarded as the province of poetics) to the global. As soon as we begin to see the construction of place as a factor of a *way of inhabiting* we see how dense and how *intense* is the rhizomic pattern of relationships in which place is located. The phenomenon of place extends from the most personal and intimate of relationships – the family group amongst whom you belong; that group which provides the first and most powerful context for identity; the people with whom you sit down every day to eat; the daily habits of existence – to the most attenuated: those myriad global effects on living which you may or may not appropriate in particular ways.

Bourdieu's term *habitus* may be useful here. Habitus, 'the durably installed generative principle of regulated improvisations' (1972: 78), is a term which suggests the extent to which 'place' may be seen to be a 'practice' rather than a visual, geographic or topographic location. In Bourdieu's formulation habitus refers to the way in which each individual lives out his or her life through a series of repetitive actions – habits – which are nevertheless governed by certain parameters. It is produced by 'the material conditions of life, and . . . pedagogic action' (Bourdieu and Passeron 1972: 63–4), and is linked to the notion of cultural capital which each individual acquires in the process of self-formation. As we saw, Bourdieu and Passeron suggest that habitus comes about from students internalizing the cultural principles learnt during teaching so that they may be perpetuated and reproduced (1972: 31). This reproduction is not always necessarily intentional, but operates as a way of giving the individual's life a coherent direction: 'The habitus is the universalizing mediation which causes an individual agent's practices, without either explicit reason or signifying intent, to be none the less "sensible" and "reasonable"' (79).

The orchestration of habitus produces a commonsense world endowed with an objectivity secured by the consensus of the community (80). Put simply, what you do is related to where you are, what you have learned, and who you are with, a relationship that is circulatory, reinforcing and interchangeably identifying. Habitus connects 'habitation' with 'habit' so that the 'practice' of place, or group or class habitus is a network of unconscious actions in a system of undirected agreement. Habitus is therefore not only a practice but a *relational* practice. It describes the practical ways in which an individual may make choices that utilize some of the cultural capital of a dominant power or ideology: a practical mediation of the pressure of ideology with the strategies of self-fashioning. An exploration of the habitus 'tends to pull analysis towards material practices rather than away from them, as investigation of "subjectivity" tends to do' (Holden 1998: 7).

Such a relational practice can be critical in post-colonial experience. Seeing imperial discourse as producing cultural capital, and the colonized subject as one who may actively acquire such capital, not as a passively interpellated colonial subject, but as an agent making choices, reveals the circulatory and relational nature of the colonial habitus. Although Bourdieu and Passeron do not focus on place as such, the interrelation between location and habitus is obviously crucial both in classroom and family environment. The transformation of colonial space into post-colonial 'life-place' occurs through the interaction of habitation and representation. On one hand habitation may be seen to be a term loosely collecting together the discourses of mapping, geography, enclosure and boundaries, with their material consequences extending from the domestic space to the nation state to the geographical world itself. Representation, on the other hand, appears to encompass those aspects by which space is conceived and presented: visuality, perspective, surveillance, language.

However, the benefit of making such a division is to understand its artificiality: all the discourses of habitation are intimately connected to the processes of representation. We have seen, in the last chapter, how the discourse of mapping emerges from the ocularcentrism of Western culture and in turn generates the perspectival method of Renaissance representation. Similarly, geography was a discipline deeply implicated in empire because it enacted and embedded the act of surveillance. The very provisionality of a 'boundary' between habitation and representation hints at the possibility of a transformation of space. The processes of transformation, by which place is either 'reclaimed' or re-inscribed, require a conceptual connection between the discursive and material which we could describe by the term 'habitation *as* representation' – our ways of being in a place are so intimately connected to our ways of representing it that habitation may be seen to be a way of representing. This implies a habitation which transcends seeing, constituting place as a network of actions, practices and relationships.

The notion of the palimpsest has been almost indispensable in demonstrating the way in which space is transformed into place. Paul Carter's demonstration of the ways in which naming and subsequent renamings turn putatively 'empty' space into place (1987) has been important for understanding the significance of place in colonial experience. But how do we conceptualize place as a constantly negotiated network of relationships? In talking about space, place and gender, Doreen Massey develops an argument for constituting social space 'in terms of the articulation of social relations which necessarily have a spatial form in their interactions with one another' (1994: 120). If we accept this idea that social relations have a spatial form, then 'one way of thinking about place is as particular moments in such intersecting social relations, nets of which have over time been constructed, laid down, interacted with one another, decayed and renewed'. More importantly, some of these relations 'will be, as it were, contained within the place; others will stretch beyond it, tying any particular locality into wider relations and processes in which other places are implicated too' (120). That is to say, as well as the palimpsestic process of inscription and erasure by which place comes into being, there is a *rhizomic* network by which place maintains its dynamic, emergent identity (see Ashcroft and Salter 1994). It is not only 'the "changing fortunes" of an area which must be understood by locating it within a wider context, but also the character of the place itself . . . the very formation of the identity of a place – its social structure, its political character, its "local" culture – is also a product of interactions' (Massey 1994: 120). The interactions with the global which contribute to the very construction of the local are themselves an important part of the interpolating process, as we shall see, but also indicate how extensive these interactions might be. The nature of the interpolating process determines the nature of the relationship between the global and the local, and thus distinguishes different places. The rhizome of place is increasingly global and this makes the interactions of global and local an imperative aspect of the construction of place. 'Thinking of places in this way', says Massey, 'implies that they are not so much bounded areas as open and porous networks of social relations' (121).

The increasingly familiar issue of globalization has a spatial dimension which impacts the identity of 'place' in much the same way that imperial discourse and colonial occupation changed the nature and experience of the local habitus. Economic globalization means more than the increasing spatial reach of a particular group of companies, it also means 'the stretching out over space of relations of power, and of relations imbued with meaning and symbolism' (158). But more importantly, perhaps, these relations of power can themselves undergo a transformation as they take on a new spatial form. As we shall examine later, local culture is not simply a passive recipient of global influences, the appropriation of global forms can be instrumental in the construction of local identity. But critical in this reconstruction of habitus, this transformation of colonial space into life-place, are the strategies by which the local culture deals with boundaries.

## Boundaries

In the previous chapter we saw the importance of surveillance in Coetzee's allegory of the colonial occupation and control of colonial space, *Dusklands*. In particular, boundaries are critical to the organization of such surveillance and their absence most threatening to the civilizing gaze. The protagonist Jacobus Coetzee states that 'In the wild I lose my sense of boundaries' (Coetzee 1974: 78). Boundaries are critical in the colonial taming of the wild and the control of space. The sense of boundlessness, of that which had not been, and could not be surveyed, lent to the imperial view of the unexplored places of the Earth a fervent need for imaginative control. The presence of 'blank' places on the map, even into the late nineteenth century, called European explorers to be filled with names, and to colonizers to 'develop' that land. 'Primitives' who did not 'develop' the land and its resources were invariably viewed as having no right of possession. This attitude, formalized in maps and supported by the iconography of light and dark, is repeated throughout the world in the progress of imperial expansion because the colonizing powers brought with them a particular view of land which had a philosophical, legal and political provenance as well as an economic justification. The key to it can be found in the idea of 'enclosure' which had come to underlie the Western concept of property. Connected to, and perhaps stemming from, the principles of spatiality, of perspectival perception as a universal truth, of space existing objectively separate from the perceiving subject, a quantity which can be mapped with mathematical precision, the idea of enclosure, or property, has dominated colonizers' views of place. In turn such a concept has stimulated many of the struggles and contests over the constitution and experience of place in post-colonial societies.

John Locke's discussion of property in the *Second Treatise of Government* (Book II, Chapter 5) outlines the rationale for the expropriation of lands by the 'advanced' agrarian communities from hunter-gatherer societies. For Locke, the very mark of property is the enclosure: the defining, or bounding of a place that signals its settlement or cultivation, and, consequently, marks the frontier between the savage and the civilized. Although nobody has an exclusive dominion over nature, says Locke, since the 'Fruits' of the Earth and the 'Beasts' were given for the use of men, there must be a way to appropriate them before they can be of any use to a particular man. Such usefulness is achieved and regulated by enclosure (Locke 1690: 330). Because it is man's labour which removes the products from nature and makes them his, '*As much Land* as a Man Tills, Plants, Improves, Cultivates and can use the Product of, so much is his *Property*. He by his Labour does, as it were, inclose it from the Common' (1690: 332). For God 'gave it to the use of the Industrious and Rational (and *Labour* was to be *his Title* to it)' (333).

It is this philosophical history which lies embedded in Salim's statement when he buys a lot in Naipaul's *A Bend in the River*: 'I thought, "What a place to live in!" I could hear the river – the development wasn't too far from the rapids. I listened to the river and looked up at that sky and I thought: "This isn't property. This is just bush. This has always been bush"' (1979: 29). Clearly the concept of enclosure leads to an emotional relationship with place which exceeds the simple marking of a boundary. The difference between 'property' and 'bush' is a complex one. But the effect of the distinction between enclosed property and 'wild' bush was to invalidate the claims over land of any people whose relationship with it did not involve agricultural 'improvement' and its requisite enclosure. So powerful was the concept of property as a mode of inhabiting place that the social reformer Thomas Fowell Buxton could say in the mid-nineteenth century that only the Bible and the plough could lead Africa on to a higher level of existence: for 'plough' meant agriculture, and agriculture meant property, and property meant civilization (Baumgart 1982: 14).

Other colonists, of course, had a very different idea about the rights of African ownership of land, and the ideology of Social Darwinism, as well as the long history of race thinking, provided a justification for the long history of European land theft. In 1856 Charles Kingsley wrote: 'Each people should either develop the capabilities of their own country, or make room for those who will develop them. If they accept that duty, they have their reward in the renovation of blood, which commerce, and its companion, colonization, are certain to bring' (1860, vol. 2: 21–2). This is a fascinating compilation of the certainties and assumptions of imperial culture: all people 'should' develop the capabilities of their country (why, we are not told); such 'development' means invariably the production of wealth (any other form of land tenure is *ipso facto* undevelopment); failure to develop justifies the entry of colonizers ('blank' spaces by their very 'blankness' justify colonization); acceptance of the duty to develop will, curiously, bring racial renovation (confirming the racial impetus of imperialism). Kingsley's overweening confidence is an uncanny repetition of Mercator's confidence that Europe, by virtue of its greater civilization, is the world's mother (Rabasa 1993: 193–4). The occupation of geographical space is driven by the same moral authority that drives the *mission civilatrice*.

Boundaries are fundamental to European modernity, deeply implicated in the Western privileging of visuality. The regulation of space by physical boundaries is a metonymy for the regulatory practices of Western epistemology itself. The philosophy of enclosure, like the creation of the map, is related to a perspectival view of space. It is not simply a rationale for dividing land but reflects a fundamental aspect of Western thinking. The ocularcentrism of Western discourse is marked by the complementary, though opposed, concepts of horizon and boundary. Whereas the horizon adumbrates the region of imaginative possibility which the method of thinking attempts to regulate, boundaries organize visual space in ways that enable the method of perspectival vision to dominate thinking. Whereas horizon has been an evocative metaphor in literature and philosophy, particularly phenomenology, its allusion to possibility and open meaning has had at best an ambiguous *epistemological* function in Western thought. Boundaries, on the other hand, are crucial because they explicitly defer to the 'will to truth' which dominates Western discourse.

We use spatial metaphors to define concepts through their extension or intension, 'we use them to provide the setting for mathematical and logical arguments, and we make them explicit when talking about "a field of research," "the frontiers of knowledge," "the boundary between world-views," "the distance between cultures," "the limits of reason"' (Reichert 1992: 90). We have only to think of the prominence of frontiers, boundaries of race and ethnicity, of nation, of gender and class, the binaries of centre and margin, to see how deeply the trope of the boundary embeds itself in Western thinking. To this extent, space and place reveal themselves to be metonymic of the expansion and impact of imperial culture throughout the world. Locke's philosophy of enclosure is merely a formalized extension of the most fundamental boundary in Western epistemology: that between the subject and object, a boundary which became fundamental to the perception of space.

Perhaps more profound in the development of modernity was the construction of a boundary between civilized self and primitive other. It has become a truism since Saussure that the self cannot be signified outside its difference from the other, that without the 'margin' their can be no 'centre'. But few have considered just how necessary this construction of other was to Europe. Modernity was Europe's monumental project of self-realization, and could not occur without that 'other' constructed in imperial discourse, nor the other *produced* in the discourse of exchange which underlay the development of capitalism. The rhetoric of spatial difference worked its way into European philosophy (as in the metaphors of architecture and travel in Descartes's *Discourse on the Method*) during this time but it was nowhere clearer than in the difference asserted in the representation of the colonized. In all forms of discourse, literary, geographical, economic, this representation was 'a presentation which signalled the distinctiveness, and therefore the lack, of the colonial when compared to the presence of the European' (Stratton 1990: 145). In colonial representation the boundary of signification emerged with almost inviolable certainty, since it was essential to the production of Europe's 'presence'.

We can see how spatial thinking continues to operate as metonymic of racial, political and cultural power within colonialism. In *Dusklands* Jacobus Coetzee, seated on his ox-wagon, encounters a Hottentot:

> There he stands, inhabiting the prescribed place four paces away and three feet down, resignation is in the air, we are now going to live through gifts of tobacco and words of peace, directions to water and warnings against brigands, demonstrations of firearms, murmurs of awe, and eventually a lifetime of the pad-pad-pad of naked feet behind us. The devious pursuit ending in the frank straight line, the transformation of savage into enigmatic follower, and the obscure movement of the soul (weariness, relief, incuriosity, terror) that comes with this familiar transformation, we feel as a fated pattern and condition of life.
>
> (1974: 81)

The trope of seeing is connected to the metaphor of space within which the colonial subject is separated, defined, demarcated. The man occupying his 'prescribed place' will engage in the ritual of engagement, until the 'devious pursuit' ends in the preferable 'frank straight line' of the colonizer. What seems to be a fated condition of life is nothing other than the rigidity of the political and epistemological boundaries of colonialism: boundaries enforce and organize Jacobus Coetzee's surveillance, his capacity to see. In this dismal prophecy of the 'transformation of savage into enigmatic follower' we see how surveillance situated in space extends into the temporal trajectory of history, both dominated and regulated by the gaze of the colonizer.

On his rough ox-wagon Jacobus Coetzee is supported by nothing less than a primary metaphor of the Enlightenment. Indeed the trope of the boundary has become inextricable from the trope of seeing in Western epistemology. 'It is particularly in the best works in social theory, philosophy and human geography that this becomes clear: the extent to which thinking is bound in the picture of the geometrical line' (Reichert 1992: 88). Consequently, this binds thinking within the discourse of spatiality, within the trope of the boundary. 'Is this spatial metaphor appropriate for the subject matter they are concerned with?' he asks:

> Does it not, relying on the logic of the eyes, on visual things rather than on invisible relations, lay the basis for the very reification they seek to undermine? Does it not, implying a particular, physical idea of being, force thoughts into the very coherence and historical stability it seeks to question?
>
> (88)

Paradoxically, the trope of the boundary, which, by this analysis, focuses the contradictions of Western thought, becomes the very tool of reification by which it can order and regulate any opposition to its contradictory power. If the trope of the boundary means limitation and contradiction, it also means control.

Coetzee articulates the importance of boundaries to the 'civilizing' project:

> We cannot count the wild. The wild is one because it is boundless. We can count fig-trees, we can count sheep because the orchard and the farm are bounded. The essence of orchard tree and farm sheep is number. Our commerce with the wild is a tireless enterprise of turning it into orchard and farm. When we cannot fence it and count it we reduce it to number by other means.
>
> (1974: 80)

Here the mathematical configuration and bounding of space are shown to be critical in the colonizing project, by 'enclosing' with both physical and epistemological means. Indeed the mathematical co-ordinates of spatial boundaries were crucial to the growth of Renaissance mapping. As we see in those maps preceding Mercator's, those spaces which cannot be mapped, because they are unknown, are *ipso facto* 'wild' – wildness and boundlessness become the ultimate tautology.

Furthermore, the concept of enclosure is a philosophy which has extensive ramifications in the contemporary production of space: the growth in the importance of private property and private production; the growth of capital; the emergence of defined boundaries of social experience. The ability to influence the production of space is an important means to augment social power, says Harvey:

> In material terms this means that those who can effect the spatial distribution of investments in transport and communications, in physical and social infrastructures, or the territorial distribution of administrative, political, and economic powers can often reap material rewards. The range of phenomena to be considered here is vast indeed – it varies all the way from one neighbour inciting another to help improve local property values by painting the porch . . . to the interest of military contractors in exacerbating geopolitical tensions . . . as a means to ensure bigger and better armaments contracts.
>
> (1990: 233)

Clearly the economic basis of colonization relied heavily on this capacity to effect the spatial distribution of investments. Colonized space, whatever the particular nature of the colony, became a reservoir of raw materials and labour and a market for manufactured goods. In this way the economic control of space maximized the dominance of mapping, perception, surveillance, turning the 'life-place', the place of habitation, into a space which, both in representation and exploita-tion, was dominated by European assumptions and spatial tech-nologies. Place was reorganized into colonial space through the carving out of estates, plantations and grazing properties, the building of roads, railways, tunnels and bridges. In places like some Caribbean islands, which were turned into virtual sugar production factories, the effect was total and catastrophic, but in all colonies the reorgan-ization of space changed every aspect of local social and individual existence.

### The prison house of empire

Given the extensive metaphoric function of boundaries in imperial discourse and in Western thinking in general, it is useful to consider first the most concrete, oppressive and brutal form of boundary control, that of the prison. For when we observe the dramatic effects of imprisonment as a tool of colonial dominance, and the discursive response to incarceration by the colonized – what we might call, in the broadest sense, the 'practice of inhabiting' – we see the prison, and the representation of imprisonment by the incarcerated, as the most extreme metonym of colonial occupation. A prison is the most concrete model possible of the coercive and surveillant power of a dominant authority, and when we observe the responses of political prisoners, particularly in South African prison writing, we find a concentrated example of transformative responses to imperial boundaries.

This is not to equate colonization with imprisonment but rather to see the prison as the most concentrated and punitive model of spatial control – a system of comprehensive surveillance, a system of total physical control, a system for inducing certain kinds of thinking in prisoners. The prison metaphor has a twofold function: it reveals the strategies by which boundaries construct subjectivity; and, more importantly, it reveals – in the response of those prisoners who invent particular forms of habitation, and engage in particular forms of writing – a powerful example of transformation. While the cultural boundaries erected by imperial control may be relatively notional and often apparently benign, the structure of relations they form can be illuminated by the aggressive and programmatic incarceration of the prison.

The first element in the function of the prison boundary is to construct a space that is literally 'placeless', a carceral space in which the dominant relationship is that between the imprisoning gaze and a featureless, undefined subject. It might not be an exaggeration to see in this a metaphor for the authority of an imperial surveillance in which the colonized place, like colonial subjectivity, exists as marginal to the universal space of the world map or the globe, and is identified by that relationship. The dominant elements of this strategy are, on one hand, the suppression of identity by a sense of isolation and, on the other, the reproduction of identity by the imperial boundaries which are represented by the prison walls and the dehumanizing strategies of imprisonment. The key to resistance here, of course, is the capacity to produce one's own identity through representation. The fascinating discovery we can make from prison memoirs is that prisoners' strategies of rejection or disregard for prison authorities, because they are vulnerable to the ceaseless power of the prison, are ultimately less effective than those forms of representation which appropriate some of the material and psychological features of the imprisonment itself, and transform them into strategies of identity formation.

In an analysis of South African prison writings J. U. Jacobs (1991) describes the most common *processes* by which the prisoners are deprived of their identity, those processes most regularly recorded in prison memoirs: stripping, interrogation, and torture. The stripping of the subject's identity is performed literally on entry into prison. This symbolic ritual removes all vestiges of the prisoner's individual characteristics. In *Bandiete* Hugh Lewin explains the significance of this stripping:

> You are stripped bare of everything that you can call your own, constantly stripped bare of anything that you make your own; you are stripped bare in an endless process of peeling off your protective covering and leaving you naked. So they can watch you. So that you, like the corridor, are without decoration, without covering, with nothing behind which to hide, with nothing they can't see into and watch.
>
> (1981: 41)

The link between surveillance and the negation of identity is very clear. As we saw, surveillance implies the authority to survey, and objectifies the subject of the gaze. Physical stripping was a dramatic enactment of the apartheid system in South Africa whereby a group of people was identified purely by skin colour and kept separate, stripped by the pass laws of both dignity and individual identity. The pass laws, significantly, also controlled movement and location – they were the means by which the apartheid state regulated the times, routes and destination of travel for pass holders and determined the situation of their place of residence. Such laws, along with those which allowed detention without trial,[6] represent the most authoritarian form of 'stripping', but, in a more subtle and perhaps less directly punitive sense, this could be seen also to be a feature of the imposition of colonial cultural boundaries in the process of identity formation. Simple acts of resistance, such as the political prisoners' refusal of a rectal examination, are signs of a broader establishment of communal identity, a resistance to bodily invasion, which becomes more elaborate and more focused through the representation of the experience in writing.

The second prevailing feature in accounts of imprisonment, according to Jacobs, is interrogation. The way in which pain leads to truth – truth always being the gaoler's truth – is described by Colonel Joll in

Coetzee's *Waiting for the Barbarians*. Training and experience have taught him to recognize the tone that enters the voice of a man who is telling the truth: 'I am speaking of a situation in which I am probing for the truth, in which I have to exert pressure to find it. First, I get lies, you see – this is what happens – first lies, then pressure, then more lies, then more pressure, then the break, then more pressure, then the truth' (1980: 5). 'Pain is truth, all else is subject to doubt' is the magistrate's deduction from this. The ultimate goal of interrogation is to produce a preconceived truth. Thus the interrogation process can be seen to be a model for the function of imperial history.

That power which appears, by incessant questioning, to be extracting the truth is *producing* it by negating the subjectivity of the imprisoned, as effectively as it does by stripping them naked. Interrogation and history become a boundary as tight as the prison walls themselves, because the discourse of history produces a 'truth' which comes to locate the very identity of the subject. The magistrate in *Waiting for the Barbarians* says: 'I wanted to live outside history. I wanted to live outside the history that Empire imposes on its subjects, even its lost subjects. I never wished it for the barbarians that they should have the history of Empire laid upon them' (1980: 154). Ironically, neither the agent of empire, the magistrate, nor its 'othered' objects, the barbarians, can live outside the history that empire lays upon them. The history produced through the interrogation and torture of the prisoners also imprisons the magistrate by imposing its 'truth'.

The centrality of pain in the extraction of truth is a telling reminder of the material effects of such discursive activities as imperial historiography, and introduces the third element in the dehumanizing function of the prison: torture. Torture degrades the subject into the *abject* of the imperial gaze. Pain is, psychologically, an occasion of extreme isolation, and torture removes any fellow feeling or sense of community, any sense that the tortured abject is part of a community, even a community of suffering. But, apart from this physical isolation, torture reflects the dominant discourse's attack upon language itself. What makes torture a significant metaphor for colonial boundaries is that, whether or not it involves physical pain, the experience of being held in captivity is itself torture, according to Ngugi. Detention without trial should be seen not only as a punitive act of physical and mental torture, but as 'a terrorist programme for the psychological siege of a whole people' (Ngugi 1981b: 14). It is important to remember that Ngugi was imprisoned in an independent Kenya: the prison as a model for ideological and political control is not limited to imperial discourse. The torture of detention is a natural extension of the carceral function of political boundaries. The inscription on the body performed by physical torture occurs also upon the mind in the psychological torture of incarceration. In Soyinka's testimony *The Man Dies* he says: 'I testify to the strange, sinister byways of the mind in solitary confinement, to the strange monsters it begets. It is certain that all captors know it; that they create such conditions especially for those whose minds they fear' (1972: 12).

However, it is the *responses* by captors in their prison writings which provide the most fascinating demonstration of the link between resistance and transformation. These features of incarceration – surveillance, stripping, interrogation and torture – are not simply rejected, but are in some sense appropriated and transformed. The narratological elements of prison memoirs include:

• a narrative by a subject whose identity is established by the experience of imprisonment. Whereas surveillance is designed to produce a subject who identifies with the prisoning power by seeing himself or herself as a prisoner, in prison memoirs this identity becomes the authoring subject, the focus of a discursive resistance. In the same way the subject of the imperial gaze – the colonial subject – uses that identity as the focus of a post-colonial authorship, transforming the imperial language as a tool of resistance.

• a narrating subject who engages in a stripping down, a baring of the soul, in a curious rehearsal of the dehumanizing experience of physical stripping, which *re-establishes* the humanity negated by that process. Such 'stripping down' need not be limited to a process of psychological examination and exposure, but suggests the various ethnographic and cultural functions by which post-colonial writing may 'reveal' and communicate a different experiential reality through the dominant language.

• a narrating subject who interrogates himself or herself as well as the prison system and the social structure for which it stands. Once we see interrogation – the process of extracting a fore-ordained 'truth' – as a model for the operation of imperial history, we can see the self-interrogation of the prisoner as a strategy of interpolating that history. The writer enters the interrogative mode, for the purposes of producing a different truth, a different history. Thus the dominant 'truth' is resisted by means of the very process by which the subjectivity of the prisoner was negated.

• a narrating subject who speaks for a community, not only to present a collective subject but to reinstall that sense of communal experience which is explicitly removed by torture. Whereas the prison boundaries, by isolating the subject, attempt to remove any sense of community, this attempt is reversed by a strategy which suppresses individual identity beneath a stronger desire to speak for an oppressed community. As with the first strategy, this involves the recuperation of a language, even when that language is appropriated from the imprisoning discourse.

## Inhabiting boundaries

Although the prison provokes the most striking examples of transformative response, the boundaries of colonial discourse are inevitably more subtle and pervasive. The capacity to appropriate, renegotiate, realign and replace boundaries, not merely as spatial division but as epistemological limit, is deeply implicated in the transformative process operating in a wide variety of circumstances, cultures, societies. But as soon as we make this tropic connection between spatiality and epistemology, between the boundaries of space and those of knowledge, we are drawn inexorably to the issue of power. At this point the discourse of habitation reveals its importance, because just as we inhabit a network of relations which constitutes, or underlies, our sense of place, just as we can see that to inhabit space is to some extent to inhabit boundaries of knowledge, so we begin to understand that the critical condition of post-colonial experience is the habitation of power itself. To inhabit place is, in a variety of ways, to inhabit power. To transform one's place is to engage the 'boundaries' of power.

These boundaries are by no means static: in a well-known lecture Foucault urges that power is not simply oppressive but productive:

> Power must be analysed as something which circulates, or rather as something which only functions in the form of a chain. It is never localised here or there, never in anybody's hands, never appropriated as a commodity or piece of wealth. Power is employed and exercised through a net-like organisation. And not only do individuals circulate between its threads; they are always in the position of simultaneously undergoing and exercising power. They are not only its inert or consenting target; they are also always the elements of its articulation. In other words, individuals are the vehicles of power, not its points of application.
>
> (1980: 98)

The principle of interpolation hinges on subjects' active occupation of this 'net-like organisation'. They are not inert, they articulate power, act as its vehicles. But they also operate as the vehicles of the *disarticu-lation* and transformation, the redirection and utilization of specific forms of power. The productive and circulatory nature of power is absolutely critical to the process of transformation. It is this circulatory dynamic which enables the simple resistance to power to be itself transformed into a process of cultural, political and material change.

Such a process may be seen in an example given by Renee Pittin, who examines the ways in which boundaries are negotiated by Hausa women in Katsina City, Nigeria. Under Islamic law Hausa women are secluded in the family compound, which usually contains the dwellings of a husband and several wives. These gendered boundaries have a close affiliation with those boundaries erected by imperial power and may be seen to demonstrate the same principles of categorization, enforcement and surveillance. Both are patriarchal boundaries which stand as the material expression of a range of cultural and political formations. The initial Western reaction to this form of seclusion might be to see the boundary around the compound as a form of actual and metaphoric prison wall inhibiting the free movement, free expression and self-development of women. However, seclusion in rural areas has often had enormous economic benefits for women, says Pittin, as:

> they are thereby no longer required to labour on 'family' farms, the produce of which is never under their control; they are relieved of all extradomestic fetching and carrying and of labor on any farms and gardens; and they are thereby 'freed' to engage in income-earning activities within the home, the proceeds of which are inalienably their own.
>
> (1996: 181)

Strikingly, considering the gender relationships which lead to the requirement of seclusion in the first place, some Hausa women have taken their husbands to court to demand seclusion within the boundary of the home compound. The boundaries in this case are a combination of cultural and religious sanctions, but they may be seen as metonymic of the power which operates in the colonizing process. Here we find a specific instance of a spatial relationship – a boundary designed, some might say, as a property demarcation – transformed into a spatial sign of personal empowerment. We may see the circulation of power in this instance as complex and attenuated, and a good example of the operation of power *through* people as well as *upon* them. But taking one's husband to court is a very specific utilization of power, a utilization of the extant social structures, which makes it difficult to see the individual as simply 'an effect of power' as Foucault contends (1980: 98).

This does not escape Foucault's basic premise, that in any society there are 'manifold relations of power which permeate, characterise and constitute the social body' (1980: 93) and that these relations cannot exist without the functioning of a discourse. The Hausa women function within the discourse of Islam and their agency operates within certain limits; the exercise of their power is implicated in the production of (Islamic) truth. But the spatial dimension, the discourse of boundaries, demonstrates that the appropriation of power may be represented as a process of *inhabiting* power. The women's use of the legal system – their interpolation of institutional power – is a very direct demonstration of the practice of habitation. When we consider the fact that the world map, the maps of continents, and to some extent the European names of places, are accepted as universal representations; when we consider the fact that time has been disembedded from place almost as much for these Hausa women today as for New York stockbrokers, we begin to understand the extent, and indeed the *necessity*, of this habitation. Spatiality is a discourse of power which must be inhabited. How it is inhabited becomes a question of how power itself is inhabited.

This process of inhabiting power is itself a constitutive element of place, for the habitation is linked to the transformative way in which place comes to be both spatial location and a location of identity. The compound boundaries become more than spatial signs of a cultural enclosure for the Hausa women. The process of negotiation which transforms them may be usefully described as an inhabiting of the spatial frames of power. This habitation of power is also located in that network of rhizomic connections through which place is constituted. The relationship between agency and power in this instance raises the same issues as are raised in any example of interpolation, namely: Where does agency begin and end? How free is the subject? Where is power *located* in the interpolating process? Yet the idea that power can be inhabited suggests the possibility of conceptualizing the difficult relationship between subject, power and discourse. It may help resolve some of the difficulties in understanding how much freedom the subject may have within discourse. The subject does not passively inhabit this matrix of perceptions, appreciations and actions but may utilize it at specifically determined moments: this action is the key to the 'practice' of habitation.

Consider the multiple ways in which people may constitute their identity in terms of the congregations of organizations they inhabit: scholarly, ethnic, sporting, commercial, religious. Individuals may switch from one to the other in rapid succession without confusing their different roles in each; indeed the term 'role' is a useful synonym for 'self' in the course of any subject's social existence. This reveals not only that the subjects who shift like this from role to role are heterogeneous but that the specific aspects of identity which we experience within these different circumstances depend upon how we inhabit the specific locations and social settings of those roles. Not only is identity constructed but it is variable and provisional. Thus when considering the concept of 'imagined communities', whether ethnic, national, supranational or professional, those communities which we inhabit according to circumstance, we should beware of referring to them as though they were homogeneous entities with a recognizable unity. This of course is a habitual mistake in references to that abstract construction 'the nation' for which Benedict Anderson's term 'imagined communities' was coined. In colonial nationalism the myth of a recognizable or representable identity is the natural consequence of the attempt to construct authentic identity. This attempt is paradoxically regulated by the most material evidence of colonial control: national boundaries.

## The boundaries of the state

Habitation extends to the furthest limits of one's 'place', even to those boundaries created by the European colonization and its dominance of the map – the nation. Such boundaries suggest the need for caution to such commentators as Cooper and Stoler, who object that postcolonial theory runs the risk of overemphasizing the importance of colonialism to people in the contemporary world (1997: 34). Yet we can hardly overemphasize something which has determined the very shape of the world. The profound geo-political consequences of colonial boundary-making have been obvious. Colonization robbed colonized countries of their 'place-ness', replacing or overlaying the 'life-place' of a people with 'colonized space' (Gotlieb 1992: 464–6). The consequences of the (often arbitrarily drawn) line on a map have been profound and almost uniformly repressive to formerly colonized states. The colonial boundary, which has been so catastrophic to the material and political life of colonized states, demonstrates both the material and ideological force of the trope of the boundary. Whatever the nature of the place in which a people makes its home, it is these boundaries, the boundaries of the state, which present the most urgent political, cultural, economic and social problems to post-colonial societies.

Perhaps nowhere are the effects of this imperial boundary-marking shown so catastrophically as in the partition of India and Pakistan. A separation between Hindu and Muslim established by the Raj to perpetuate the principle of *Divide et imperia* resulted in a genocidal catastrophe which is no less galling for the incompetence with which it was carried out. Shashi Tharoor's *The Great Indian Novel* satirizes the absurdity and horror of this process. A political geographer who had never set foot in either India or 'Karnistan' demonstrates how easy it all is:

> One takes a given cartographical area – there – one checks the census figures for religious distribution and then one applies the basic principles of geography choosing natural features as far as possible for the eventual boundary, studying elevation and relief . . . then one draws one's boundary line v-e-r-y carefully, like this.
>
> (1989: 224)

> 'Congratulations, Mr Nichols!' A veteran administrator named Basham rose to his feet. 'I have worked in that very district for the last ten years and I must take my hat off to you. You have just succeeded in putting your international border through the middle of the market, giving the rice-fields to Karnistan and the ware-houses to India, the largest pig-farm in the zilla to the Islamic state and the Madrassah of the Holy Prophet to the country the Muslims are leaving.'
>
> (224–5)

Indigenous communities are divided, renamed and reconstituted, caught within geographical areas which have no relation to their social make-up, traditions or needs. These geographical areas come to be known as nations, and, arbitrary though they may be, they become crucial in post-colonial perceptions of personal identity. The appalling tragedy of partition is only a more obvious, more brutal example of the destructiveness of imperial mapping, but it is a story that has been played out time and again in the colonial world, with the establishment of boundaries that have been capricious at best, often absurd and, in many cases, catastrophic. The most lasting effects are those which are less visible: lines on a map have become the determining parameters of being itself. How post-colonial peoples inhabit these spaces signifies the ways in which they interpolate power.

The example of Africa is particularly instructive. Perhaps no other continent has been so clearly fragmented by colonial boundaries.

Newly independent post-colonial states simply occupied the spaces which had been negotiated between colonial powers during European expansion, and thus have no more cultural and communal logic than they had as colonies. Where state boundaries have cut through the territories of ethnic groups, these boundaries have remained, institutionalizing ethnic tension and communal violence. The problem for post-colonial societies has been that 'the continuity of colonial boundaries served to indigenize colonized space rather than to rectify it' (Gotlieb 1992: 462). The boundary of the post-independence state remains an arbitrary but inescapable trace of a colonial past. A gloomy assessment of the particular vulnerability of the African state is provided by Verhelst:

> Nowadays, it has become obvious that most Africans hardly recognise themselves in the states their colonizers have bequeathed to them. Since the state sees itself as the driving force of development, the latter consequently finds itself profoundly handicapped. The frequency of *coups d'état* reveals not only the behind-the-scenes intrigues of neo-colonialism, but also the shallowness of the regime's roots in society, the unsuitable nature of their methods of government and the very nature of their power.
>
> In reality, the post-colonial 'state idolatry' is equalled only by the profound absence of legitimacy of the authorities. An artificial entity, from the points of view of both its frontiers and history, the African state, far from being the product of a long and spontaneous process of nation-building, exists in itself, and very often for itself and for the bourgeoisie which has taken control of it. The people are elsewhere and define themselves by a sub- or trans-state identity . . . As an elderly Mossi man put it, 'To me Mali is just tax.' Nothing more.
>
> (1990: 38)

The spatial significance, and the frequent paradox, of colonial nationalism becomes obvious when we consider the amount of emotional and political energy expended in the name of such artificial, detached and culturally erroneous boundaries. The question of how post-colonial peoples are to inhabit the space defined by these boundaries, how they are to retrieve the 'place-ness' of such a space, lies at the heart of the political realities of the post-colonial state.

Two possibilities offer themselves: to alter these boundaries, or to inhabit them in a different way. To date, the first alternative has seemed impossible and the second improbable. The case of stateless people, such as the Kurds and the Roma, of the territorially ambiguous, such as the Karamajong of Northern Uganda and Kashmir, which has been the site of a boundary war since partition, all demonstrate how intractable the concept of national boundaries has become. The prospect of inhabiting state boundaries in a different way seems equally problematic. For such spaces have been inhabited in terms of the ideological discourses inherited from Europe, principally that of nationalism, which, like the boundary itself, divides ethnic groups, fragments peoples, separates families. The nation is also buttressed by the more insidious ideology of global capitalism, with its expectation of an 'ordered' (meaning nationally structured and internationally subservient) economy. Such ideologies and expectations have been kept in place by the strictures of the IMF and World Bank, and, as with people in countries around the globe, constituted as elements of an economy rather than members of a society. Such states become the sites of protracted 'boundary wars' as questions of nation, of ethnic, cultural and racial identity, locality and community, become orchestrated by the spatial trope of the boundary itself and its most subtle and resilient expression – difference.

However, for the ordinary people who cross borders every day in African states the reality of the national boundary is already being transformed because it is accorded a very different meaning. Like the service station in Mbarara, the boundaries of the state are inhabited differently by different people, different groups, at different times. For whom do these boundaries exist in Africa? Not for the local fishmonger who walks across the border each day to trade. Not for the family visiting relatives in the next country. For ordinary people, the national border means nothing, and the traffic of local people, who may not even have heard of passports, is rarely policed. At the level of ordinary experience, the boundary is already being transformed. It is kept in place by the set of global requirements and still has a material reality at the level of international politics (and indeed as a source of tourist income), but as a definition of self, or a description of one's 'life-place', it is less significant.

What purchase on freedom does an African nation have? Certainly we have, as yet, found no alternative to the state, but can a nation exist without a centripetal, exclusionary and monolithic mythology of identity?

It would appear not. Nations merely take over the role of empire and reinstate the centrality of imperial power in the already created colonial élites. As Fanon says, 'National consciousness, instead of being the all-embracing crystallization of the innermost hopes of the whole people . . . will be in any case only an empty shell, a crude and fragile travesty of what it might have been' (Fanon 1961: 148).

Fanon describes the way in which the newly created middle class will 'look toward the former mother country and the foreign capitalists who count on its obliging compliance'. But this merely puts into practice the structural reality which colonialism installs and which the nation cannot escape. The issue has only recently been revealed in Rwanda in all its material horror. That this is an evidence of the reinstating of empire is pointed out again by Soyinka:

> One hundred years ago, at the Berlin Conference, the colonial powers that ruled Africa met to divvy up their interests into states, lumping various peoples and tribes together in some places, or slicing them apart in others like some demented tailor who paid no attention to the fabric, colour or pattern of the quilt he was patching together.
>
> One of the biggest disappointments of the OAU when it came into being more than 20 years ago was that it failed to address the issue. Instead, one of its cardinal principles was non-interference and the sacrosanctity of the boundaries inherited from the colonial situation. And now we see in Rwanda what that absence of African self-redefinition has wrought. If we fail to understand that all this stems from the colonial nation-state map imposed upon us, there will be little chance to correct the situation over the long term.
>
> (1994: 31)

Clearly the 'practice' of habitation involves much more than simply passively occupying colonial boundaries. The dysfunctional consequences of these arbitrary divisions are horrifyingly demonstrated by the Rwandan example.

When does the issue of nationality matter? The meaning of nation for individuals is intermittent, fragmentary, variable, depending on their situation. People are drawn into the nation automatically when they enter the exchange economy. Money is, apart from anything else, a signifier of national distinctiveness. People may also choose to identify themselves with the nation at times such as war or international sport. But the activity of ordinary life at any 'Third-World' border shows that the pattern of nations is a matrix, a boundary network regulating what is in fact a rhizomic pattern of habitation. This rhizome offers many disjunctive points at which the idea of nation might be appropriated for some purpose. But it also shows many other arborescences which push the boundary of nation back behind a dense network of other exigent realities. If the boundaries of states are provisional, the boundaries around such concepts as 'Africanness' are even more so. Diasporic contributions to various forms of 'Africanness' completely deconstruct geographical and racial boundaries.

As an alternative to the post-colonial state Gotlieb proposes the establishment of geo-ethnic regions: 'territories defined by anthropological, economic and ecological continuities, not by the borders of former colonies' (1992: 469). These would attempt to reverse the fragmentation of colonization by mirroring continuities of language, culture, modes of production and ecological setting, providing a common cultural space, a common political space and a common economic space (469). Such an idea seems extremely attractive in continents such as Africa, where colonial boundaries clearly divide ethnic groups. But Gotlieb himself detects a problem with the notion of an anthropological commonality, for, clearly, no such homogeneity exists in contemporary societies, even in 'traditional' societies in Africa. How one might then establish a region based on a spurious sense of homogeneity is not explained. No attempt is made to answer the questions: Who will decide the new boundaries? Who will draw them? Who will enforce them? The Eurocentrism of the discourses of identification – anthropology, economy, ecology – suggests a more subtle but nevertheless equally colonizing boundary-making process. But what of the wishes of local communities? If these regions are notional spaces overlapping several states, how would the autonomy of the region be negotiated? If these problems emerge for the continent apparently most amenable to such change, how would one begin to put such an idea into effect outside Africa?

Such regions might, however, present an opportunity to inhabit colonial boundaries in a new way. Ultimately, it may not be the geo-political boundaries of the nation which matter, but the conceptual boundaries of ethnocentrism and nationalism (which often gain their authority by appending themselves to the boundaries of the state) which must be dismantled. For this to occur, physical boundaries, the present borders of nation states, as well as conceptual boundaries, would need to be rendered porous and flexible, and, critically, be loosened from the ideological identification which keeps them in place. Boundaries are, indeed, becoming more flexible on a global scale as the authority of the nation state itself becomes increasingly blurred. Many boundaries reveal themselves to be border zones within which, as Nederveen Pieterse puts it, *hybrid* sites and spaces emerge, meeting places of different organizational modes: Free Enterprise Zones and off-shore banking facilities; overseas military facilities and surveillance stations; ethnic border lands; global cities; ethnic mélange neighbour-hoods (Nederveen Pieterse 1995a: 51). In some respects the borders of African nations today are like the borders of the Hausa compound: whether they exist as signs of entrapment or empowerment depends upon the will and determination of the inhabitants, and the discourse within which they are located.

The question of the colonized response to boundaries is a critical one in post-colonial discourse, because it hinges on the distinction between opposition and transformation. There are other ways of dealing with boundaries than by simply (and perhaps futilely) rejecting them, and the most subtly transformative way lies in the mode of their habitation. It is through habitation that the *concept* of boundary, so fundamental to European epistemology, may be deconstructed in post-colonial discourse, as the tenuousness of its symbolic spatial function is exposed. Boundaries are a sign of the need to resolve ambivalence, to regulate and categorize difference. Yet they are always subject to slippage and provisionality, which makes their deep implication in Western modes of thinking and being so fascinating. Rather than simply rejecting boundaries, perceiving their provisionality may be the key to a more subtle dismantling. For it is in its opposite – the horizon – that the colonial boundary is disrupted by post-colonial discourse.

# 8  Horizon

Habitation describes a way of engaging colonial boundaries which neither ignores them nor rejects them but occupies them in a way which redeploys the power they administer. The corollary of this is a mode of thinking which transforms boundaries by seeing the possibilities – the horizon – beyond them. Boundaries of various kinds and forms of boundary-marking are central to the colonial relationship, from the most material forms of spatial enclosure to the most abstract modes of Western thinking. None of these boundaries is easy to ignore, and the ultimate force of imperial hegemony lies in their invisibility, for boundaries, erected as forms of conceptual enclosure and social regulation, become ways of understanding 'how things are'. The transformation of colonial space therefore involves several processes: the recognition of boundaries, a practice of inhabiting which uses them to the benefit of the inhabitants, and the development of a mode of thinking which disrupts and transcends them.

The earnestness with which resistance discourse clings to category boundaries such as 'nation', 'race' and 'class' demonstrates how powerful and self-perpetuating are the modes of thinking installed by Western epistemology. The inability to escape these boundaries is the endemic problem of much resistance rhetoric, demonstrated in the establishment of the nation as a replica of the colonial administration, or in Senghor's belief, for instance, that 'the emotions are black as reason is Greek'. Francophone *négritude* (a theory of the distinctiveness of African personality and culture) is possibly the best-known demonstration of this occupation of an imperial boundary, and Soyinka's response to the phenomenon is instructive:

> Sartre . . . classified [*négritude*] as springing from the intellectual conditioning of the mother culture; he rightly assumed that any movement founded on an antithesis which responded to the

Cartesian 'I think, therefore I am' with 'I feel, therefore I am' must be subject to a dialectical determinism which made all those who 'are' obedient to laws formulated on the European historical experience. How was he to know, if the proponents of the universal vision of Négritude did not, that the African world did not and need not share the history of civilisations trapped in political Manicheisms?

(1976: 135–6)

Despite Soyinka's warning, however, some of the most vigorous and sophisticated African theory simply reinstates political Manichaeisms, confirming the African as both unitary and other. JanMohamed's concept of the Manichaean allegory of colonialist discourse (1983, 1985) articulates the binary itself very well, but his criticism of those texts which he calls 'symbolic' and 'imaginary' (after Lacan) actually reproduces the binary rather than offering a way to disrupt it.

Yet effective resistance to the concept of the boundary is not another boundary but its opposite: what we may term *horizonality*. It is in horizonality that the true force of transformation becomes realized, for whereas the boundary is about constriction, history, the regulation of imperial space, the horizon is about extension, possibility, fulfilment, the imagining of post-colonial place. The horizon is a way of conceiving home, and with it identity, which escapes the inevitability of the imperial boundary. Horizonality is, possibly, the *only* way in which the predominance of the boundary in Western thought can be resisted.

## The concept of horizon

The word 'horizon' is derived from a Greek verb meaning 'to circumscribe'. Thus while the horizon 'circumscribes' the limit of our view of the Earth, it bisects our field of vision, providing us with a permanent sign of spatial possibility. Language is familiar with this horizon which surrounds us and which can be very near or very far. In general we can say that the horizon is an unattainable line, something which science sees as an optical illusion but which we understand as the constant limit of vision, the always present yet always receding 'boundary' of perception. The horizon became a key concept in phenomenology when it first appeared in Husserl's *Ideen* (1913) referring to the circumference in which all things, real and imaginable, are bound to appear 'spread out in space endlessly, and in time becoming and become, without end' (101).

In Husserl's phenomenology the horizon is the principle by which both meaning and its open possibilities appear to us. While the boundary remains central to Western epistemology it is the horizon, with its merging of location and possibility, which offers itself as the most productive principle of post-colonial subjectivity. Critically, horizon is a principle which does not dispense with boundaries altogether but inhabits them, utilizes them, incorporates them in a different way. Phenomenology has become the *bête-noir* of post-structuralist theory, because the attempt to define the processes of consciousness by locating 'things in themselves', the actuality of objects free of any mediating influences (Husserl's *noema*), seemed to most commentators, after Derrida, to be a logocentric and increasingly anachronistic hermeneutics. But the key to phenomenology is the recognition that the 'things in themselves' *never* appear in unmediated form. The objects of consciousness are always known and understood according to their place in a particular horizon.

The hermeneutic possibilities of the horizon may be demonstrated by the example of a simple perceptual object, say a cup on a table. When I look at the cup, all I actually see of the object, all the actual visual data available to me, is a curved shape, and yet in the act of consciousness I *intend* it as a cup. I may take the cup in my hand and turn it around, looking at its base, its inside, its handle. When I do this, I bring to consciousness all that lies on the *inner horizon* of the cup, that is, the horizon of its physical dimensions as an object, those dimensions which I intend, or assume, when I first observe it. (It is this act of intending a three-dimensional object which makes the phenomenon of perspective of such interest to Merleau-Ponty.) But the cup is also on the saucer, on the left-hand corner of the table, the table is by the wall of the kitchen and so on. All these other possible contexts in which the object may be seen constitute the *outer horizon* of the cup. This is the circumference, the aggregation of possible contexts in which the cup may be located, in which it may have an existence, a use, and hence a meaning.

For any perceptual object the outer horizon provides an increasingly specific spatial location. Any discussion of the setting (*entourage*) of the perceived enables us to see more clearly the perceived itself. The wider the horizon, the more information we obtain about the location of the object, the more determinate its meaning. But this location, this locating process, is the model for understanding any object of meaning. For if we see meaning itself as the location of an object within a horizon of contexts or uses, the potentiality of meaning is limited only by the extent of the horizon in which we place it. When we think of textual meaning, the similarity of this notion to Derrida's concept of *différance* becomes clear. In practice, convention provides a horizon to specific words that is 'bounded' by the rules of the discourse in which they occur. Yet while the outer horizon provides a seemingly endless extension of contextual meaning, such meaning must also exist as a *relation* between the object and a specified horizon or context. Thus the dominant feature of horizonality is possibility rather than meaninglessness. For meaning is always relational, always a function of practice. Crucially, the horizon itself is created in language. As Wittgenstein says, '*the limits of my language* mean the limits of my world' (1922: no. 5.6). The object, determined by its relation to a horizon, a context, is therefore an object determined in language, as is the very notion of objectivity. If I am building a wall and say 'Brick!' to my helper, then not only does this stand as a sentence without the need of any translation into a longer command, but on the horizon of the command lies the range of possible further sentences making it more explicit. While this example occurs between two interlocutors with a specifically shared knowledge, the same principle applies to all meaning. The word means according to its location in a horizon. This principle is crucial in literary writing, for the horizons of the writing can be said to be 'co-intended', that is, *constituted* by the interaction of the writer and reader functions. Horizon is both spatial and temporal because the contextual horizon initiates a *process* of traversal by the act of consciousness: we do not only see that the horizon is there (in metaphoric space) but move through it (in time) in the process of contextualizing the object of meaning. This linking of space and time leads to the further conclusion that consciousness is so linked to language that the two become virtually inseparable. Language predicates consciousness, as we have seen, although the two are not synonymous, nor do they represent incommunicable worlds.

One of the most interesting things about the concept of horizon is that in the act of mundane perception it is a permanent, taken-for-granted aspect of our relationship to the world. Consequently, it is the cultural insistence on *boundaries* rather than the perception of horizonality which seems anomalous or imposed. By regulating perception, such boundaries have actually limited human knowledge of the interrelatedness of things. Yet boundaries have become the automatic, culturally installed determinates of perception. The horizon is something I normally take for granted in everyday life, and is 'the ground of all praxis,' says Husserl, 'not only the praxis of life but also the theoretical axis of cognition' (1913: 30). It exists as the background of all my perceptions. Any experience always has a horizon of possible experiences of the same, and these exist submerged, rather than explicitly seen as possibilities, within the experience. Clearly, in the context of language and the meaning of texts, this suggests a pluralist hermeneutics closer to post-structuralism than many would assume.

But the function of horizon in post-colonial studies lies in its engagement with *conceptual* boundaries as well as the boundaries of meaning.
When we look at the major mechanisms by which world reality has
been structured by European society – the projection map, the mechanical clock, the Gregorian calendar – we see that all of these depend for
their very existence upon the installation and preservation of strict
boundary markers in space and time. The prominence of certain horizons, certain boundaries, the privilege of certain meanings, is largely
directed by the discourse of culture with its firmly bounded rules of
inclusion and exclusion, and this applies to all cultures, colonizing and
colonized. Horizonality therefore implies the use of mundane experience as a transgressive principle of resistance, a principle that, when
used to disrupt a dominant culture, must be used also to reconsider
one's own. It does not mean the replacement of one boundary for
another, one cultural limit for another, but puts the nature of inherited
boundaries themselves in question. Consequently post-colonial
approaches to identity, subjectivity, ethnicity, nationality may well
assume a disturbing iconoclasm in their negotiation of the edges of
these apparently 'natural' characteristics.

As we have seen repeatedly, it is the inability to contest the dominance of politically installed boundaries which undermines the project
of post-colonial resistance. Not only does ethnic, racial or cultural
opposition fall into the boundaries erected by imperial discourse but,
more often than not, any questioning of those boundaries upon which
the formation of identity relies so heavily is felt to be scandalous. Yet
a recognition of the regulatory power and discursive function of
boundaries is an essential basis for the development of post-colonial
horizonality. Throughout the world, formal modes of organization,
institutions, metaphorically bounded sites, are traversed by informal
spaces, inhabited by diasporas, migrants, exiles, refugees, nomads.
These are sites of what might be called 'interstitial emergence' but it is
an emergence that functions by means of the act of habitation, through
which identity construction takes place.

Perceiving the horizons beyond the boundaries of 'difference' represents one of the greatest challenges to the transformative process,
because these boundaries are so ubiquitous and so internalized. Speaking of a night journey on a train towards the state border, David
Malouf says, 'What I was hungry for was some proof that the world
was as varied as I wanted it to be; that somewhere, on the far side of
what I knew, difference began, and that point could be clearly recog-
nised' (1985: 127). It is the pressing need for such borders between
identity and difference which leads to their power and prevalence.

Individuals and communities seem to long for a clear border beyond which the 'not me' and the 'not us' can be identified. Whether those borders are the geo-political borders of colonial states or imaginative boundaries erected by discursive representations of difference, they share a need to move from defensive spatial conceptions – resistance as oppositionality – to horizonal conceptions of difference in which the trope of the boundary itself is questioned: resistance as transformation. Said's warning about the potential imperialism of the concept of difference is salutary:

> The fetishization and relentless celebration of 'difference' can therefore be seen as an ominous trend . . .
> In short what is now before us nationally, and in the full imperial panorama, is the deep, the profoundly perturbed and perturbing question of our relationship to others – other cultures, other states, other histories, other experiences, traditions, peoples and destinies. The difficulty with the question is that there is no vantage *outside* the actuality of relationships between cultures, between unequal imperial and nonimperial powers, between different Others.
> (1989: 213, 216)

The problem with the spatial metaphor of difference is that there is no 'outside' from which to view this relationship. Said's remark demonstrates the simultaneous irresistibility and inadequacy of spatial metaphors. Spatial boundaries survive fully articulated to describe the most pressing concerns of cultural relationships in the post-colonial world. But, while there is no 'outside' from which to view these relationships, there is a conceptual horizon beyond them within which they can be viewed.

Some of the most controversial features of contemporary post-colonial theory, such as ambivalence and hybridity, are what we might term *horizonal*. These two concepts, theorized extensively by Bhabha and demonstrated lavishly in the work of Salman Rushdie, are specific demonstrations of the complexity of subjectivity and the potency available to any questioning of boundaries. The problems surrounding them have not come from their attempt to transcend boundaries so much as from their apparent failure to take into account the material status of the operation of power. The question of hybridity, for instance, is very different in Latin America – where the ideology of the mestizo has been seen by some as obscuring the continuing oppression of indigenous Americans – from the way it might appear in diasporic and migrant societies. According to Ella Shohat, 'A celebration of

188 Post-Colonial Transformation

syncretism and hybridity *per se* if not articulated in conjunction with questions of hegemony and neo-colonial power relations, runs the risk of appearing to sanctify the *fait accompli* of colonial violence' (1992: 109). Horizonality allows us to see the blurring of boundaries as a strategy of empowerment, for the *conjunction* of hybridity and power relations which Shohat talks about becomes more than an occasion for resentment, it becomes the source of transformation.

Considering the pervasiveness of the boundary, what, we might ask, would consciousness be like if freed of these enclosing spatial co-ordinates? A clue to this lies in language. One consequence of the structuralist analysis of language in Saussure's linguistics, for instance, is the erection of a boundary between the signifier and signified. Perhaps one of the few characteristics uniting the theory of signs with the positivist theories such as Frege's distinction between sense and reference is the presence of the spatial metaphor of the boundary. But, asks Reichert, 'could not some thoughts or ideas be defined by others, in which they are included? Are signifiers and signifieds solid entities, homogenous regions a distance scale may be held on to? Do they not dissolve as we try to get hold of them . . . ?' (1992: 90). Indeed, when we look at that post-colonial writing produced from an oral culture, we enter into a world in which signifier and signified, sense and reference, representation and 'reality' may in fact dissolve into each other. Language embodies its referent, the signifier dissolves into the signified. Consider Gabriel Okara's description of the sacred power of words in *The Voice*:

> Spoken words are living things like cocoa-beans packed with life. And like the cocoa-beans they grow and give life. So Okolo turned in his inside and saw that his spoken words will not die. They will enter some insides, remain there and grow like the corn blooming on the alluvial soil at the river side.
>
> (1964: 110)

Language becomes an activity with a tangible force and manifests the actual capacity of fertility and growth.

But how does this power inhering language predicate a way of experiencing reality in which the notion of boundary is diminished? When Chinua Achebe describes the celebration of the ritual of the *egwugwu* in his village we witness a powerful demonstration of the slippage between performance and being. The *egwugwu* are the ancestral spirits of the clan. It is clear to all that they are humans dressed up for the ritual, but in the act the boundary between human actor and spirit disappears:

Okonkwo's wives, and perhaps other women as well, might have noticed that the second *egwugwu* had the springly walk of Okonkwo. And they might also have noticed that Okonkwo was not among the titled men and elders who sat behind the row of *egwugwu*. But if they thought these things they kept them within themselves. The *egwugwu* with the springly walk was one of the dead fathers of the clan. He looked terrible with the smoked raffia body, a huge wooden face painted white except for round hollow eyes and the charred teeth that were as big as a man's fingers. On his head were two powerful horns.

(1958: 63–4)

The knowledge of the performance does not lessen the terror of being in the presence of the spirits. Although Achebe's account reinstalls a boundary in the guise of an ethnographic irony, when he considers the recognition of Okonkwo by his wives, the critical feature of the occasion is the description of an experience in which the spatial distinction between acting and reality, the human world and the spirit world, has dissolved. 'The land of the living was not far removed from the domain of the ancestors' (1958: 85), suggests Achebe. But clearly, in their performance the *egwugwu* dissolve this boundary completely. This experience is itself contingent upon an experience of language in which signifier and signified have dissolved into one another. The effect of this dissolution of linguistic boundaries upon the conceptions of place and identity is obviously profound and intimately linked to their transformative possibilities.

Horizonality may be installed as a cultural product of the text through the literary representation of pre-colonial cultures, as we see in this example. But this capacity to control representation, so to speak, is itself a fundamentally horizonal practice, because it constantly disrupts the centrality of the cultural assumptions underlying the colonizing language. Horizonality is a function of *both* production and consumption in post-colonial literary discourse. Because the meaning event is constitutive, as we saw in Chapter 3, the interaction of the writer and reader functions in the text must always be a matter of dynamic interchange and transformation, particularly when it is characterized by cultural difference. For this difference, rather than producing polarity and incomprehension – further boundaries – becomes the basis for the dissolution and transformation of those boundaries. This is perhaps the most exciting feature of the horizonality of these texts.

The dissolved boundary between the human world and spirit world in Achebe's 'pre-colonial' vision is only one form of the horizonality possible in the contest between post-colonial discourse and European ontology. Despite its grounding in the visual, the term 'horizonality' may describe the dismantling of ocularcentrism itself. As we have seen, the visual, bounded, objectification of nature, which had as its ultimate effect the enclosure of property, was a fundamental feature of European settlement. The Cartesian separation of subject and object on which this was based was catastrophically alien to the indigenous conception of space in which time, space and identity intermingle in a continuous present. The Australian poet Les Murray, who has no recourse to a pre-colonial consciousness (apart from being the sole surviving speaker of the Katangala language), nevertheless attempts to break down the various boundaries of the natural world in a 'New World' form of vision 'struggling to emerge from under successive impositions of neo-aristocratic style inherited from abroad' (Murray 1992: 176). Such a 'field' in which inner and outer, human and animal, foreground and background are interrelated is itself a state of 'Equanimity':

> From the otherworld of action and media, this
> interleaved continuing plane is hard to focus: we are looking into
>     the light −
> it makes some smile, some grimace.
> More natural to look at the birds about the street, their life
> that is greedy, pinched, courageous and prudential
> as any on these bricked tree-mingled miles of settlement,
> to watch the unceasing on-off
> grace that attends their every movement.
> the same grace moveless in the shapes of trees
> and complex in our selves and fellow walkers: we see it is
>     indivisible
> and scarcely willed. That lights us from the incommensurable
> we sometimes glimpse, from being trapped in the point
> (bird minds and ours are so pointedly visual):
> a field all foreground, and equally all background
> like a painting of equality. Of infinite detailed extent
> like God's attention. Where nothing is diminished by perspective.
>                                                     ('Equanimity' 1994: 181)

The equanimity of perception reflects a controversial alliance in Murray's poetry with indigenous forms of representation. But in this case the balance is one which specifically contests the dominance of perspective and that Eurocentric objectification which encloses and commodifies space. Such a disruption of spatiality itself is the ultimate paradox of post-colonial horizonality.

## Horizon and writing

In a putative discussion of Shelley's unfinished poem 'The Triumph of Life' Derrida remarks:

> I wish to pose the question of the *bord*, the edge, the border, and the *bord de mer*, the shore . . . The question of the borderline precedes, as it were, the determination of all the dividing lines that I have just mentioned: between fantasy and a 'reality', an event and a non-event, a fiction and a reality, one corpus and another, and so forth.
>
> (Kamuf 1991: 256)

As we have seen in the previous chapter, the conception of a boundary is critical to representation: both European presence and colonial otherness are represented through their difference from each other. The borderline, the moment of difference, is also the moment necessary to the production of knowledge. But this border is historically also located in writing, firstly because it is, above all, in the *texts* of imperialism that otherness is constructed, and secondly because it is the absence of writing by the colonized other which constitutes that other as lack.

This location of writing itself at the border becomes an occasion of productive instability for Derrida's theory. Writing is the deferral of presence which constantly subverts the border, each sign the trace of another: signification deferred. The concept of *différance* subverts the boundary of writing totally, but a border crossing such as Derrida's becomes problematic for post-colonial writing. The challenge is to subvert the notion of the boundary, to conduct this most radical subversion of European epistemology, without deferring the urgent desire of the colonized to represent the real conditions of colonization. The problem with this is, of course, that the 'real' is itself a boundary of considerable influence, its separation from fantasy and fiction, as Derrida suggests above, seeming, at least from the Western perspective, to be an unavoidable and necessary requirement. How is post-colonial writing to challenge the boundary that determines and defines knowing without challenging the apparent boundary of the real?

A clue to this is provided in the example above where Achebe talks about the *egwugwu* in Umuofia, which operate as *both* signifier and signified of the spirits, both representation and embodiment of the other world. The apparently compulsory boundary between signifier and signified is shown to be absent (or negotiable) in the language and world view of Umuofia, but this absence is itself represented in the text in a language of representation – English – which operates according to such binary division. By such use of language the post-colonial text reveals its capacity to occupy an interstitial space which blurs the boundary of representation, which suggests the horizon of signification without dispensing with the reality of experience. This capacity to appropriate the colonial language and represent an experience which radically disrupts the precepts of that language is possibly the clearest demonstration of the horizonal capacity of post-colonial writing.

But the horizonal capacity is demonstrated also in the disruption of the boundary which occurs in hybrid subjectivities. Gloria Anzaldua suggests that the very condition of being a mestiza disrupts boundaries of all kinds. The chicana who inhabits the 'borderlands' is in an unparalleled position to see the porousness of those borders. The first thing to address is the pejorative way in which hybridity is viewed – a contamination, a weakening. On the contrary, to Anzaldua, this blurring of genetic boundaries is a form of strength: 'At the confluence of two or more genetic streams, with chromosomes constantly "crossing over," this mixture of races, rather than resulting in an inferior being, provides hybrid progeny, a mutable more malleable species' (1987: 77). But much more than the racial strength she claims is the mestiza's capacity to inhabit the space of the boundary in a way that constantly subverts it:

> She has discovered that she can't hold concepts or ideas in rigid boundaries. The borders and walls that are supposed to keep the undesirable ideas out are entrenched habits and patterns of behavior; these habits and patterns are the enemy within. Rigidity means death. Only by remaining flexible is she able to stretch the psyche horizontally and vertically . . .
>
> The new *mestiza* copes by developing a tolerance for contradictions, a tolerance for ambiguity. She learns to be an Indian in a Mexican culture, to be a Mexican from an Anglo point of view . . . Not only does she sustain contradictions, she turns the ambivalence into something else.
>
> (79)

The writer in the borderlands negotiates this fragile space of experience and possibility perhaps more directly than any other:

When I write it feels like I'm carving bone. It feels like I'm creating my own face, my own heart – a Nahuatl concept. My soul makes itself through the creative act. It is constantly remaking and giving birth to itself through my body. It is this learning to live with *la Coatlicue* that transforms living in the Borderlands from a nightmare into a numinous experience. It is always a path/state to something else.

(73)

Here then is the ambivalence of writing in the borderlands, a writing metonymic of the post-colonial – it is both the carving out of the soul, and the path to something else, the conversion of the nightmare into the numinous. This is the essence of post-colonial transformation, the location of an experience and an identity that is always pushing beyond itself. Into the horizon.


## Verandas

Horizonality, with all of its metaphoric implications, may take on explicitly material forms. One of the most suggestive of these is the architectural example of the veranda. The veranda became – particularly in Australia, which imported the idea from colonial India – more than an attachment to the building to provide shade and coolness in the hot climate. It came to represent the ambivalence of a certain kind of cultural outwardness. While the presence of England was manifest throughout its empire in its architecture, the veranda represented the surplus, the interstitial, outward-looking and, above all, dissolving boundary between the house, with its representation of permanence, solidity, tradition and continuity, and the outside, an outside bounded by the psychic line of the horizon. It is the region of discovery, of possibility and flight:

A verandah is not part of the house. Even a child knows this. It is what allows travelling salesmen, with one foot on the step to heave their cases over the threshold and show their wares with no embarrassment on either side, no sense of privacy violated. It has allowed my mother, with her strict notion of the forms, to bring a perfect stranger in off the street and settle her (for ever as it happens) in one of our squatter's chairs. Verandahs are no-man's-land, border zones that keep contact with the house and its activities on one face but are open on the other to the street, the night and all the vast, unknown areas beyond.

(Malouf 1985: 20)

In terms of Malouf's exploration of the childhood house as our first sense of spatiality and place, the veranda is a crucial trope in the child's discovery of the ambivalence and possibility of habitation in a post-colonial setting.

Verandas are the space of transition, and consequently of transformation. They capture the sense of dissatisfaction with the sturdiness, the conventionality represented by the house, which is, ultimately, a dissatisfaction with the containment which comes as the price of protection. Verandas become the potent metaphor of that continual tension between boundary and horizon which characterizes post-colonial discourse. They suggest, and indeed embody, a concept of 'home' which escapes the confinement of boundaries, a *heimlichkeit* which embraces outwardness and possibility. If we see this outwardness as an easy familiarity with, and an acceptance of, change, then it clearly goes beyond the post-colonial and reveals itself as a quotidian feature of global culture in its everyday consumption. But the very problematization of 'home' which colonial displacement engendered underlies that outward and transformative form of cultural habitation which characterizes global culture.

The dissatisfaction with boundaries can be demonstrated in the creative dissatisfaction with inherited models of cultural production that characterizes much post-colonial creativity. Tom Thompson's *Annunciation with a Distant Town* is a fine demonstration of the veranda as the setting for a counter-discursive reply to European art. Based on the Annunciation tradition of Renaissance painting, Thompson's painting is most reminiscent of Domenico Veneziano's *Annunciation*, and pictures the angel Gabriel, dressed as a local man, appearing to Mary seated on a wide, country-style veranda. 'This is an ideal veranda,' says Drew, 'which Thompson constructed from memory, composed of a number of verandas the artist remembered. By universalizing his veranda, Thompson makes it symbolize the transformation of Australian culture' (1994: 78–9). However, more importantly for our purposes, the veranda, with its sense of the interstitial, is an ideal representation of the operation of counter-discourse itself. The veranda is not merely the scene of the painting but is also, metaphorically, the scene of the transformative interaction of dominant and local cultures. This interaction, this counter-discourse, is not one of exclusion and polarization, as we might normally expect of 'countering' activity, but of engagement and re-articulation. 'Writing back' to the traditional model, so to speak, this painting inhabits the conceptual and imaginative boundaries of the canonical original in a way that opens up a different horizon, both visually and metaphorically.

In colonial experience verandas are a more faithful model of the porous nature of both physical and conceptual boundaries. According to Paul Carter, 'The settler's proliferating boundaries are not simply physical necessities: they serve the symbolic function of making a place that speaks, a place with a history' (1987: 155). The act of enclosure 'permeates the entire structure of settler society' (155–6). But, as we have seen, it is not just the settler for whom boundaries operate as a founding principle, for boundaries are not just fixed edges which create the concept of place by defining difference, but shifting, debatable areas which are not just zones of uncertainty but places where communication can occur. Edges are areas of possibility, ranging from fences, in the case of new settlers, to areas of no-man's land between Aboriginal tribes where negotiation can take place. This does not necessarily lessen the emotional power of boundaries. But in the actual negotiations of post-colonial life the veranda stands more evocatively for the zonal and interactive possibilities of boundaries, for the horizonal potential of individual interactions with conceptual limits.

For these reasons, the veranda can be seen as the defining metonym of transculturation. Verandas are the very model of the 'contact zone' where inhabitants and strangers may meet with ease. They are the space in which 'inside' and 'outside' interact, and not only do they reveal the provisionality of such apparently unnegotiable boundaries but they represent that space in which the inner and outer may change and affect one another. Metaphorically speaking, verandas represent that space in which discourse itself is disrupted and the very identities of the 'inner' and 'outer' become negotiable. This metaphor of the contact zone had practical effect in colonial India where the veranda was the place for a kind of interaction with servants different from that which occurred inside the house. In other places the veranda was always the place where the meeting of strangers, the negotiation with outsiders in various ways could be conducted without the defining restrictions of convention. The extent to which the knowledge gained changed the colonizer or host varied greatly, but the space of interaction was nevertheless there.

The alternative, something perhaps ubiquitously attempted by colonizing populations, is what Alex Miller refers to as 'extraterritoriality' – a term used to describe foreign nationals in China. In *The Ancestor*

*Game*, Lien, the daughter of a renowned classical scholar, is told that extraterritoriality:

> merely denoted the continued jurisdiction of their country of origin over foreign nationals resident in the International Settlement . . . Did this mean, then, she had wished to know, that these people had travelled to the far side of the world from their ancestral homelands and yet had managed to remain at home?
>
> (1992: 93)

This is a question we may well ask of the colonial process as a whole: At what point does the colonial, enslaved or diasporic subject leave home? For just as it is impossible to leave home entirely behind, is it also impossible to remain untouched by a new place? Transculturation does not necessarily guarantee occasions of personal transformation from the colonial experience, but it does suggest the urgency of change presented to those in cross-cultural interaction. It is apparent to Lien, when considering these people, that they 'had not emerged intact from their acquisition of the condition of extraterritorialness, but had forfeited a precious aspect of their humanity in the process . . . Partly dead, indeed, was how she had come to think of the foreigners' (93).

As a trope, the veranda suggests the inevitability of horizonality in colonial relations. The contact zone is a region, a curiously porous and indistinct border within which change must take place: change that, in fact, requires an extremely heavy expenditure of cultural energy to prevent. Yet such energy is expended constantly to erect and reconfirm the borders of identity. The boundaries continually erected and re-erected in cultural discourse are signs of a tendency to stay within the walls of the house, where 'inside' and 'outside' are more clearly defined. Emotionally, the veranda is a dangerous place to live. But, metaphorically, the veranda is the place of post-colonial habitation because it is here that the horizonality of home and the transculturality of place are most clearly realized.

## Horizon and 'home'

Verandas, so potent a sign of the space between, so ambivalent a border zone of habitation, call into question the very nature of home, for nothing seems more resistant to horizonality, more protective of emotional and psychological boundaries than 'home'. Clearly, the interactive and horizonal possibilities of verandas, so resonant in metaphor, do not always emerge in real life. It is in the establishment of a home that the possibilities of horizon are most clearly tested. What does 'home' mean in the disrupted world of colonial space? How can 'home' become the transformative habitation of boundaries? For certainly that *unheimlichkeit*, that 'unhousedness' or 'uncanniness' which characterizes much colonial displacement, is a primary force of disruption in post-colonial life.

Bell hooks argues that the very meaning of the term 'home', in terms of a sense of place, has been very different for those who have been colonized, and that it can change with the experiences of decolonization. In times of estrangement, 'home is no longer just one place. It is locations . . . One confronts and accepts dispersal and fragmentation as part of the constructions of a new world order that reveals more fully where we are, who we can become' (1991: 148). One might say that, ironically, one of the consequences of the disruptions and displacements of colonization has been that 'home', like 'place', becomes freed from a simple spatial concept of location. It becomes a way of seeing, a way of inhabiting and, ultimately, transforming global discourses of power by being 'at home' in them whatever local appropriations that may entail.

For the diasporic person, for the immigrant, 'home' is deeply embedded in memories that are not one's own. This sense of home rests deeply in a sense of 'imagined community' which now has nothing to do with nation, but with a shared sense of loss which becomes the constant horizon of one's practice of habitation. The Australian son of a Jewish refugee from the Nazis says on returning to his father's town in Poland:

> While the old man talks I am overcome by an uncanny feeling that there are many of us at this moment – sons, daughters, nieces, nephews, grandchildren – wandering country roads and city streets, or picking our way through forest undergrowth to uncover mould-encrusted tombstones. Perhaps this is how it has always been for descendants of lost families: we search within a tangle of aborted memories, while stumbling towards a mythical home which seems to elude us as it recedes into false and dead ends.
>
> (Zable 1991: 74)

This imagined community of seekers defines home by its absence, by its situation as the focus of desire. This may be intensely so for the diasporic subject. But the mythical and elusive nature of home is possibly that which embeds it so strongly in the imagination. The power of home to ground the psyche can be matched by the equally disruptive sense of its absence, by the sense of an ancestral place which by its very elusiveness creates an unwelcome yearning: 'It seems to have always been with me, the knowledge that somewhere on this planet there was an ancestral village called Orla where, centuries ago, my forebears had emerged after years of wandering to begin life anew' (Zable 1991: 97). This ancestral village, located in the dimly apprehended mists of memory, is itself a disruption of the essential and bounded concept of home. For the diasporic subject home is projected into the various discourses inhabited by the subject.

How does home come to be home? How does 'our place' come to be? Above all, how can home be a habitation which dispenses with the boundaries of an inherited Western epistemology? Consider a party of American Negroes, described in Toni Morrison's *Paradise*, descended from freed slaves, driven from their home in Haven, trekking across America in a grim parody of the American pioneering spirit, refused entry into black towns, entirely avoiding white towns, some of which have signs at their perimeters saying 'no Negroes'. What does, what *can* 'my place' mean for these people? How will 'home' come to have a meaning? These might be founding questions for any diasporic peoples, and possibly unanswerable, but at the very least *asking* them reveals how important place might be. This group of invisible pioneers, their women pregnant, their children exhausted and dying, must delve deep into the spirit to find their place. For these people, the discovery and nurturing of place will go hand in hand with the nurturing of history, with the inevitable struggles for authority between those who wish to claim it as their own. But the history of the discovery of their place has all the character of myth: because it explains more than the past, it defines the way the world is.

Paradoxically, this party of benighted and displaced Negroes is enacting the allegorical journey of the Pilgrim Fathers who escaped to and settled America. This is only one narrative in this compelling novel, but perhaps the most resonant. As so often in history, the settlement of a paradise by those escaping persecution, a settlement built on the most resounding humanitarian motives, the strongest sense of community, results in the re-erection of the very conditions, the very restrictions, the animosities, the hostilities – the boundaries – they are escaping. This is the point at which the horizon of possibility into which the travellers have launched themselves becomes bounded and constricted by the limitations of the ways they have learned to know the world, ways which contrast deeply with their spiritual beliefs and aspirations.

Zechariah, the leader of the group, followed by his son Rector, goes into a wood one night to pray for guidance, humming a prayer in 'the sweetest, saddest sounds Rector ever heard'. Eventually they see a man walking away from them, leading the way:

> Together they watched the man walking away from the palest part of the sky. Once, he lingered to turn around and look at them, but they could not see the features of his face. When he began walking again, they noticed he had a satchel in his left hand.
>
> (Morrison 1998: 97)

'He is with us', said Zechariah. 'He is leading the way.' They follow the sound of his footsteps, and months go by before they see the man again. This time, Rector sees him unpacking his satchel:

> The walking man was there, removing items from his satchel and putting others back. Even as they watched the man began to fade. When he was completely dissolved, they heard the footsteps again, pounding in a direction they could not determine; in back, to the left, now to the right. Or was it overhead? Then suddenly it was quiet . . . Not a thing in sight. Only a depression in the grass. Big Papa leaned down to touch it. Pressing his hand into the flattened grass, he closed his eyes.
>
> 'Here,' he said. 'This is our place.'
>
> (98)

Exiled, dispersed, wandering, searching: where else could one's place be but the location of the spirit, the location divinely ordained for Big Papa and the nine exhausted families? But that is only the beginning of the story. For it is not their place. It belongs to Indians who have both a traditional, cultural and a contemporary legal right over the land. Yet in that moment when Zechariah says, 'This is our place', the question of ownership is invisible. For both the Indians and the black refugees from Haven, the question of place is the question of belonging. Belonging can be invented, nurtured or given. But it is out of belonging that habitation acquires the power to *form* place. It is out of belonging that a people can 'inhabit' power and transform both their lives and perhaps the forces of exclusion and dominance which have driven them to this place. Morrison's novel goes on to describe the insidious ways in which such a community can unravel by turning inward, by inhabiting a place in such a way that the horizon is obscured, the eyes looking only inward and backward until the arrival becomes the myth of authenticity and anyone not of the nine original families is subtly excluded.

Above all is the desire to invest in 'home' the certainty of belonging, the solidity of antiquity. This desire for home emerges with the force of a cultural characteristic of black America:

> 'This is their home; mine too. Home is not a little thing.'
> 'I'm not saying it is. But can't you even imagine what it must feel like to have a true home? I don't mean heaven. I mean a real earthly home. Not some fortress you bought and built up and have to keep everybody locked in or out. A real home. Not some place you went to and invaded and slaughtered people to get. Not some place you claimed, snatched because you got the guns. Not some place you stole from the people living there, but your own home, where if you go back past your great-great-grandparents, past theirs, and theirs, past the whole of Western history, past the beginning of organised knowledge, past pyramids and poisoned bows, on back to when rain was new, before plants forgot they could sing and birds thought they were fish, back when God said Good! Good! – there, right there where you know your own people were born and lived and died. Imagine that. Pat. That place. Who was God talking to if not to my people living in my home?'

(213)

The story of the town called Paradise is about people who did not know how to transform the boundaries of an adopted home, did not know how to inhabit in such a way that boundaries became something more than a recapitulation of their own marginality. The consequences of this failure – in terms of intolerance of those who are different, in terms of the capacity to develop and change, to accept, to nurture, to let live – is catastrophic, a recapitulation of all that those boundaries of habitation represent; a repetition of all they are trying to escape; a 'fortress' they have 'bought and built up and have to keep everybody locked in or out'. Their habitation is a myth of identity with which they are trying to combat the myth of American society itself, and thus that identity is captured by the myth. Richard's desire for a home established at the beginning of the world is a desire for a *sense* of home that can be constructed only in the imagination. But it is no less powerful for that. Perhaps such a sense of home is the only one that can be established by the diasporic community. Certainly the illusion of permanence and antiquity constructed by the founders of the town of Paradise is doomed to fail because it represents, on the contrary, a *failure* of the imagination, a failure of horizonality.

# Imperial boundaries and post-colonial possibility

This failure of the imagination can affect a whole society, when the possibilities of habitation fail to be realized, when the transformative potential offered by post-colonial space fails to be grasped by those who come to occupy it. Boundaries were essential to imperial attempts to organize and regulate cultural space. Their success may be seen in the extent to which they prevented such transformation. In David Malouf's *Remembering Babylon* (1993) we see clearly the ways in which the boundary of enclosed property operates as a fragile and ambivalent metonymy of imperial attempts to organize colonial culture according to the boundaries and limits of visual perception. In demonstrating the intractability of the boundaries erected by the habits of European dwelling, and their tight hold on the colonial imagination, the novel offers a sense of the possibility of a different way of inhabiting colonized space. This example reveals also that, far from dismissing conceptual or cultural boundaries, horizonal consciousness, which understands their importance, is perhaps the best means of their articulation.

In *Remembering Babylon* a small Scottish community of settlers in Queensland is visited by Gemmy, a white castaway who has grown up with Aboriginal people. Gemmy is first discovered hovering like a bird on the fence which marks the enclosure of the settlement and thus the enclosure of civilization:

> out of a world over there, beyond the no-man's land of the swamp, that was the abode of everything savage and fearsome, and since it lay so far beyond experience, not just their own but their parents' too, of nightmare rumours, superstitions and all that belonged to Absolute Dark.
>
> (2–3)

Perhaps nothing could more clearly signify the coercive power of colonial boundaries than these rough fences surrounding the settlement. To be able to look beyond them and see the possibilities inhabiting the 'Absolute Dark' signifies that horizonality which is so difficult to achieve. The fence on which Gemmy hovers symbolizes not only the separation of the 'civilized' from the 'primitive' world but also the border between two incommensurable discourses, two modes of habitation, two entirely different ways of being in the world. And it is these two ways of being which his very presence offers to bring together, thus potentially nullifying the boundary which is regulated by imperial discourse. Gemmy is a living conundrum of authenticity. In this his own perception of the moment of contact is revealing:

> It was a question of covering the space between them, of recovering the connection that would put the words back in his mouth, and catch the creature, the spirit or whatever it was, that lived in the dark of him, and came up briefly to torment or tease but could be tempted, he now saw, with what these people ate and the words they used.
>
> (33)

Gemmy's subjectivity, developed so differently within the discourse of Aboriginal life, is now made to enter the ambivalent marginal state between cultures, the edges of the empire, the region in which subjectivity itself comes into question, where its potential for transformation is realized. It is the desperate fragility of this boundary, coupled with its profound significance, which makes it of such strategic interest to post-colonial discourse. For the examination of the ambivalent boundaries of subjectivity is precisely where the concept of horizonality becomes effective.

Gemmy had 'started out white. No question' (40). But the frightening question for the settlers is, 'had he remained white? Could you lose it? Not just language, but *it. It*' (40). In this question lies the complete uncertainty of racial purity, a concept which nevertheless becomes embedded in the discourse of race which imperialism unleashes. And inevitably this notion of 'race' is reduced to the ultimate ontological boundary: the egregious binarism of 'black' and 'white', a boundary within which the apparent exploratory initiative of colonial expansion is circumscribed. It is the comfortable sense of identity which rests upon the certainty of difference which becomes undermined by Gemmy, because:

> you meet at last in a terrifying equality that strips the last rags from your soul and leaves you so far out on the edge of yourself that your fear now is that you may never get back.
>
> It was the mixture of monstrous strangeness and unwelcome likeness that made Gemmy Fairley so disturbing to them, since at any moment he could show either one face or the other; as if he were always standing there at one of those meetings, but in his case willingly, and the encounter was an embrace.
>
> (43)

Can there be such a thing as a white Aboriginal? The idea undermines the concept of race on which is based not only imperial control but also its opposition. But this doesn't mean that Gemmy's hybridity is not oppositional. Its subversiveness represents the very different, *transformative* oppositionality of post-colonial discourse.

Malouf received severe criticism from some quarters for this apparent disregard for the political importance of authenticity. But it is clear that horizonality represents one of the most transformative principles of post-colonial discourse, because it disrupts, blurs and dismantles spatial and conceptual boundaries of all kinds. As well as problematizing the boundaries of ethnicity, Malouf's novel offers a different kind of horizonality, which we could call, after Glissant, a 'prophetic' vision of the past. As we have seen, fences do not merely enforce the philosophy of enclosure, they represent a cultural orientation, a habit of thought. Malouf attempts to disrupt these boundaries by invoking the vision of an Australian society which might have inhabited the land differently, have developed a less confrontational and anxious concept of place. When Mr Frazer follows Gemmy, learning the Aboriginal names for the land, learning a different way of knowing and thus inhabiting place, he writes in his journal:

> We have been wrong to see this continent as hostile and infelicitous, so that only by the fiercest stoicism, a supreme resolution and force of will, and by felling, clearing and sowing with the seeds we have brought with us, and by importing sheep, cattle, rabbits, even the very birds of the air, can it be shaped and made habitable. It is habitable already.
>
> (1993: 129)

The issue, for Mr Frazer, is one of *seeing*. He thinks of the early settlers surrounded by plenty, a wealth of flesh, fowl and fruit but unable to see it with their English eyes:

> since the very habit and faculty that makes apprehensible to us what is known and expected dulls our sensitivity to other forms, even the most obvious. We must rub our eyes and look again, clear our minds of what we are looking for to see what is there.
>
> (130)

The long and lyrical entry into his diary from which this is taken is an account of the ecological blindness which language has produced in settler societies and against which their literature and art have been in constant struggle. His vision is that by breaking out of this language the land might reveal its secrets 'so that what spreads in us is an intimate understanding of what it truly is, with all that is unknowable in it made familiar within' (131). The picture of Gemmy leading the parson through the bush, giving him the Aboriginal names for what they discover, is a beautiful demonstration of the very different ways in which the land is conceived. What is required for this new kind of understanding is a different kind of language, a language in which the human occupants themselves might be different. But it is also clear that the 'true' way of seeing place is not some fixed pre-existing Aboriginal conception but a hybrid encompassed by the different kind of language, a language towards which post-colonial writing works:

> There was no way of existing in this land, or of making your way through it, unless you took into yourself, discovered on your breath, the sounds that linked up all the various parts of it and made them one. Without that you were blind, you were deaf, as he had been, at first, in their world.
>
> (65)

The operative phrase here is 'took into yourself': the process of taking in to oneself is always provisional, overlapping, syncretic. Gemmy's encounter with Mr Frazer represents a crucial 'Adamic' moment in the development of a post-colonial society, a moment in which Gemmy's offering of a horizonal capacity to see beyond the boundaries of vision might have led to a transformation of that society's future. But the impossibility of Mr Frazer ever communicating a different way of viewing the country to the absurd colonial administration (an impossibility brilliantly demonstrated in the political nuances of the Governor's dinner party) shows why the transformation could not take place.

Mr Frazer's utter failure to convince the colonial administration of the hidden bounty of the land reveals a cultural horizon that was not entered, a way of inhabiting the land which was prevented by an intractable attachment to imperial cultural boundaries. This is one area in which the literary text maintains an advantage over others. For the vision of 'what might have been' could seem dismal and futile in a political or historical text, yet the investigation of cultural possibilities, the imagination of a cultural horizon, is the recognition of the reality of a post-colonial future. The possibility Malouf conceives, of a different place, a different way of inhabiting place, is both imagined and offered in the concept of horizon. Post-colonial habitation is never simply shelter, never simply residence, but a process of outwardness, a transformation of boundaries which constantly tends towards the problematization of limits. The horizon is the unbounded boundary, the limit of the gaze kept in a tension with the possibility of change, a tension in which the world is held intact.

It remains the gift, the surplus, of writing to see beyond the boundaries which continue to imprison consciousness, and this vision extends even to the boundaries of writing itself. It is often the writer, seeing beyond the boundaries of words, who can best articulate their limitations. At the end of Coetzee's *Foe*, which 'writes back' to Defoe's imperial classic, *Robinson Crusoe*, exposing its patriarchal and imperialist bases, and thus deconstructing the founding assumptions of English literature, an unnamed narrator dives to the wreck:

> But this is not a place of words. Each syllable, as it comes out, is caught and filled with water and diffused. This is a place where bodies are their own signs. It is the home of Friday.
>
> He turns and turns till he lies at full length, his face to my face. The skin is tight across his bones, his lips are drawn back. I pass a fingernail across his teeth, trying to find a way in.
>
> His mouth opens. From inside him comes a slow stream, without breath, without interruption. It flows up through his body and out upon me; it passes through the cabin, through the wreck; washing the cliffs and shores of the island, it runs northward and southward to the ends of the earth. Soft and cold, dark and unending, it beats against my eyelids, against the skin of my face.
>
> (Coetzee 1986: 157)

This novel, so powerful in its disruption of limitations, so wide-ranging in its dialogue with feminism and colonialism, comes to the point at which it sees language itself as the final boundary. The slow stream of Friday's body, itself its own sign. 'The words are purposes. The words are maps', says Adrienne Rich in 'Diving into the Wreck' (1976: 54), but beyond words is the horizon which only words can intimate. This is the horizon. The horizon of the body. Beyond the map.

# 9   Globalization

How far does the horizon extend? Here we encounter the horizon of
this book itself. For those colonial boundaries which enclose consciousness, that imperial power which is resisted and transformed, that
horizon into which the post-colonial imagination progresses, may now
be seen to extend beyond historical imperialism and its continuing
effects. What has been common among the many disparate post-
colonial cultures, with their very diverse experiences of colonization, is
the use of similar – though differently articulated – strategies in the
transformation of colonial power. It is in analysing these strategies that
post-colonial theory may throw light on the relationship between the
local and the global in contemporary cultural life. Despite the long and
effective record of literary writing as a method of interpolating imperial
discourse, the consumption of dominant forms of representation is
nowhere more evident than in the pervasive and unselfconscious
involvement of local communities in global culture. The provisionality
of inherited boundaries, the fluidity of the concept of 'home' which we
find to be characteristic of post-colonial habitation, extends, in contemporary times, into a global system of cultural interactions. The
strategies by which colonized communities have coped with, resisted
and consumed the cultural capital presented to them by imperial
culture are recapitulated on a global scale in local communities
throughout the world.

  Globalization proves to be an endless source of cultural surprise. In a
story about his travels to Egypt, Amitav Ghosh discovers that the male
members of an isolated traditional village are as travelled as any metropolitan jet-setter.

  The men of the village had all the busy restlessness of airline
  passengers in a transit lounge. Many of them had worked and

travelled in the sheikhdoms of the Persian Gulf . . . some of them had
passports so thick they opened out like concertinas.

(1986: 135)

The traditional, rural village as airline transit lounge. It is hard to
imagine a better figure for postmodernity, says James Clifford: a new
world order of mobility, of rootless histories. But the figure has a
material grounding which is very much inflected with colonial history.
For the places to which these travellers go to find work are almost
always other Middle East, Islamic, 'Oriental' locations. This habit of
travel is not new to the village; the grandparents and ancestors and relatives of these people had travelled too. 'The wanderlust of its founders
had been ploughed into the soil of the village,' says Ghosh; 'it seemed
to me sometimes that every man in it was a traveller' (1986: 135). This
'postmodern' image is profoundly ambivalent: while it suggests the
surprising mobility of the global, it is still dominated by, inherits, and
perpetuates an imperial construction of the world. Globalization does
not exist outside history, in a kind of universal postmodern space, but
reveals itself as the site of practices and strategies which have been
developed by local communities over many centuries.

The paradox of global culture is that it makes itself 'at home' in
motion rather than in place. Clifford's book *Routes* examines the
extent to which practices of displacement 'might be *constitutive* of
cultural meanings rather than their simple transfer or extension'
(1997: 3). The crucial question here, as it is in our consideration of
writing (Chapter 3), is how individual subjects might participate in
such constitutive practices. When we address the complexities of global
culture, of the mobility of cultural formations, we need to alert ourselves to the historical, grounded engagement between cultural subjects
and those forces within which local identity must be constituted. The
startling discovery we make when we see how local communities
acquire modes of representation is that their constant and often
unheralded consumption of global culture becomes the very way in
which that culture is transformed. But more obviously, global culture
becomes the object of a tactical appropriation by which the character
of local identity is strengthened.

What, we might ask, is the place of post-colonial studies in this global
phenomenon? How can this field be seen to continue to emphasize the
materiality of local experience, and the significance of colonial relations, while addressing the increasing importance of social and cultural
issues which appear to have little apparent connection to the material
fact of European colonialism? The answer to this question is twofold:

firstly, we cannot understand globalization without understanding the structure of global power relations which flourishes in the twenty-first century as an economic, cultural and political legacy of Western imperialism. Secondly, post-colonial theory, and particularly the example of post-colonial literatures, can provide very clear models for understanding how local communities achieve agency under the pressure of global hegemony. There are many globalisms: sociological, economic, political, cultural, depending on the discipline from which the phenomenon is approached. But all of them may be addressed in terms of the model of power relations developed over several centuries of European imperialism.

One reason for addressing global culture in terms of a post-colonial model is to develop strategies for handling the relentless economic devastation which globalization wreaks on smaller economies. A common view among theorists in the developing world is that globalization is simply recolonization:

> It seeks to integrate every economy into a single world system under the direction of global corporations. Thus, its proponents seek to eliminate national and territorial borders to enable their products to avail of unlimited market access without paying the usual high tariffs. This way, too, a country's natural resources may be exploited without much hindrance.
>
> (Constantino 1998: 1)

The policies by which the colonies were forced to serve the industrial centres of Europe during the nineteenth and early twentieth centuries are well known. In a strenuously worded version of the 'homogenization thesis' Constantino argues that this situation becomes even worse in global economics:

> Under the old system of colonialism, colonies like the Philippines exported raw materials to the mother countries and imported these back as finished products. Under the new system, the role of countries like ours is to produce labor-intensive, low-technology, and/or semi-manufactured products needed by the North, while the rich countries concentrate on knowledge-intensive and high technology production. This is so because the South, collectively regarded as the poor countries, has an abundance of cheap labor, workers whose wages are a mere fraction of the wages workers in the North receive.
>
> (1998: 3)

It is difficult to transfer this view of global economics, however persuasive, into a political analysis. The word 'imperialism', says Nederveen Pieterse, 'may be adequate in relation to US actions in Panama or Grenada, but less so to describe the Gulf War' (1995b: 59). There is little argument that the IMF and World Bank, transnational corporations and regional investment banks have a heavy influence on the domestic policies of countries from Brazil to the Philippines. But 'the actors are not states and the foreign policy of the countries involved are [*sic*] not necessarily affected' (59). The power dynamic between 'North and South' is very reminiscent of historical relations between imperial centres and dominated states, but globalization has diffused the situation immensely. There is no question that the filiations and interests of those directing and forming the foreign policies of post-colonial states cannot be isolated from the economic influence of the major powers, particularly the USA, which provides a inexorable push towards free trade, monetarism and 'economic rationalism'. But the issues of intention, government policy and national goals have been radically destabilized by globalization. It is in the area of global *culture* that the key to local agency may be found.

The engagement of local communities with global culture is marked by a far greater degree of self-determination than we find at present in global economic relationships. The message of local responses to global culture is the same message delivered by colonial experience: no matter how oppressive the system, or how ubiquitous its effects, it is not immune to appropriation and adaptation by local communities for their own benefit. There is no question that the underlying pressure of the global economy, like the imperial economy before it, is to render the post-colonial world a mere instrument in the enrichment of the North. But this situation is neither inevitable nor irreversible. The experience of the post-colonial world shows that change is not going to occur by futile attempts to establish fortress societies or to abolish globalism, but rather by strategies to transform it as global *culture* has been transformed by appropriation and adaptation. Certainly defensive economic strategies, such as the control of speculative capital, will always be necessary. But the model of post-colonial societies reveals that local empowerment comes by means of the creative interpolation of the dominant, and increasingly a globally dominant, discourse.

## Imperialism and globalism

Theories of globalization have moved, over the last half century, from expressions of the process as 'cultural imperialism' or 'neo-imperialism' to analyses of the 'hybridization', 'diffusion', 'relativization' and inter-relationship of global societies, the 'compression of the world and the intensification of the consciousness of the world as a whole' (Robertson 1992: 8). This sense that imperialism has been superseded as a model for global processes and replaced by a more sophisticated view of the systems which operate in global culture stems, invariably, from an extremely limited view of imperialism itself. The classic definition of imperialism as the establishment of an empire by a nation which exerts a centripetal and hierarchical power over a number of colonial terri-tories says nothing about the *circulation* of that power within the empire, nor anything about the transcultural exchanges involved, since it tends to see the subjects of empire as the passive objects of imperial dominance. This simple view becomes radically destabilized by the description above (see Chapter 2) of imperialism as a rhizomic and unprogrammed structure of connections and engagements. When we observe the actual complexities of the *cultural* interchanges in imperial relationships and, in particular, the activities of the supposed passive subjects of imperialism, we find the beginnings of existing global energies for interchange, circulation and transformation.

Both imperialism and contemporary globalism are grounded in the discourse of modernity. Both find their origins, their teleology, their ideology and technologies in the rise of modernity itself, both as a specifically European historical phenomenon and as a discursive forma-tion. Modernity is generally regarded as referring to modes of social organization which emerged in Europe from about the sixteenth century, broadly represented by the discovery of the 'new world', the Renaissance and Reformation (Habermas 1981: 5). Modernity was seen to be a distinctive and superior period in the history of humanity, a notion which became habitual as successive generations saw their own 'present' as enjoying a prominent position within the modern. As European power expanded, this sense of the superiority of the present over the past became translated into a sense of superiority over those premodern societies and cultures which were 'locked' in the past – primitive and uncivilized peoples whose subjugation and 'introduction' into modernity became the right and obligation of European powers. The emergence and dominance of reason as a philosophical mode (see Habermas 1987) and the radical restructuring of time and space became the most powerful discursive tools in the European construction of a modern world reality. These aspects of the modern, and, more generally, the *idea* of the modern itself, remain critical in the operations of globalization.

The concept of modernity is therefore significant in the emergence of colonial discourse. Modernity is fundamentally about conquest, 'the imperial regulation of land, the discipline of the soul, and the creation of truth' (Turner 1990: 4), a discourse which made possible the large-scale regulation of human identity within both Europe and its colonies. The emergence of modernity is co-terminous with the emergence of Eurocentrism and the European dominance of the world effected through imperial expansion. In other words, modernity emerged at about the same time as European nations began to conceive of their own dominant relationship to a non-European world and began to spread their rule through exploration, cartography and colonization. Europe constructed itself as 'modern' and constructed the non-European as 'traditional', 'static', 'pre-historical'. The imposition of European models of historical change became the tool by which these societies were denied any internal dynamic or capacity for development.

In addition to models of historical change, and the teleological assumptions on which these were based, the cultural energies of modernity were very early directed into economic development. Wallerstein's claim that capitalism has been the world system since the sixteenth century (1974a; 1976b) leads to the conclusion that capitalism is the economic discourse of modernity, the natural concomitant of European imperialism. However, while the *mode* of imperialism as a policy is economic, its historical *energy* is profoundly cultural. The link between globalism and the imperial dominance of subject nations can be traced back to Adam Smith, who is perhaps the first globalist. Smith's view of the role of commodities in distinguishing the civilized from the barbarous is deeply embedded in the ideology of empire. For him the social body is a body composed of things, a web of commodities circulating in an exchange that connects people who do not see or know each other. These things make it a 'civilized' body. Having an abundance of 'objects of comfort' is the litmus test that distinguishes 'civilized and thriving nations' from 'savage' ones, 'so miserably poor' they are reduced to 'mere want' (1776: lx). It is trade that has caused certain parts of the world to progress, leaving others (such as Africa) in a 'barbarous and uncivilized state'.

What we see in the example of Adam Smith is how the teleological and civilizing rhetoric of imperialism becomes the rationale for a global view of the world. We do not need to make a category leap from imperialism to globalism, for not only are both embedded in the idea of modernity but both hinge upon a hegemonic world view which is captured in the metaphor of colony itself. *Colonus* in Latin is a term for a small farm. 'Colony' is related to the idea of farming an area, making it productive, 'cultivating' it. This transfers effortlessly into rhetoric such as Smith's even when the political and geographical reality of the colony is not at issue. Cultivation becomes a powerful discursive strategy of imperialism: it has the dual implication of nurture and improvement, of productive exploitation and civilization. This not only enforces the idea of 'enclosure' as the only efficient way to occupy space but confirms the underlying principle of the *mission civilatrice* itself. To Nederveen Pieterse, who argues against the significance of modernity in the emergence of contemporary globalization (1995b), we would have to insist upon the importance of modernity's mode of self-realization and distribution – imperialism – as the key function in this emergence.

Globalism and imperialism are grounded in a similar discursive orientation towards the world, a similar naturalization of the historical reality of power relations. But there is a specific moment when nineteenth-century imperialism transfers from one English-speaking imperial centre to another and hence transfers from a geographical empire (however diminishing) to a globalization process without spatial boundaries. This defining moment in the movement of imperialism from Britain to the USA may be metonymically represented by Teddy Roosevelt's speech on the eve of his election to the Presidency in 1901.

> It is our duty toward the people living in barbarism to see that they are freed from their chains . . . and we can free them only by destroying barbarism itself. Exactly as it is the duty of a civilized power to scrupulously respect the rights of weaker civilized powers . . . so it is its duty to put down savagery and barbarism.
>
> (Beale 1956: 32, 34)

This speech, which perhaps marks the apex of imperialism and the beginning of the USA's serious appropriation of the concept as a policy, confirms the effortless way in which the ideology of imperialism with its huge contradiction of nurture and exploitation transfers into the twentieth-century global economy. Indeed, the key to the link between classical imperialism and contemporary globalization in the twentieth century has been the role of the United States, which enthusiastically assumed command of imperial rhetoric. More importantly, United States society during and after this early expansionist phase initiated those features of social life and social relations which today may be considered to characterize the global: mass production, mass communication and mass consumption. During the twentieth century these spread transnationally, 'drawing upon the increasingly integrated resources of the global economy' (Spybey 1996: 3).

Nederveen Pieterse argues against this view of globalization as the extension of European modernity, suggesting that this conflates Westernization with globalization. He says: 'The implication of the modernity/globalization view is that the history of globalization begins with the history of the West. But is not precisely the point of globalization as a perspective that globalization begins with world history?' (1995b: 47). But where does world history, where does the *idea* of 'the world' begin but in Western history? This is precisely the point of the significance of imperialism in modernity, and it reconfirms the power of Western history to construct world reality. This does not mean that globalization must be seen as a simple replacement for Western imperialism, as Tomlinson suggests: 'the distribution of global power that we know as "imperialism" . . . characterised the modern world up to, say, the 1960s. What replaces "imperialism" is "globalization"' (1991: 175). But it does confirm two important links between imperialism and globalization: both are grounded in systems of domination that emerged from, and characterize, European modernity; and both can be seen to be affected by similar processes of local transformation and worldwide circulations of culture.

In fact, the circulatory energies of globalization reflect the transcultural nature of imperial discourse, a fact which confirms, ironically, that globalization *must* be more than a simple extension of geographical imperialism since imperialism itself is so very multifaceted and circulatory. Globalization is the radical *transformation* of imperialism, continually reconstituted, and interesting precisely because it stems from no obvious imperial centre. While it is often understood in terms of large-scale phenomena, its homogenizing tendencies are effected in a heterogeneous array of local situations. This continues to be a source of confusion, for while globalism is grounded in the history of imperialism it is by no means as directed, centripetal and organized as imperial expansion: the constitutive energies of globalism are far more rhizomic, circulatory and diffuse. Globalism obtains its energy from its very diffusion, global culture making itself at home in motion rather than in a place, quite unlike the energy of imperial control.

Globalism has most often been invoked to demonstrate the processes of supranational movements of capital, transnational corporate power and the diffusion of the global economy. When examined objectively, the macro-economic consequences are quite ambiguous, for while globalization 'has often perpetuated poverty, widened material inequalities, increased ecological degradation, sustained militarism, fragmented communities, marginalized subordinated groups, fed intolerance and deepened crises of democracy', it may also be seen to have had a positive effect in 'trebling world per capita income since 1945, halving the proportion of the world living in abject poverty, increasing ecological consciousness, and possibly facilitating disarmament, while various subordinated groups have grasped opportunities for global organisation' (Scholte 1996: 53).

But what is much more intriguing, and perhaps difficult to comprehend, is the peculiar phenomenon of *global culture*. For how can a culture be global? How can one speak of a global society when our ideas of society and culture have been heavily dominated by the nation state? How can we develop a global political theory when we have no concept of a world society, and when all classical political theory has dealt with the state–society framework? Where does global culture emanate from and what exactly does it mean for local communities? How can they resist it? Should they want to? It is precisely these questions which invoke the energies and interests of post-colonial theory. For post-colonial experience demonstrates that the key to the resistance of the global by the self-determination of the local lies not in dismissal, isolation and rejection but more often in engagement and transformation. The diffuse and interactive process of identity formation proceeds in global terms in much the same way as it has done in post-colonial societies, and it is the model of post-colonial appropriation which is of most use in understanding the local engagements with global culture.

Two broadly different approaches dominate globalization theory, and these are associated with two very different views of culture. On the one hand culture is seen to be essentially territorial, the possession of a particular society or social group; on the other hand it is seen to be a malleable array of strategies for negotiating a group's reality, a *trans-local* learning process. According to these positions culture is either endogenous or exogenous; organic or diffuse; formed by societies and nations or transformed by diasporas and intercommunication. These views of culture are not incompatible, but they do generate very different assessments of cultural relations. The first tends to see globalization as homogenizing, the second sees it as heterogenetic; the first sees it as hegemonic, the second as interpenetrating. But there is a sense in which these oppositions are unnecessarily polarizing and take too little account of the energies of local groups. As an analysis of post-colonial transformation reveals, when we look closely at imperialism itself, we discover that it is by no means as hierarchically structured and downward-directed as many assume. The reason for this is that colonized communities are more than simply the objects of imperialism.

The very obvious hegemony of imperial rule is itself affected by a transcultural interdependence which presents an interesting model of contemporary global relations.

## Global culture, local identity and transformation

The cultural interchange between the local and the global appears to incorporate a power imbalance even more significant, and more diffuse, than that characterizing imperial relations. The *diffusion* of global influence makes the relationship between the local and the global all the more complex, because when we examine local cultures we find the presence of the global within the local to an extent that compels us to be very clear about our concept of the local. Robertson suggests (1995) that the term 'glocalization' more adequately describes the relationship between the local and the global as one of interaction and inter-penetration rather than of binary opposites. 'It makes no good sense', says Robertson, 'to define the global as if the global excludes the local' (34). Clearly the world as a whole has some systemic properties beyond the units within it, such as modernity itself and its major systems: capitalism and imperialism. But 'such units themselves are constructed in terms of extra-unit processes and actions, in terms of increasingly global dynamics' (34). Global analysis confirms something that has become increasingly clear in our present examination of post-colonial discourse: that the dominant and the subaltern do not exist in a simple and incontrovertibly oppositional mode. Neither is their inter-penetration a one-way process of 'contamination' from an imperial discourse to a colonized subject. 'There is no good reason', says Robertson, 'to define globalization largely in terms of homogenization' (34). The view that the local and the global should not be seen as simple opposites, but that the local contributes to the character of the global, is widely held. But how this occurs is less clear, and it is precisely this process that the phenomenon of post-colonial transformation illuminates.

To begin to consider the post-colonial approach to globalization, let us settle on a definition of the 'local' as a *sub-national* community of consumers. When we speak of the local we speak of a community which operates transversely to, or below the level of, those state apparatuses which organize representation in the interests of national identification. It might be one identified with a spatial location, but it might also be identified with an ethnic, gendered or cultural 'location'. It is a com-munity small enough not to need to be 'imagined' as the nation, or any wider community of identification must be. The reasons for theorizing the site of the local below the level of the nation are: that nations have clearly and historically defined structures of relationships to an 'international' collectivity; that nations continue to exert a hegemonic pressure of their own upon the production of culture; and that nations have sometimes become locked within what Barber calls the axial principles of our time: 'tribalism' and 'globalism' – a 'McWorld' of homogenizing globalization versus a 'Jihad world' of 'lebanonization' (Barber 1992: 54). That is, many post-Cold-War national movements have generated a particularly bounded and xenophobic version of locality as a collection of coercive tribal pressures. This is only a more extreme version of the cultural homogenization of nationally constituted societies which has been proceeding since the eighteenth century (co-terminous with the rise of the concept of the 'international'). But it continues the general trend of the nation towards what we might call a suppression of locality.

As we have seen, literary writing demonstrates that resistance, and the agency of the local, is most powerful when it is transformative. By 'taking hold' of writing, whether as novel, history, *testimonio*, by appropriating political discourse and political structures, by interpolating educational discourse and institutions, transforming conceptions of place, culture, even economics, the post-colonial subject unleashes a rapidly circulating transcultural energy. That is to say, the subject exhibits agency to the degree that he or she participates in a circulation of influence between the global and the local. Contrary to assumptions about the limited distribution and impact of literary writing, literature, because it has been wedded so closely to a historical notion of élite culture, has often been the means by which colonial politicians, writers and intellectuals have been able to appropriate the cultural capital invested in imperial discourse and redeploy it for local purposes.

However, post-colonial transformation also operates powerfully in the volatile interactions of mass, folk and popular culture. If folk culture, in its traditional form, largely disappears, or becomes suppressed, with the spread of modern media, the same cannot be said for popular culture, which demonstrates an energetic tendency towards localization. Popular culture has often become the mode of a transformation of mass culture, in much the same way as 'local' writing in colonized societies interpolated the ideology and assumptions of English literature, and gradually began to transform the concept of literature itself. But popular culture becomes critical in the engagement of the global by the local because it is already devoid of that particular hierarchy of value which characterizes the consumption of high culture such as canonical literature. In this respect the protean and adaptable power of the visual image and of music become marked (see Hall 1991b: 27). This is not to say that popular culture is not also subject to the tyranny of fashion and to a different kind of snobbery, but it has regularly shown itself to be more malleable and adaptable to local usage.

The question remains whether this consumption of Western advertising, music and other forms of mass culture is simply another form of neo-colonialism. This is a familiar question, of course, and is dominated by the contested issue of identity, for we find that identities are constructed in a globalized world by a continual, and ever more widening, process of interaction, appropriation and change. If globalism is not simply a result of top-down dominance but a transcultural process, a dialectic of dominant cultural forms and their appropriation, then the responses of local communities become critical.

We find these responses, these global effects, even in societies that might be regarded as extremely isolated. As far back as 1934 F. M. Keesing found that Hollywood films were having a profound effect in Samoa.

> The influence of motion pictures upon Samoan youth cannot be overestimated. In Apia alone something like 1,000 natives attend the theatres weekly . . . Their special passion is for 'wild west' pictures, with horses, guns, and fighting . . . According to the manager of one theatre the Samoan audiences are learning English rapidly through the medium of the sub-titles (they were silents), and gaining an increasing 'comprehension' of what the stories are about. This must be counted as now the greatest educational influence in Samoa other than the schools.
>
> (1934: 441)

This was not American Samoa, so it is clear that the global reach of American popular culture had been well under way even before the development of 'talkies', and even into the furthest reaches of the British Empire. The evidence that movies were having a greater educational impact than schools could be seen in the following description of the popularity of Hollywood heroes.

> Early actors such as Tom Mix (Toma Miki) and Harold Lloyd (Ara Loiti) became local Wild West heroes and later Oki Mefi (Audie Murphy) and Chon Wein (John Wayne). Kek Taklas (Kirk Douglas) and Toni Ketis (Tony Curtis) became favourites in *Spartacus of Rome* and *The Vikings*. In the seventies Clint Eastwood

westerns were extremely popular and he was simply referred to as *le pulupulu* – 'the cape' under which his various firearms were concealed and provided much of the action and suspense.

(Va'ai 1997: 162)

The transliteration of the names here is a sign of a process of extensive appropriation which accompanies the consumption of global cultural forms in countries like Samoa. The question of whether popular consumption is a function of global homogenization or local hybridization continues to be argued in the Samoan press as heatedly as it is everywhere else. But clearly, in areas such as popular music, radio and television serials, a rigorous adaptation of Western (mainly US) characters and images to Samoan life in local productions demonstrates the resilient inventiveness of local communities. Popular media culture interweaves local and imported traditions, influences, genres and practices, and whether in song, dance or story unselfconsciously uses whatever material comes to hand.

## Paradise

This inventiveness, this free-wheeling propensity for hybrid adaptation, conflicts continually with essentialist myths of authenticity, particularly those by which the Western world keeps its 'others' marginalized. In *Routes* James Clifford examines a London museum display of a New Guinea Highland village called 'Paradise'. Paradise is a term which is, in this context, deeply ironic, because it is the cliché which most regularly represents the exotic otherness of the primitive. In the context of this exhibition, a hybrid mixture of 'traditional' and received artefacts, the term is itself deconstructed. The exhibition includes a replica of the village's general store:

> The store, beside a hand-operated coffee mill and a coffee tree, is made of corrugated iron and wood. Through a window and doorway, you observe: 'PARADISE Kokonas'; 'Bik Pela / SPEAR / coarse cut / tobacco sticks'; Coke bottles, shirts on hangers (the most visible one bearing a 'Los Angeles County Sheriff' patch); printed cloth – 'PNG,' 'Jesus . . . ,' tropical scenes; 'Cheese flavoured / TWISTIES / Baim nau'; mats, pots, spices; 'HIGH MOUNTAIN Instant Coffee'; mirrors, hats, acrylic yarn, sardines, tea, rice, sugar, batteries, cassettes, hair dye . . . Paradise.
>
> (Clifford 1997: 146)

The hybridity of this general store is an evocative sign of 'the postmodern' to most commentators. It is as if this 'inauthentic', destabilized representation of the meeting of globalism and Highland village is a sign of the worldwide influence of a postmodern West. In Stewart and Shaw's *Syncretism/Anti-Syncretism* they suggest that 'we have recently acquired an englobing appetite for the irony of apparently incongruous cultural syntheses', and conclude that in 'our enthusiasm for deconstructing synthetic traditions we may have invented another kind of intellectual imperialism' (1994: 180). But who are 'we'? What makes a cultural synthesis 'incongruous'? To whom is it incongruous? The assumption that 'we', the Western producers and definers of culture, have the authority to speak, while the local villagers are the passive recipients of syncretic culture, is itself a startling recapitulation of the ethnocentric biases of classical imperialism.

Clifford's analysis suggests rather that this hybridity is a sign of a constructive cultural evolution. But his primary interest is in the nature of museums, and the inexorable way in which this exhibition reveals how the boundary between the 'traditional' and the modern dissolves in the various activities of daily life. What is even more interesting is that the village transgresses the very principles on which modernity itself is distinguished from the 'premodern', 'traditional' or 'primitive' culture. What about the *users* of these commodities? we might well ask. What are they doing, for instance, when they come to regard colourful plastic as an 'essential' feature of a traditional headdress? Clifford's analysis fails to ask, or to ask clearly enough, what exactly might be the nature of the agency involved in the appropriation of images, commodities, materials, ideas, which represent both colonial and global dominance.

This ambivalence opens up an aporia in Clifford's text when he uses the word 'permit'.

> Change in the New Guinea Highlands is not portrayed on a before/after axis, with a 'traditional' baseline preceding the arrival of 'outside' influences. Rather, we are thrown into the midst of transformations. Modernity's effects are immediately and dramatically registered in the diverse commodities of the trade store. An influx of new wealth *permits* the Wahgi to compensate battle deaths, to make bride-wealth payments.
>
> (1997: 154)

This very astutely undermines the distinction between modernity and primitivism. But the word 'permit' causes us to wonder what the act of consumption means in this context. Is the word 'transformation' a noun or a verb? Does modernity 'permit' the confirmation of traditional verities or does it 'enable' New Guinea Highlanders to employ modern means to constitute their cultural identity? It seems a small distinction, but it is critical to understanding how individuals locate themselves in modernity. What is happening, for instance, when a man uses an enlarged and elaborate representation of a South Pacific Lager label as the model for the decoration of his shield? (Clifford 1997: 172). Is this a sign of an enslavement by capitalism, of the insidious power of advertising, a sign of the capture of traditional society by the forces of commodity production? What is the function of beer in Papua New Guinea society? What is the specific function of the pattern and colour being incorporated into the shield? Beer itself has a peculiar place in these villages, because a party which supplies plenty of South Pacific Lager is a sure sign of a 'bikman', a man of influence and power, and so the signifier of the shield is an incorporation of an advertising design into the culture in a particular way.

But this incorporation is also deeply ironic because the enlargement of the beer sign and its inscription on a shield locate it far from its function as advertisement. The decoration of a shield in this way employs what to the maker of the shield is an exotic, colourful and intricate design in such a way as to *empty* the representation of all content and *refill* it in a way that asserts its local and cultural function. Far from being a slavish advertisement for South Pacific Lager, the shield confirms the endless appropriability of signification. Like the Papua New Guinea writer who writes in English to produce a decolonizing text, the maker of the ceremonial shield demonstrates in a visual way the power of the local society to appropriate the signs of global commodity production for a specific confirmation of local identity. The political, cultural and economic features of global culture traverse at some point the critical plane of representation.

We can see how clearly the 'Paradise' collection demonstrates the inventive and adaptable processes of post-colonial habitation. The transformation of that material culture presented to it as 'dominant' or 'civilized' is a sign of a surprisingly potent and even gleeful capacity for self-fashioning in colonized societies. A similar example occurs in South Africa, where the plastic shopping bags so prevalent in supermarkets have been appropriated by inhabitants of the townships as a resource for an entire new industry. The plastic is woven into hats – hats of astonishing variety and of sometimes remarkable delicacy and sophistication. Material which is little more than non-degradable landfill is re-used for productive purposes. The situation is somewhat different from the Paradise example because one might see the township hat industry as saving an environment put under threat by a white middle class. Nevertheless, paradoxically, the hats come to operate as the signs of a particular kind of adapted cultural authenticity.

Another example of the appropriation of Western material culture to actually *confirm* cultural identity can be seen in the weaving of traditional sleeping mats in Samoa. The sleeping mats are woven with pandanus and edged with a pattern of brightly coloured woollen yarn. This imported yarn is used purely for the decoration which identifies them as authentic Samoan sleeping mats. Asked whether it were possible to use something other than the yarn, since it was expensive and imported, a weaver replied: '*A ave ese le vulu ua le koe fala Samoa ae ouke leiloa poo se a* If you take away the wool – it is no longer a Samoan mat – I wouldn't know what it is' (cited Va'ai 1997: 167).

This capacity for transformation extends well beyond the re-use and refashioning of material resources. By appropriating strategies of representation, as well as strategies of organization, communication and social change, through access to global systems, local communities and marginal interest groups can both empower themselves and influence those global systems. Although choice is always mediated by the conditions of subject formation, the *belief* that one has a choice in the processes of changing one's own life or society can indeed be empowering. In this sense the appropriation of global forms of culture may free one from local forms of dominance and oppression or at least provide the tools for a different kind of identity formation.

## Signs of the times: Tom Jones in Penang

The beer label shield in 'Paradise' operates as a sign, complex enough to be read as a text of transformation. Even more potent signifiers, therefore, are billboard signs themselves, signs which may be read as cultural texts signifying much more than they advertise. The key element of these texts is the *consumption* they both demonstrate and promote. The critical observation we make in all examples of habitation is that the act of consumption is the first, and possibly most transformative means in which local communities engage dominant culture. For the act of consumption reduces the consumed product, and through it the consumed culture, to its most fragile state, a state of pure potentiality. Consumption precedes the radically transformative acts of post-colonial production, because the moment of consumption is the moment at which the power of the consumed culture is most provisional.

The following example of a billboard sign, a 'text' created by appropriating global culture, reveals two things. Firstly, globalization disrupts internal histories of genre, relocating the narrative of that history spatially as well as culturally. Genre may be seen here to refer to the 'genre' of billboard signs themselves, as well as to the genre of the cultural activity they advertise. Secondly, the agency of identity construction may proceed through processes which engage dominant images and forms in sometimes quite ambivalent ways. Without examining the cultural history in which these texts are embedded, without knowing the specific processes, the individual decisions which led to the conception and erection of these signs, they may be read as *metonyms* of identity construction.

The sign in question is a startling and almost disorienting billboard in Penang, Malaysia, advertising a Tom Jones song-singing competition. The phenomenon of pop idol Tom Jones already has a history before it reaches Penang. His Welshness, his mythic representation of the melodic tradition of the Celtic fringe of the United Kingdom, compromises the notion of the singer's simple signification of 'Western music'. Before Tom Jones gets to Penang the music and the image have already been transformed in a particular way.[7] When we discover Tom Jones in Penang we see that the competition is not for tourists or Westerners, but for 'all amateur Malaysians 18 years and above'. The competition is indisputably local, but the sign is only anomalous to the viewer who has essentialized the 'genre' of Tom Jones's music.

What exactly is being consumed here? we ask ourselves. What exactly is the representative status of Tom Jones in Penang? How, and how much, has the product been changed at the point of consumption? The format of the competition derives from the tradition of *karaoke*, a Japanese form which itself has had a meteoric rise in popularity in bars throughout the world. But consider the sponsorship of the competition by a local Danish brewery and what appears to be a Chinese firm of chartered accountants. In such a text cultural stereotype finds little purchase, not only because of the palimpsestic nature of the image but because consumption itself, the location, the purposes and meanings of the consumption, operate in a mode of ironic reconstitution. The text disrupts our sense of the movement of genre, of the 'rightness' of certain images in certain places. But it also disrupts our ideas about cultural authenticity. Our immediate reaction to this sign may well be that it is a classic example of cultural contamination, just as it might be when we consider the way colourful plastic has become an essential component of the *authentic* Highland headdress, or woollen yarn the sign of an authentic Samoan sleeping mat. But what does contamination or

adulteration mean in the context of the fluid and free-wheeling appropriations of local culture? Salman Rushdie asks: 'If the young people of
Iran now insist on rock concerts, who are we to criticize their cultural
contamination?' (1999: 32). This disruption and transgression is itself a
disruption of stereotypical notions of cultural identity. But curiously it
is a disruption already made possible by the displacements of global
culture.

This sign announces a competition which already exists in a
hybridized context. One of the most popular bars in Penang is a reggae
bar called Ziggy Stardust's on Koh Samui Road. Despite the hegemonic
impetus of globalism, the identity of global culture is itself hybridized,
circulating and transcultural. This text shows us that we cannot see
the relationship of a dominant West and the Third World as a simple
function of the downward pressure of neo-colonialism. Not only is this
modified by the circulation of popular images represented in these
signs, but we can conclude that indeed this circulation is itself globalism:
this constant interchange between the 'local' and the 'global' is itself
the key to the transcultural process of globalization.

## The T-shirt

The Penang billboard, being located in a formerly colonized city, shows
how the strategies of post-colonial consumption can be adapted to
global commodification. Even more suggestive of the relationship
between individual choice, rhizomic agency and transformative
textuality, and more global in its reach, is the phenomenon of the
T-shirt, which seems to demonstrate perfectly the extravagant openness
of representation to local or personal signification. The T-shirt is
possibly the one universal item of clothing which *advertises* the dominance of sign value over use value. Its utility as clothing is well attested
globally, but its reason for existence almost seems to lie entirely in its
value as a sign.

The question of the T-shirt as a sign of the global dissolution of
barriers of distance and identity is raised by Homi Bhabha in a discussion at the Cultural Studies Conference in 1990 (Grossberg et al.
1992). Commenting on Clifford's theory of travel, Bhabha suggests
that the T-shirt focuses the principle of global hybridization as an
impossibility to move, rather than travel, and a compensatory act
which prevents circulation and movement. He gives as examples the
Urbana, Illinois, or Harvard T-shirts seen on the streets of Bombay, or
of particular kinds of sunglasses, or television programmes or music,
which operate as images of travel, and elaborate around them 'a text

which has not to do with movement and displacement, but with a kind of fetishization of other cultures, or of the elsewhere, or of the image and figure of travel' (114). This idea of the 'fetishization of elsewhere' is a compelling one but, like most responses to the link between global economy and the Third World, is inclined to see the local subject as a captive of dominant forces, overlooking the actual complexity of the T-shirt's significatory possibilities and also the possibilities of agency which exist in the appropriation of the sign value of the T-shirt.

The fact remains that in places as diverse as Bombay, Lagos or a Papua New Guinea village the overt inscription of the T-shirt, which in a capitalist economy is assumed to be equivalent to its sign value, being the message which accords status or group identity may be completely disregarded. This is not because it operates as a generalized sign of modernity but because, like the linguistic sign, the image may have deep layering of meaning functions. Replying to Bhabha, Clifford mentions the Kanak militant in a Tarzan T-shirt or the Lebanese militiaman in a Rambo T-shirt. 'Is this a fetishization of other cultures?' he asks, 'or is it a way of localizing global symbols for the purposes of action?' (114). The evidence from a range of examples is that it is most often the latter. 'Action' may not need to refer to political or military action, but describes that range of acts which 'resist' domination by transforming the modes of its discourse.

For this reason the T-shirt operates as the strongest symbol of the process of representation occurring in all the above examples of transformation. For the T-shirt, such an obvious investment in sign value, demonstrates the importance of cultural capital in the subject's engagement with global culture. In a sense, the T-shirt mimics the cultural capital it signifies. (We can see this same mimicry in the fake Cartier watches and Gucci bags to be found in markets throughout Asia.) But the mimicry, while being 'menacing', because it is both economically subversive and vaguely parodic, reveals a further dimension: such menace does not diminish the currency of the cultural capital the subject employs as a sign of empowerment. Paradoxically, this empowerment often includes the freedom to wear the T-shirt as clothing, with no regard at all for its sign value. Because the wearing of a T-shirt requires such a variety of different decisions it is perhaps best read as a text. But the *process* represented by the T-shirt's consumption is one which we see in post-colonial cultures as much as in 'glocalization' – the disarticulation of mimicry, which occurs the moment the cultural capital of the dominant culture is appropriated, is also the disarticulation which propels the consuming subject from emulation to transformation.

This very disarticulation occurs in even the most controlled and elaborate appropriation, such as the literary text. The menace of mimicry never diminishes the power of the cultural capital being employed, nor the transformative potential of the consumption. In this paradox we find located the political agency of interpolation, that intervention into, and simultaneous disturbance and utilization of, the cultural capital represented by the dominant discourse. When we see the acts of consumption by which global culture is adapted to local needs, we see the truly global reach of the strategies operating in postcolonial habitation, and the extent to which interpolation, habitation and transformation are interlinked. At this point also, we see the global dimensions of the discourse of resistance with which we began. For that resistance which always operates to contest and disturb the dominant is fully effective only when it utilizes the capacity of culture for change and adaptation, when it fulfils its own potential to transform.

# Notes

1 On 6 February 1840 forty-six Maori chiefs from the northern regions of New Zealand 'signed' a document written in Maori called 'Te Tiriti o Waitangi', 'The Treaty of Waitangi'. According to the English versions of that document, they thus ceded to Her Majesty the Queen of England 'absolutely and without reservation all the rights and powers of Sovereignty' which they exercised over their respective territories. That trick of language, in which sovereignty, or *mana*, was substituted for governance or *kawanitanga*, became the substantive ground of British sovereignty over New Zealand.

2 The objection might be raised that this confirms Spivak's point: the appropriators all end up as class élites rather than subalterns; 'representers on behalf of' rather than 'representers of'. But there is no subaltern who is a fixed and perfectly authentic representation of the subaltern position; the experience of class and oppression may vary from subject to subject. Subalterneity and appropriation are both located on a continuum.

3 I discovered this in an experiment conducted some years ago, in which participants were offered progressive lines of separate poems selected randomly in the belief that they were progressively reading a single poem. Respondents of high professional competence revealed great ingenuity in interpreting the 'poem' and in all cases directed their response to a constructed intentionality generally identified as 'the poet'.

4 In 1884, by international agreement, the meridian defined by the cross hairs in the eye-piece of Airy's 'Transit Circle' telescope at Royal Greenwich Observatory was designated the prime meridian, and all points along it located at 0° longitude. All other points on the Earth have longitudes ranging from 0° to 180°E or from 0° to 180°W. Except where it is changed to account for populated areas, the international date line lies along the 180° meridian. Meridians of longitude and parallels of latitude together form a grid by which any position on the Earth's surface can be specified.

5 Yorkshireman John Harrison invented the revolutionary marine chronometer which solved the problem of finding longitude at sea. However, he was involved in a protracted struggle with Parliament over rewards due to him from the Board of Longitude for solving the problem. After many long trials, Harrison, at the age of eighty, was finally granted a sum of money slightly larger than the mentioned reward.

6 The pass laws were concerned with social control and were activated by the police daily. Detention without trial laws were instituted to imprison political activists such as the ANC guerrillas and communists.

7 It is still not unusual to find Tom Jones films featured on flights by Asian airlines. There is an extensive Tom Jones fan club network throughout Asia, and the music and films have a cult status in Hong Kong. Why this should be so might be the subject of a different, but extremely fascinating study.

# Bibliography

Achebe, Chinua (1958), *Things Fall Apart*, London: Heinemann.

Achebe, Chinua (1964), *Arrow of God*, London: Heinemann.

Acton, John Emerich Edward Dalberg (1906), *Lectures on Modern History*, London: Macmillan.

Alberti, Leon Battista (1956), *On Painting* (trans. J. R. Spencer), London: Routledge.

Aldrich, Robert (1996), *Greater France: A History of French Overseas Expansion*, New York: St Martin's.

Alexis, J. S. (1956), 'Of the Marvellous Realism of the Haitians', *Presence Africaine* 8–10.

Ankersmit, F. R. (1983), *Narrative Logic: A Semantic Analysis of the Historian's Language*, The Hague: Martinus Nijhoff.

Anzaldua, Gloria (1987), *Borderlands/La Frontera: The New Mestiza*, San Francisco: Aunt Lute.

Appiah, Anthony Kwame (1992), *In My Father's House: Africa in the Philosophy of Culture*, London: Methuen.

Arteaga, Alfred (1994), *An Other Tongue: Nation and Ethnicity in the Linguistic Borderlands*, Durham, NC, and London: Duke University Press.

Ashcroft, Bill, Gareth Griffiths and Helen Tiffin (1989), *The Empire Writes Back: Theory and Practice in Post-Colonial Literatures*, London: Routledge.

Ashcroft, Bill, Gareth Griffiths and Helen Tiffin (1995), *The Post-Colonial Studies Reader*, London and New York: Routledge.

Ashcroft, Bill and John Salter (1994), 'Australia: A Rhizomic Text' in Livio Dobrez (ed.), *Identifying Australia in Postmodern Times*, Canberra: Australian National University Press.

Attwell, David (1990), 'The Problem of History in the Fiction of J. M. Coetzee' in Martin Trump (ed.), *Rendering Things Visible: Essays on South African Literary Culture*, Johannesburg: Ravan.

Austin, J. L. (1962), *How to Do Things with Words*, Oxford: Clarendon.

Baldick, Chris (1987), *The Social Mission of English Criticism 1848–1932*, Oxford: Clarendon.

Barber, B. R. (1992), 'Jihad vs. McWorld', *The Atlantic* 269 (3).

Barthes, Roland (1957), *Mythologies*, London: Jonathan Cape (1972).

Barthes, Roland (1971), 'From Work to Text' in Rick Rylance (ed.), *Debating Texts*, Milton Keynes: Open University (1987).

Baumgart, Winfried (1982), *Imperialism: The Idea and Reality of British and French Colonial Expansion 1880–1914* (trans. Ben V. Mast), Oxford: Oxford University Press.

Beale, Howard (1956), *Theodore Roosevelt and the Rise of America to World Power*, Baltimore: The Johns Hopkins University Press.

Bernasconi, Robert (1997), 'African Philosophy vs. Continental Philosophy' in Emmanuel Chukwudi Eze (ed.), *Postcolonial African Philosophy: A Critical Reader*, Oxford: Blackwell.

Beverley, John (1989), 'The Margin at the Center: On *Testimonio* (Testimonial Narrative)', *Modern Fiction Studies* 35 (1) (spring): 11–27.

Beverley, John and Marc Zimmerman (1990), *Literature and Politics in the Central American Revolutions*, Austin: University of Texas.

Bhabha, Homi K. (1983a), 'The Other Question', *Screen* 24 (6): 18–35.

Bhabha, Homi K. (1983b), 'Difference, Discrimination and the Discourse of Colonialism' in Francis Barker et al. (eds), *The Politics of Theory*, Colchester: University of Essex.

Bhabha, Homi K. (1984), 'Representation and the Colonial Text: Some Forms of Mimeticism' in Frank Gloversmith (ed.), *The Theory of Reading*, Brighton: Harvester.

Bhabha, Homi K. (1985), 'Signs Taken for Wonders: Questions of Ambivalence and Authority under a Tree outside Delhi, May 1817', *Critical Inquiry* 12 (1): 144–65.

Bhabha, Homi K. (1994), *The Location of Culture*, London: Routledge.

Bickerton, Derek (1973), 'On the Nature of a Creole Continuum', *Language* 49 (3): 640–69.

Bourdieu, Pierre (1977), *Outline of a Theory of Practice*, Cambridge: Cambridge University Press.

Bourdieu, Pierre and Jean-Claude Passeron (1972), *Reproduction in Education, Society and Culture* (trans. Richard Nice), London and Beverly Hills: Sage.

Brantlinger, Patrick (1988), *Rule of Darkness: British Literature and Imperialism 1830–1914*, Ithaca, NY: Cornell University Press.

Brathwaite, Edward Kamau (1974), 'Timehri' in Orde Coombes (ed.), *Is Massa Day Dead? Black Moods in the Caribbean*, New York: Doubleday.

Brennan, Timothy (1989), *Salman Rushdie and the Third World: Myths of the Nation*, New York: St Martin's Press.

Cabral, Amilcar (1973), *Return to the Source: Selected Speeches* (ed. African Information Service), New York: Monthly Review Press.

Capel, Horacio (1994), 'Geography and the Spanish Empire' in Godlewska and Smith 1994.

Carey, Peter (1985), *Illywhacker*, London and Boston: Faber.

Carey, Peter (1988), *Oscar and Lucinda*, St Lucia: University of Queensland Press.

Carter, Paul (1987), *The Road to Botany Bay*, London: Faber.

Césaire, Aimé (1969), *Une Tempête: d'après 'La Tempête' de Shakespeare – Adaptation pour une théâtre nègre*, Paris: Editions de Seuil.

Chakrabarty, Dipesh (1992), 'Postcoloniality and the Artifice of History: Who Speaks for "Indian" Pasts?' *Representations* 32 (winter): 1–26.

Chambers, Ross (1991), *Room for Maneuver: Reading (the) Oppositional (in) Narrative*, Chicago: University of Chicago.

Clifford, James (1997), *Routes: Travel and Translation in the Later Twentieth Century*, London and Cambridge, MA.: Harvard University Press.

Coetzee, J. M. (1974), *Dusklands*, Harmondsworth: Penguin.

Coetzee, J. M. (1980), *Waiting for the Barbarians*, New York: Penguin.

Coetzee, J. M. (1986), *Foe*, Harmondsworth: Penguin.

Conrad, Joseph (1902), *Heart of Darkness*, Harmondsworth: Penguin (1986).

Constantino, Renato (1998), 'Globalization is Recolonization', Asia Pacific Solidarity Conference: www.peg.apc.org/-apiaustralia/apsc-rc.htm.

Cooper, F. and Stoler, A. L. (ed) (1997), *Tensions of Empire: Colonial Cultures in a Bourgeois World*, Berkeley: University of California Press.

Cormack, Lesley B. (1994), 'Geography and the State in Elizabethan England' in Godlewska and Smith 1994.

Crawford, Robert (1992), *Devolving English Literature*, Oxford: Clarendon.

Crush, Jonathan (1994), 'Post-Colonialism, De-Colonization, and Geography' in Godlewska and Smith 1994.

Cudjoe, Selwyn R. (1980), *Resistance and Caribbean Literature*, Athens, OH, and London: Ohio University Press.

Cudjoe, Selwyn R. (1993), *Eric Williams Speaks: Essays on Colonialism and Independence*, Wellesley, MA: Calaloux.

Davidson, Basil (1973), *Black Star: A View of the Life and Times of Kwame Nkrumah*, London: Allen Lane.

Davidson, Basil (1983), *Modern Africa*, London: Longman.

de Certeau, Michel (1984), *The Practice of Everyday Life* (trans. Steven F. Randall), Berkeley: University of California Press.

Deleuze, Gilles and Félix Guattari (1972), *Anti-Oedipus: Capitalism and Schizophrenia* (trans. Robert Hurley, Mark Seem and Helen R. Lane), Minneapolis: University of Minnesota Press (1987).

Deleuze, Gilles and Félix Guattari (1980), *A Thousand Plateaus: Capitalism and Schizophrenia* (trans. Brian Massumi), Minneapolis: University of Minnesota Press (1983).

de Man, Paul (1980), *Allegories of Reading*, New Haven: Yale University Press.

Derrida, Jacques (1976), *Of Grammatology* (trans. Gayatri Chakravorty Spivak), Baltimore and London: Johns Hopkins.

Derrida, Jacques (1978), *Writing and Difference* (trans. Alan Bass), London: Routledge.

Descartes, René (1964), *Philosophical Writings* (trans. and ed. by E. Anscombe, P. T. Geach and A. Koyré), London: Nelson.

Dirlik, Arif (1994), 'The Postcolonial Aura: Third World Criticism in the Age of Global Capitalism', *Critical Inquiry* 20 (winter).

Donnell, Alison and Sarah Lawson Welsh (1996), *The Routledge Reader in Caribbean Literature*, London: Routledge

Drew, Philip (1994), *The Coast Dwellers*, Ringwood, Vic.: Penguin.

Driver, Felix (1992), 'Geography's Empire', *Environment and Planning D. Society and Space* 10: 23–40.

Edgerton, Samuel (1976), *The Renaissance Re-Discovery of Linear Perspective*, New York: Basic Books.

Ellison, Ralph (1964), *Shadow and Act*, New York: Random House.

Eze, Emmanuel Chukwudi (ed.) (1997), *Postcolonial African Philosophy: A Critical Reader*, Oxford: Blackwell.

Fanon, Frantz (1952), *Black Skin, White Masks* (trans. Charles Lam Markham), New York: Grove (1967).

Fanon, Frantz (1961), *The Wretched of the Earth*, London: MacGibbon and Kee (1965).

Field, Barron (1825), *Geographical Memoirs on New South Wales: By Various Hands*, London: John Murray.

Foucault, Michel (1969), 'What Is an Author?' (trans. J. V. Harari) in J. V. Harari (ed.), *Textual Strategies: Perspectives in Post-Structuralist Criticism*, London: Methuen (1979).

Foucault, Michel (1970), *The Order of Things*, London: Tavistock.

Foucault, Michel (1971), 'Orders of Discourse', *Social Science Information* 10 (2): 7–30.

Foucault, Michel (1972), *The Archaeology of Knowledge*, London: Tavistock.

Foucault, Michel (1977), 'What Is an Author' in *Language, Counter-Memory, Practice*, Oxford: Blackwell.

Foucault, Michel (1980), *Power/Knowledge: Selected Interviews and Other Writings 1972–1977*, New York: Pantheon.

Freeman, Edward A. (1898), *The Growth of the English Constitution from the Earliest Times to the Present*, London: Macmillan.

Frye, Northrop (1982), *The Great Code: The Bible and Literature*, New York: Harcourt Brace Jovanovich.

Gandhi, Leela (1998), *Postcolonial Theory: A Critical Introduction*, Sydney: Allen & Unwin.

Ghosh, Amitav (1986), 'The Imam and the Indian', *Granta* 20 (winter): 135–46.

Giddens, Anthony (1990), *The Consequences of Modernity*, Cambridge: Polity.

Gikandi, Simon (1992), 'The Politics and Poetics of National Formation: Recent African Writing' in Rutherford 1992.

Glissant, Edouard (1989), *Caribbean Discourse: Selected Essays* (trans. with intro. by J. Michael Dash), Charlottesville: University Press of Virginia.

Godlewska, Anne and Neil Smith (eds) (1994), *Geography and Empire*, Oxford: Blackwell.

Gotlieb Yosef (1992), 'Retrieving Life-Place from Colonized Space: Transcending the Encumbrances of the Post-Colonial State', *Political Geography* 11 (5) (September): 461–74.

Grossberg, Lawrence, Cary Nelson and Paul Treicher (1992), *Cultural Studies*, New York and London: Routledge.

Gugelberger, George (ed.) (1996), *The Real Thing: Testimonial Discourse and Latin America*, Durham, NC, and London: Duke University Press.

Gugelberger, George and Michael Kearney (1991), 'Voices for the Voiceless: Testimonial Literature in Latin America', *Latin American Perspectives*, Issue 70, 18 (3) (summer): 3–14.

Habermas, Jürgen (1981), 'Modernity versus Postmodernity', *New German Critique* 22: 3–14.

Habermas, Jürgen (1987), *The Philosophical Discourse of Modernity*, Cambridge: Polity.

Hall, Stuart (1990), 'Cultural Identity and Diaspora' in Jonathan Rutherford (ed.), *Identity: Community, Culture, Difference*, London: Lawrence and Wishart.

Hall, Stuart (1991a), 'The Local and the Global: Globalization and Ethnicity' in Anthony D. King (ed.), *Culture, Globalization and the World System*, London: Macmillan.

Hall, Stuart (1991b), 'Old and New Identities, Old and New Ethnicities' in Anthony D. King (ed.), *Culture, Globalization and the World System*, London: Macmillan.

Harlow, Barbara (1987), *Resistance Literature*, New York and London: Methuen.

Harris, Wilson (1970), 'History, Fable and Myth in the Caribbean and the Guianas' in Hena Maes-Jelinek (ed.), *Explorations: A Selection of Talks and Articles 1966–81*, Mundelstrup: Dangaroo (1981).

Harris, Wilson (1983), *The Womb of Space: The Cross-Cultural Imagination*, Westport, CT: Greenwood.

Harris, Wilson (1985), 'Adversarial Contexts and Creativity', *New Left Review* 154 (Nov.–Dec.).

Harvey, David (1990), *The Condition of Postmodernity*, Oxford: Blackwell.

Harvey, David (1996), *Justice, Nature and the Geography of Difference*, Oxford: Blackwell.

Hegel, Georg Wilhelm Friedrich (1899), *The Philosophy of History*, New York: Dover (1956).

Hobson, J. A. (1902), *Imperialism* (intro. Philip Siegelman), Ann Arbor: University of Michigan (1965).

Holden, Phillip (1998), 'Complicity and Resistance: English Studies and Cultural Capital in Colonial Singapore' (unpublished paper delivered at ACLALS, Nov. 1998).

Holdich, Thomas (1899), 'The Use of Practical Geography Illustrated by Recent Frontier Operations', *Geographical Journal* 13: 465–80.

Holst-Petersen, K. and A. Rutherford (eds) (1985), *A Double Colonization: Colonial & Postcolonial & Women's Writing*, Aarhus: Dangaroo.

hooks, bell (1991), *Yearning: Race, Gender, and Cultural Politics*, London: Turnaround.

Horkheimer, Max and Theodor Adorno (1975), *A Dialectics of Enlightenment*, New York: Continuum.

Husserl, Edmund (1913), *Ideas* (trans. W. R. Boyce Gibson), London: Allen & Unwin (1969).

Jacobs, J. U. (1991), 'Confession, Interrogation and Self-interrogation in the New South African Prison Writing' in Kirsten Holst-Petersen and Anna Rutherford (eds), *On Shifting Sands: New Art and Literature from South Africa*, Portsmouth, NH: Heinemann (1992).

Jakobson, Roman and Morris Halle (1956), *Fundamentals of Language*, The Hague: Mouton.

JanMohamed, Abdul R. (1983), *Manichean Aesthetics: The Politics of Literature in Colonial Africa*, Amherst: University of Massachusetts Press.

JanMohamed, Abdul R. (1985), 'The Economy of Manichean Allegory: The Functions of Radical Difference in Colonialist Literature', *Critical Enquiry* 12 (1).

Jay, Martin (1993), *Downcast Eyes: The Denigration of Vision in Twentieth-Century French Thought*, Berkeley: University of California Press.

Kachru, Braj (1986), *The Alchemy of English: The Spread, Functions and Models of Non-Native Englishes*, Oxford: Pergamon.

Kamuf, Peggy (ed.) (1991), *A Derrida Reader: Between the Blinds*, New York and London: Harvester.

Kanafani, Ghassan (1982), *Literature of Resistance in Occupied Palestine: 1948–1966*, Beirut: Institute for Arabic Research (in Arabic).

Kasaipwalova, John (1987), 'Betel-nut is Bad Magic for Aeroplanes' (1971) in G. Powell (ed.), *Through Melanesian Eyes*, Melbourne: Macmillan.

Keesing, F. M. (1934), *Modern Samoa: Its Government and Changing Life*, London: Allen & Unwin.

Kellner, Hans (1987), 'Narrativity in History: Post-Structuralism and Since', *History and Theory* 26 (Sept.).

Kimbrough, Robert (ed.) (1988), Joseph Conrad, *Heart of Darkness*, New York: Norton.

Kingsley, Charles (1860), 'Mansfield's *Paraguay, Brazil and the Plate*' in *Miscellanies*, 2 vols, London: Parker.

Kirby, Andrew (1994), 'What Did You Do in the War, Daddy?' in Godlewska and Smith 1994.

Kroestch, Robert (1974), 'Unhiding the Hidden: Recent Canadian Fiction', *Journal of Canadian Fiction* 3.

Lamming, George (1992), *The Pleasures of Exile*, Ann Arbor: University of Michigan Press.

Lazarus, Neil (1990), *Resistance in Postcolonial African Fiction*, New Haven and London: Yale University Press.

Le Riverend, Julio (1967), *Economic History of Cuba*, Havana: Ensayo Book Institute.

Lee, Dennis (1974), 'Cadence. Country. Silence: Writing in Colonial Space' *Boundary* 23 (1) (fall).

Lewin, Hugh (1981), *Bandiete: Seven Years in a South African Prison*, London: Heinemann.

Livingstone, David N. (1992), *The Geographic Tradition*, Oxford: Blackwell.

Livingstone, David N. (1994), 'Climate's Moral Economy: Science, Race and Place in Post-Darwinian British and American Geography' in Godlewska and Smith 1994.

Locke, John (1690), *Two Treatises of Government* (intro. Peter Laslett), Cambridge: Cambridge University Press (1964).

Luis, William (1981), 'Re-Writing History: César Leante's *Los Guerillos Negros*', *Journal of Caribbean Studies* 2 (3): 250–65.

Macaulay, Thomas Babbington (1835), 'Minute of the 2nd February, 1835' in G. M. Young (ed.), *Speeches*, London: Oxford University Press (1935).

McClintock, Anne (1995), *Imperial Leather: Race, Gender and Sexuality in the Colonial Contest*, New York: Routledge.

Malouf, David (1978), *An Imaginary Life*, Sydney: Picador (1990).

Malouf, David (1985), *12 Edmonstone Street*, London: Chatto & Windus.

Malouf, David (1993), *Remembering Babylon*, London: Chatto & Windus.

Mandelbaum, D. (1949), *Selected Writings of Edward Sapir*, Berkeley and Los Angeles: University of California Press.

Manwaring, Elizabeth (1965), *Italian Landscape in Eighteenth Century England*, New York: Russell and Russell.

Massey, Doreen (1994), *Space, Place and Gender*, Cambridge: Polity.

Menchú, Rigoberta (1983), *I, Rigoberta Menchú: An Indian Woman in Guatemala* (ed. with intro. by Elisabeth Burgos-Debray, trans. Ann Wright), London: Verso.

Merleau-Ponty, Maurice (1960), *Signs* (trans. R. C. McCleary), Evanston: Northwestern (1964).

Merleau-Ponty, Maurice (1961), *Sense and Non-Sense* (trans. H. L. Dreyfus and P. A. Dreyfus), Evanston: Northwestern (1964).

Miller, Alex (1992), *The Ancestor Game*, Ringwood, Vic.: Penguin.

Mintz, Sidney (1974), *Caribbean Transformations*, Chicago: Aldine.

Mitter, Partha (1994), *Art and Nationalism in Colonial India 1850–1922: Occidental Orientations*, Cambridge: Cambridge University Press.

Morgan, Sally (1987), *My Place*, Fremantle: Fremantle Arts Centre.

Morrison, Toni (1998), *Paradise*, New York and Toronto: Knopf.

Murray, Les (1992), *The Paperbark Tree: Selected Prose*, Manchester: Carcanet.

Murray, Les (1994), *Collected Poems*, Melbourne: Heinemann.

Naipaul, V. S. (1971), *In a Free State*, London: Deustch.

Naipaul, V. S. (1979), *A Bend in the River*, Harmondsworth: Penguin.

Naipaul, V. S. (1986), *The Mystic Masseur*, Harmondsworth: Penguin.

Nederveen Pieterse, Jan (1995a), *The Development of Development Theory Towards Critical Globalism*, Working Paper Series, The Hague: Institute of Social Studies.

Nederveen Pieterse, Jan (1995b), 'Globalization as Hybridization' in Mike Featherstone et al., *Global Modernities*, London: Sage.

Ngugi wa Thiongo (1967), *A Grain of Wheat*, London: Heineman.

Ngugi wa Thiongo (1972), *Homecoming: Essays on African and Caribbean Literature, Culture and Politics*, London: Heinemann.

Ngugi wa Thiongo (1981a), *Decolonising the Mind: The Politics of Language in African Literature*, London: James Curry.

Ngugi wa Thiongo (1981b), *Detained: A Writer's Prison Diary*, London: Heinemann.

Nkrumah, Kwame (1962), *I Speak of Freedom: A Statement of African Ideology*, New York: Frederick A. Praeger.

Okara, Gabriel (1964), *The Voice*, London: Heineman (1970).

Peet, R. (1985), 'The Social Origins of Environmental Determinism', *Annals of the Association of American Geographers* 75: 309–33.

Pittin, Renee (1996), 'Negotiating Boundaries: A Perspective from Nigeria' in Deborah Pellow (ed.), *Setting Boundaries: The Anthropology of Spatial and Social Organization*, Westport, CT, and London: Bergin & Garvey.

Pratt, Mary Louise (1992), *Imperial Eyes: Travel Writing and Transculturation*, London: Routledge.

Presbey, Gail (1997), 'Critic of Boers or African? Arendt's Treatment of South Africa' in Eze 1997.

Rabasa, José (1984), 'Allegories of the *Atlas*' in Francis Barker et al. (eds), *Europe and Its Others*, vol. 2, Proceedings of the Essex Conference on the Sociology of Literature, Colchester: University of Essex.

Rabasa, José (1993), *Inventing A-M-E-R-I-C-A: Spanish Historiography and the Formation of Eurocentrism*, Norman, OK, and London: University of Oklahoma.

Rama, Angel (1982), *Transculturacion narrativa en America Latin*, Mexico City: Siglo 21.

Reichert, D. (1992), 'On Boundaries', *Environment and Planning D: Society and Space* 10: 87–98.

Reynolds, Henry (1981), *The Other Side of the Frontier: An Interpretation of the Aboriginal Response to the Invasion and Settlement of Australia*, Townsville, Qld: History Deptartment, James Cook University.

Rich, Adrienne (1976), *Of Woman Born*, New York: Norton.

Ricoeur, Paul (1984), *Time and Narrative* (trans. Kathleen McLaughlin and David Pellauer), Chicago: Chicago University Press.

Robertson, Roland (1992), *Globalization: Social Theory and Global Culture*, London: Sage.

Robertson, Roland (1995), 'Glocalization: Time-Space and Homogeneity–Heterogeneity' in Mike Featherstone, Scott Lash and Roland Robertson (eds), *Global Modernities*, London: Sage.

Rogers, De Wilton (n.d.), *The Rise of the People's National Movement*, Port of Spain: De Wilton Rogers.

Rorty, Richard (1980), *Philosophy and the Mirror of Nature*, Princeton: Princeton University Press.

Rushdie, Salman (1999), 'Learning to Love Uncle Sam', *Sydney Morning Herald* (15 March).

Rutherford, Anna (ed.) (1992), *From Commonwealth to Post-Colonial*, Mundelstrup: Dangaroo.

Rutherford, Jonathan (ed.) (1990), *Identity Community, Culture, Difference*, London: Lawrence & Wishart.

Said, Edward (1978), *Orientalism*, London: Routledge.

Said, Edward (1983), *The World, the Text and the Critic*, London: Vintage.

Said, Edward (1985), 'Orientalism Reconsidered', *Race and Class* 27 (2): 1–16.

Said, Edward (1986), *After the Last Sky: Palestinian Lives*, New York: Pantheon.

Said, Edward (1989), 'Representing the Colonized: Anthropology's Interlocutors', *Critical Inquiry* 15 (2): 205–25.

Said, Edward (1993), *Culture and Imperialism*, London: Chatto & Windus.

Salih, Tayeb (1969), *Season of Migration to the North*, London: Heinemann.

Santayana, George (1928), *Realms of Being*, London: Constable.

Sapir, Edward (1931), 'Conceptual Categories in Primitive Languages', *Science* 74.

Saussure, Ferdinand de (1916), *Course in General Linguistics* (trans. W. Baskin), Glasgow: Collins (1974).

Scholte, J. A. (1996), 'Beyond the Buzzword: Towards a Global Theory of Globalization' in E. Kofman and G. Youngs (eds), *Globalisation: Theory and Practice*, London: Pinter.

Scott, Kim (1993), *True Country*, Fremantle: Fremantle Arts Centre.

Seed, Patricia (1992), 'Taking Possession of Overseas Empires', *William and Mary Quarterly* 49 (3) (April): 183–209.

Seeley, John Robert (1890), *The Expansion of England: Two Courses of Lectures*, London: Macmillan.

Seifrid, Thomas (1998), 'Gazing on Life's Page: Perspectival Vision in Tolstoy', *PMLA* 113 (3) (May): 436–48.

Sharpe, Jenny (1989), 'Figures of Colonial Resistance', *Modern Fiction Studies* 35 (1) (Spring): 137–55.

Shaw, Gregory (1985), 'Art and Dialectic in the Work of Wilson Harris', *New Left Review* 153 (Sept.–Oct.).

Shohat, Ella (1992), 'Notes on the Post-Colonial', *Social Text* 10: 2–3 (31–2): 99–113.

Shohat, Ella and Robert Stam (1994), *Unthinking Eurocentrism: Multiculturalism and the Media*, London and New York: Routledge.

Sklodowska, Elzbieta (1982), 'La forma testimonial y la novelística de Miguel Barnet', *Revista/Review Interamericana* 12 (3): 368–80.

Slemon, Stephen (1986), 'Revisioning Allegory: Wilson Harris's *Carnival*', *Kunapipi* 8 (2).

Slemon, Stephen (1987), 'Monuments of Empire: Allegory/Counter Discourse/Post-Colonial Writing', *Kunapipi* 9 (3).

Slemon, Stephen (1988), 'Post-Colonial Allegory and the Transformation of History', *Journal of Commonwealth Literature* 23 (1): 157–68.

Slemon, Stephen (1990), 'Unsettling the Empire: Resistance Theory for the Second World', *World Literature Written in English* 30 (2): 30–41.

Slemon, Stephen (1994), 'The Scramble for Post-Colonialism' in Chris Tiffin and Alan Lawson (eds), *Describing Empire: Post-Colonialism and Textuality*, London and New York: Routledge.

Smith, Adam (1776), *An Enquiry into the Nature and Causes of the Wealth of Nations*, ed. Edward Cannan, New York: Modern Library (1994).

Smith, Neil (1994), 'Shaking Loose the Colonies: Isaiah Bowman and the "De-colonization" of the British Empire' in Godlewska and Smith 1994.

Smith, Paul (1982), 'The Will to Allegory in Postmodernism', *Dalhousie Review* 62 (1982).

Sobusobu, Akanisi (1980), 'The Taboo' in Albert Wendt (ed.), *Lali: A Pacific Anthology*, Auckland: Longman Paul.

Soyinka, Wole (1972), *The Man Dies: Prison Notes of Wole Soyinka*, London: Rex Collings.

Soyinka, Wole (1976), *Myth, Literature and the African World*, Cambridge: Cambridge University Press.

Soyinka, Wole (1994), Interview with Nathan Gardels, 'Bloodsoaked Quilt of Africa', *Weekly Mail and Guardian* (South Africa), 20–6 May: 31.

Spengler, Oswald (1926), *The Decline of the West* (trans. C. F. Atkinson), London: Allen and Unwin.

Spivak, Gayatri Chakravorty (1985), 'The Rani of Simur' in Francis Barker et al. (eds), *Europe and Its Others*, vol. 1, Proceedings of the Essex Conference on the Sociology of Literature, July 1984, Colchester: University of Essex.

Spivak, Gayatri Chakravorty (1988), 'Can the Subaltern Speak?' in Cary Nelson and Lawrence Grossberg (eds), *Marxism and the Interpretation of Culture*, London: Macmillan.

Spivak, Gayatri Chakravorty (1993), *Outside in the Teaching Machine*, London and New York: Routledge.

Spurr, David (1994), *The Rhetoric of Empire: Colonial Discourse in Journalism, Travel Writing and Imperial Administration*, Durham, NC, and London: Duke University Press.

Spybey, Tony (1996), *Globalization and World Society*, Cambridge: Polity.

Stewart, Charles and Rosalind Shaw (eds) (1994), *Syncretism/Anti-Syncretism: the Politics of Religious Synthesis*, London and New York: Routledge.

Stoll, David (1999), *Rigoberta Menchú and the Story of All Poor Guatemalans*, Boulder, CO, and Oxford: Westview.

Stratton, John (1990), *Writing Sites: A Genealogy of the Postmodern World*, Ann Arbor: University of Michigan.

Stubbs, William (1878), *Constitutional History of England in its Origin and Development*, Oxford: Clarendon.

Stubbs, William (1900), *Lectures in Early English History* (ed. A. Hassall), Oxford: Clarendon.

Tawali, Kumula (1972), *Manki Masta* in *Five New Guinea Plays*, Brisbane: Jacaranda.

Terdiman, Richard (1985), *Discourse/Counter Discourse: The Theory and Practice of Symbolic Resistance in Nineteenth-Century France*, Ithaca and London: Cornell University Press.

Tharoor, Shashi (1989), *The Great Indian Novel*, Harmondsworth: Penguin.

Tiffin, Helen (1988), 'Post-Colonialism, Post-Modernism and the Rehabilitation of Post-Colonial History', *Journal of Commonwealth Literature* 23 (1): 169–81.

Todorov, Tzvetan (1984), *Mikhail Bakhtin: The Dialogical Principle* (trans. Wlad Godzich), Minneapolis: University of Minnesota.

Tomlinson, John (1991), *Cultural Imperialism*, Baltimore: The Johns Hopkins University Press.

Toynbee, Arnold J. (1948), *Civilization on Trial*, London and New York: Oxford University Press.

Tulip, James (1990), *David Malouf:* Johnno, *Short Stories, Poems Essays and Interview*, St Lucia: University of Queensland.

Turner, B. S. (1990), *Theories of Modernity and Postmodernity*, London: Sage.

Va'ai, Emma Kruse (1997), 'Producing the Text of Culture: The Appropriation of English in Contemporary Samoa' (unpublished PhD thesis), Sydney: University of New South Wales.

Verhelst, Thierry, G. (1990), *No Life Without Roots: Culture and Development* (trans. Bob Cumming), London and New Jersey: Zed Books.

Vico, Giambattista (1968), *The New Science of Giambattista Vico* (trans. T. G. Bergin and Max Fisch), Ithaca: Cornell University Press.

Vidal, Hernan and René Jara (eds) (1986), *Testimonio y literatura*, Minneapolis: Institute for the Study of Ideologies and Literature.

Viswanathan, Gauri (1987), 'The Beginnings of English Literary Study in British India', *Oxford Literary Review* 9 (1–2): 2–25.

Viswanathan, Gauri (1989), *Masks of Conquest: Literary Study and British Rule in India*, New York: Columbia University Press.

Wallerstein, Immanuel (1974a), *The Modern World System: Capitalist Agriculture and the Origin of the European World-Economy in the Sixteenth Century*, New York: Academic.

Wallerstein, Immanuel (1974b), 'The Rise and Future Demise of the World Capitalist System: Concepts for Comparative Analysis', *Comparative Studies in Society and History* 16 (3): 387–415.

Watts, Michael (1993a), 'The Geography of Post-Colonial Africa: Space, Place and Development in Sub-Saharan Africa (1960–93)', *Singapore Journal of Tropical Geography* 14 (2).

Watts, Michael (1993b), 'Development 1: Power, Knowledge, Discursive Practice', *Progress in Human Geography* 17: 257–72.

Wendt, Albert (ed.) (1980), *Lali: A Pacific Anthology*, Auckland: Longman Paul.

West, Cornel (1990), 'The New Cultural Politics of Difference' in Russell Ferguson, Martha Gever, Trinh T. Minh-Ha and Cornel West (eds), *Out There: Marginalization and Contemporary Cultures*, Cambridge, MA: MIT Press.

White, Hayden (1980), 'The Value of Narrativity in the Representation of Reality', *Critical Inquiry* 7.

White, Hayden (1982), 'The Politics of Historical Interpretation: Discipline and De-Sublimation', *Critical Inquiry* 9.

Whorf, Benjamin Lee (1952), *Collected Papers on Metalinguistics*, Washington DC: Foreign Service Institute, Department of State.

Williams, Bernard (1981), *Moral Luck: Philosophical Papers 1973–1980*, Cambridge: Cambridge University Press.

Williams, Denis (1969), *Image and Idea in the Arts of Guyana*, Edgar Mittelholzer Memorial Lectures, Georgetown, Guyana: National History and Arts Council, Ministry of Information.

Williams, Eric (1972), *British Historians and the West Indies*, New York: Africana.

Wittgenstein, Ludwig (1922), *Tractatus Logico-Philosophicus*, London: Routledge and Kegan Paul (1961).

Wittgenstein, Ludwig (1979), 'Remarks on Frazer's *Golden Bough*' (ed. Rush Rees, trans. A. C. Miles), Retford: Brynmill.

Young, Robert (1990), *White Mythologies: Writing History and the West*, London and New York: Routledge.

Yunipingu, Galarrwuy (1980), 'Aboriginal Land Rights' in *Counterpoint Forum*, Murdoch, WA: Murdoch University.

Zable, Arnold (1991), *Jewels and Ashes*, Newham, Vic.: Scribe.

# Index

248    *Index*

standard code 65
standard language 76
Stanley, Henry Morton 142
state boundaries 177
Stoll controversy 121–3
Stoll, David 121, 123
Stubbs, Bishop 92, 96
subaltern 46, 85, 99
subjectivity 14, 35, 38–40;
    disarticulation and transformation
    173
surveillance 129, 141–4; of colonial
    space 142; 144; geographic
    mastery 149, 151, 162, 168, 169;
    technology and total institutions
    142
Symbolic Order, 38
syncreticity 108

tactics and strategies 53–5
Talented Tenth Seductioin 49
teleology 83, 98
Terdiman, Richard 32
territorialize 51
*testimonio* 18, 19, 112–23, 113; and
    control of representation 114–17;
    216
text (a social situation) 59
Tharoor, Shashi 106; *The Great Indian
    Novel* 176
*The Tempest* 33
third-world politics 19
threefold present 87
Tolstoy 137
Tom Jones in Penang 221–3
torture 119, 170; inscription of
    colonial power 120; controlling
    gaze 121
totalizing systems of representation
    150
transcultural 2, 24, 122
transformation 2, 4, 5; and
    ambivalence 22; balance with
    resistance 19; and boundaries of
    vision 204; of colonial discourse
    153; and cultural identity 220; of
    history 15, 83; of imagination 21;
    and imitation 5, 13–17; linguistic
    strategies 78; and meanability 76;
    movement between codes 77; of

place 160; strategies 74; structures
    of power 55
transformative interpolating process
    50
transforming history 99–103
Transit Circle 130
Treaty of Waitangi 19
truth 85; function 114
T-shirt 223–5; and fetishization of
    elsewhere 224

understanding 73
unfilled time 104
uninhabited land 139
universal perception 135; viewpoint
    136
Unyamwezi 142
US global power 149

veracity 122
verandas 193–6; and counter-
    discourse 194; contact zone 195
verisimilitude 122
Vico, Giambattista 79
visual perception (mathematical
    codification) 136
Viswanathan, Gauri 37
voyeurs of their own abjection 121

Walcott, Derek 100
Wallerstein, Emmanuel 211
West, Cornell 49
Western civilization 1
Western European civilization 27
Western perspectivalism 140
Western visuality 138
Westernization 23
White, Hayden 87, 89, 116, 123
Whorf, Benjamin 68
Wilde, Oscar 64
Williams, Bernard 5
Williams, Eric 57, 58
Wittgenstein, Ludwig 74, 185
world map 128; power and
    legitimacy of European civilization
    149; universal space 168
worlded 50
worldliness of texts 63–4
writer function 72–4
writing event 66